# THE EVERYTHIN[G]
## Tapas and Small Plates Cookbook

Dear Reader,

The first time I ate at a tapas bar I was impressed. Olives, cheese, ham, shrimp, fried potatoes . . . all served on little plates to share with everyone at my table. It was like a party, with a variety of tastes in small portions instead of the usual salad and entrée I was familiar with in bars and restaurants. That was in 1986, and there was only one tapas bar in town. Since then tapas have become wildly popular, and you can find tapas selections on menus everywhere, regardless of whether or not the restaurant or bar is Spanish.

The variety is stunning. Similar to appetizers, tapas, or "small plates," as they are often called, include soups, salads, vegetables, seafood, cured meats, omelets, and fried potatoes. Also included on tapas menus are snacks for nibbling, like marinated olives, nuts, cheese plates, and peppers. Bread is served by the basket, and extra-virgin olive oil is available for dipping.

Small plates have made their way from tapas bars and cafes to restaurants and clubs, which offer bar menus consisting of tapas, or sometimes a whole section of the menu will be dedicated to little jewels of appetizer-size portions in addition to the usual entrée selection. Jazz clubs often serve tapas to accompany cocktails and live music, and tapas parties are increasing in popularity. Japanese sushi, Chinese dim sum, Middle Eastern meze, and Mexican antojitos are among the selections in many restaurants now, in addition to the authentic Spanish tapas. I hope you will enjoy this vast selection of tapas-inspired recipes, from the traditional to the eclectic.

Bon Appetit!

*Lynette Rohrer Shirk*

# The EVERYTHING® Series

### Editorial

| | |
|---|---|
| Publisher | Gary M. Krebs |
| Director of Product Development | Paula Munier |
| Managing Editor | Laura M. Daly |
| Executive Editor, Series Books | Brielle K. Matson |
| Associate Copy Chief | Sheila Zwiebel |
| Development Editor | Katie McDonough |
| Production Editor | Casey Ebert |

### Production

| | |
|---|---|
| Director of Manufacturing | Susan Beale |
| Production Project Manager | Michelle Roy Kelly |
| Prepress | Erick DaCosta |
| | Matt LeBlanc |
| Interior Layout | Heather Barrett |
| | Brewster Brownville |
| | Colleen Cunningham |
| | Jennifer Oliveira |
| Cover Design | Erin Alexander |
| | Stephanie Chrusz |
| | Frank Rivera |

Visit the entire Everything® Series at *www.everything.com*

# THE EVERYTHING TAPAS AND SMALL PLATES COOKBOOK

Hundreds of bite-sized recipes
from around the world

Lynette Rohrer Shirk

Adams Media
Avon, Massachusetts

*To Jeff and Zelda, my happy tapas tasters. I love you both.*

An Everything® Series Book.
Everything® and everything.com® are registered trademarks of F+W Publications, Inc.

Published by Adams Media, an F+W Publications Company
57 Littlefield Street, Avon, MA 02322 U.S.A.
*www.adamsmedia.com*

ISBN-10: 1-59869-467-7
ISBN-13: 978-1-59869-467-3

Printed in the United States of America.

J  I  H  G  F  E  D  C  B  A

**Library of Congress Cataloging-in-Publication Data**
Shirk, Lynette Rohrer.
The everything tapas and small plates cookbook /
Lynette Rohrer Shirk.
p. cm.
ISBN-13: 978-1-59869-467-3 (pbk.)
ISBN-10: 1-59869-467-7 (pbk.)
1. Appetizers  I. Title.
TX740.S463 2007
641.8'12—dc22    2007018985

*This book is available at quantity discounts for bulk purchases.*
*For information, please call 1-800-289-0963.*

# Contents

# Acknowledgments

As always, I would like to thank my husband, Jeff, and daughter, Zelda, for their patience, understanding, and appetites while I worked on this book. Thanks also to Barbara Speer, Dena Nichols, and everyone at Stringfellow School in Coppell, Texas. And to all the Stringfellow moms who watched over my daughter during this school year, especially Lisa Hollen, who also shared her recipes. Yoga Island, Top Hat Dance Centre, Adventure Kids, and Gym Kids also provided respite for me to write while teaching my daughter how to move her body, so maybe she can flamenco dance in Madrid some day! Thanks also to the Beanlands, Conants, Stone Creek Women's Club, and Top Hat moms for various things, and to Brielle K. Matson and June Clark for providing me the opportunity to write about tapas. Finally, I would like to thank Café Madrid in Dallas for the fine tapas meals.

# Introduction

THE WORD *TAPAS* USUALLY refers to a variety of appetizers or small plates that are served in Spain at tapas bars, cafes, and restaurants, or they can be in the style of Spain but served in any country. For the purposes of this book, however, *tapas* refers to many different styles of cuisine served in appetizer portions. In some cases there are family-style portions, served on one platter for individuals to help themselves. There are traditional Spanish tapas for the purist, and modern Spanish tapas where flavors from other cuisines are used to make traditional tapas, such as Welsh Rarebit Croquettes.

The portion sizes are smaller than ordinary recipes, since tapas are meant to be served with a lot of other tapas. So if a recipe "serves 4," and there are a total of twelve finished hors d'oeuvres, that means you should make about five separate recipes that serve four people to mix and match if you intend to feed them satisfactorily. And portion sizes of recipes like paella, rice, or soup are smaller than they would be if you were to rely on the recipe as an entrée. Basically, tapas in this book are designed to be part of a tasting menu of a variety of different recipes. Keep that in mind if you want to feed four people for dinner.

There are also recipes for drinks, including sangria, and for sweets that can be served at the end or combined to form a tapas dessert menu. So don't be surprised when you find a recipe for something that wouldn't be found in the realm of tapas in the traditional sense, such as muffins, because it *can* be part of *your* tapas repertoire if you choose.

# Small Plates from Around the World

IN recent years, instead of using the designations "appetizers," "salads," and "entrees," many American restaurateurs have chosen to break up their menus into "small plates" and "large plates." These restaurants are providing a way to meet the varying needs of diners—some who may not be interested in an entrée but prefer a smaller portion, others who may have trouble deciding between several entrée selections and wish to opt for a few small plates instead of a typical entrée, and others still who may want a lot of one dish and a little of another. A do-it-yourself tasting menu is the result, and Spain is where the small plates originated in the form of tapas.

# History of Tapas from Spain

Tapas from Spain are the foundation for understanding the small plates that will be covered in this book, so it is necessary to define what they are. Spain has some of the most delicious cuisine in the world, but it is not as familiar to Americans as Mexican, Italian, French, or Chinese. Ironically, modern Mexican cuisine is derived partially from Spain, since the discovery of the New World brought an exchange of foodstuffs between the two countries.

## The Roots of Spanish Cuisine

Spanish explorers brought Old World items, such as garlic and olive oil, to the New World and brought back tomatoes, peppers, chocolate, and corn to Europe. Spanish cuisine is not as spicy hot as Mexican, but it is flavorful and bright. It is also infused with spices from the East, because the Moors occupied the country for centuries.

The Moors brought peppercorns, nutmeg, cinnamon, and cloves from the Far East to Spain via Morocco in Northern Africa. They also planted cumin, coriander, and saffron, which made a major contribution to the distinctive flavor of Spanish cuisine.

## The Birth of Tapas

The word *tapas* means "lids" in Spanish, and refers to a slice of bread being used to cover the top of a wine glass. Legend has it that such tapas were used in Spanish cafes with standing bars to prevent fruit flies and the like from getting in the wine glasses of the customers. Madrid's custom is to gather at wine and sherry bar cafes after work, before dinner. Patrons of the bars usually stand and drink their sherry and wine and enjoy selections from an extensive tapas list. This evolved from the bars offering free snacks, like a slice of ham, piece of cheese, olives, mussels, or bread. Basque tapas started on toothpicks, called *pinchos*, and eventually became something on a piece of bread, such as anchovy toasts. Gazpacho and paella are also offered in tapas bars, as well as Manchego and quince paste, flan, and *tres leches* cake.

## Learn More

If you want to explore Spanish food, start by checking out a map of Spain. Study the different regions, such as Andalusia, Catalonia, and Basqueland, which all have different local ingredients, and the great cities around Spain, like Valencia, Madrid, Barcelona, and Seville, which have their own specialties based on the diversity of raw ingredients. There are microclimates in Spain ranging from sunny coast to lush mountains that allow for the growing of wine grapes and other specialized ingredients, like the olives for olive oil, oranges, and almonds.

# Meze and Antipasto from the Mediterranean

Meze are small plates of appetizers, often served with anise-flavored liqueurs: ouzo in Greece, arrack in the Middle East, or raki in Turkey. Middle Eastern dishes such as hummus, stuffed grape leaves, and pita bread are part of the meze table.

## Meze from the Middle East

As with Spanish tapas, olives and roasted peppers are served, along with salads of eggplant and couscous. The term *meze* comes from the Persian *mazas* for "taste" and "relish." Wherever the Ottoman Empire had once been, meze dishes are still served. The countries of Egypt, Israel, Armenia, Iraq, Greece, Lebanon, Morocco, and Turkey all share the meze tradition.

Spanish tapas and the Middle Eastern meze table of small plates are similar to Moroccan feasts, which feature multiple dishes spread out. If you are serious about trying tapas and meze, you will want to buy a variety of small plates to serve the vast array of "small plates" on.

## Antipasto from Italy

Antipasto are served as appetizers before the pasta course in an Italian meal. *Antipasto* literally means "before the pasta" in Italian. A table full of Italian appetizers to eat while drinking wine is basically Italian tapas. Some popular small plates of antipasti are prosciutto-wrapped melon; caponata (eggplant relish); a variety of roasted, grilled, and pickled peppers; bruschetta; and olives. Wine, Sambuca (anise-flavored liqueur), grappa, or aperitifs such as Campari or Cinzano are enjoyed with Italian antipasto.

## All-Important Olive Oil

Olive oil is used extensively in the Mediterranean cuisines of Spain, France, Italy, Greece, and Turkey, and also North Africa and the Middle East. It appears in those cuisines in various forms—in a dish for dipping, combined with garlic and spices as a sauce for pasta, and as a medium for cooking meat and vegetables, to name a few.

The aspect of olive oil that often confuses people is the difference between "extra-virgin," "virgin," and regular olive oil. Extra-virgin olive oil comes from the first pressing of the olives, has the most intense flavor, and is the most expensive. Use this for salads and for dipping breads. Virgin olive oil is from the second pressing. Less expensive than extra-virgin, it can be used for the same purposes. "Olive oil" indicates it is from the last pressing; this is the oil to use for cooking since it does not burn as easily at high temperatures.

While these guidelines are helpful, there is another more hands-on approach to comparing the quality of different olive oils. Simply pour a few drops on your palms and rub them together to warm it. Then cup your palms under your nose to smell the aroma of the oil. Every time you get a new bottle do this to build up your olfactory inventory. It's kind of like wine tasting. You'll find that extra-virgin olive oil has more bouquet than subsequent pressings, and you will get to know the varieties of olives used to make olive oils in different countries.

# Dim Sum from China

*Dim Sum*, translated as "point heart" or "heart's delight," is classic Chinese teahouse food. It is not ordered from a menu, but pointed to on carts that are circulated throughout the dining room by waiters. The waiters roam the room and appear tableside with a cart full of freshly prepared dishes from the kitchen. There are steamer baskets filled with dumplings, and plates with small portions of baked buns and fried tidbits. The idea is that you point to your heart's delight from the cart. The dishes stack up at the table, and the bill typically is figured from the empty plates. Pork and shrimp are ubiquitous in the dim sum repertoire as fillings for dumplings and buns. Chicken wings cooked in foil packets are a favorite, and wonton soup and tea accompany the dim sum.

QUESTION?

**What is the best occasion to have a dim sum party at home?**
Dim sum makes the perfect late-morning, early-afternoon fare, also known as "brunch." You don't have to push the food around on a cart; just place it on a sideboard or table, buffet-style, for a baby shower, graduation luncheon, or any occasion where you would serve brunch.

Alcohol is typically not served with dim sum or Chinese food in general, although there are Chinese beers available. If you prefer wine to drink with dim sum, a slightly sweet white wine, such as Riesling, Gewurtztraminer, or a late-harvest-style wine is suggested. Sometimes a Pinot Noir, Merlot, or Zinfandel will pair nicely with Chinese cuisine if you desire red wine. Try Pinot Noir with pork dishes, Merlot with duck, and Zinfandel with anything spicy. Sherry makes a nice accompaniment with some Chinese food too, especially at the end of the meal with dessert.

# Chaat from India and Pakistan

*Chaat* is Indian Street Food, small plates of savory snacks originally based on fried dough. *Samosas*, potato turnovers traditionally made in a triangular shape, are a favorite. They are spicy, so they are eaten with mint, coriander, or tamarind chutney, for a cooling effect. Fried or baked chaat snacks are often served with tea or coffee. *Chapatti*, *poori*, naan, onion *kulcha*, *pappadams*, and *pakoras* are all examples of chaat. In the United States they are served as appetizers or starters in Indian and Pakistani restaurants.

Curry is not chaat, but it could be served tapas-style since it is served with a variety of condiments in small dishes that complement it. Some of the popular condiments served with curry are chopped peanuts; raisins; chutneys; shredded coconut; diced limes; chopped eggs; and chopped fruits such as bananas, pineapples, and apples.

# Izakaya from Japan

*Izakaya* are gathering places where sushi is served with sake. These sushi bars serve sushi as after-work drinking food (just like tapas in Spain). Izakaya differ from restaurants, where sitting on tatami mats at low tables to eat instead of standing is the practice. Sake shops, where people went to drink, eventually started serving food and turned into restaurants, whereas the sushi bar is the place to drink and have a little sushi while standing and chatting. Miso soup and pickled vegetables are also served along with sushi.

If you are serving warm sake with your sushi, you will need a set of porcelain sake cups, available in Japanese markets, some Asian markets, and stores that sell tea supplies. If you are serving your sake chilled in the summer, you can get a type of sake cup that is a square wooden box, which is filled to overflowing by the host/ess for the guests. The chilled sake is drunk from a corner of the sake box. Sake etiquette to remember is to never fill your own cup.

# Antojitos and Bar Food from the Americas

There is some duplicity between bar food in North America and antojitos in Central and South America. That's because of the New World ingredients they have in common. Corn tortilla chips and peanuts are the snacking icons of cantinas and taverns alike.

## Antojitos from Mexico

*Antojitos* means "little whims," and it refers to Mexican finger foods, appetizers, and snacks. Some examples of antojitos are flautas, nachos, taquitos, chili con queso, tamales, enchiladas, empanadas, guacamole, and chips and salsa. Tequila drinks, such as the Margarita, and cerveza (beer) are the beverages most often served with antojitos. Soups, such as menudo, black bean, and tortilla soup, are also part of the selection of antojitos. Miniature versions of burritos and chimichangas are also popular.

The influence of Aztec, Spanish, and Caribbean cuisine combine to make Mexican cuisine. Spanish conquistadores brought rice, meat, garlic, and onions to the New World, which were mixed with ingredients indigenous to the Americas, such as corn, tomatoes and chili peppers, and fish and tropical fruits of the Caribbean, which evolved into a unique hybrid cuisine that is Mexico's pride.

## Bar Food from the United States

The tradition of serving food with drinks in public taverns, saloons, and hotel bars is a long-standing one in the United States. Every time you see a bowl of mixed nuts at a bar remember that, and the tapas connection as well. Colonial taverns served as roadhouses to nourish travelers who would stop for refreshments in the form of ale and some kind of hearty fare to fortify them.

The tradition of bar food evolved in the United States, borrowing from the Irish and English public houses. British "pubs" serve such fare as bangers and mash, pickled sausages, bubble and squeak, scotch eggs, and shepherd's pie to go with a few pints of Guinness or Bass Ale. The American "happy hour" seems to be a descendant of the Spanish tapas tradition too, with drink specials and some food available "on the house." Salty snacks, such as pretzels and nuts, are often served with an ulterior motive, to encourage more drink sales as the patrons get thirsty from the salt. American saloon keepers in the 1800s would offer a so-called free lunch to patrons if they would buy one drink, betting that they would buy more than one. From drinking houses in New Orleans to the bars of the fancy hotels along the "cocktail route" in San Francisco, this "free" lunch, similar to the original concept of tapas in Spain, was served daily to drinking patrons. It was not an offering of small plates though; in fact it was often a veritable all-you-can-eat buffet, with oyster stew, carved meats, potatoes, bread, and butter.

The "free lunch" was outlawed in New York in 1896 under the umbrella of the Raines Law. This law was passed under pressure from the temperance movement, which claimed the "free lunch" encouraged drinking alcohol. The law was amended shortly after in 1897 to allow the "free lunch" to return.

# Classic Spanish-Style Tapas

# Potatoes Brava

**SERVES 4**

*1 pound russet potatoes*
*2 cups extra-virgin olive oil*
*Salt to taste*
*Brava Sauce (page 11)*

Potatoes are a favorite all over Spain, and these crisp potato nuggets fried in extra-virgin olive oil are one of the most popular tapas there.

1. Peel the potatoes and cut them into 1-inch chunks. If you won't be frying them right away, save them in water so they don't turn brown. Be sure to drain and blot them dry before frying so they won't splatter.

2. Heat the olive oil in a deep, heavy-bottom pot or a deep fryer to 275°F. Check with a candy thermometer for correct temperature.

3. Carefully lower the potato chunks (blotted dry) into the olive oil with a slotted spoon and poach them for about 10 minutes. This is to precook them, so they shouldn't turn golden in color yet. Drain the poached potatoes on paper towels and set aside.

4. Raise the temperature of the olive oil to 350°F. Carefully lower the poached potatoes into the olive oil again and fry them until they are crisp and golden brown. Drain the potatoes and sprinkle them with salt.

5. Serve hot with Brava Sauce drizzled over the top and more on the side for dipping.

### Alternate Potato Prep . . . . . . . . . . . . . . . . . . . . . . .
Poaching the potatoes ahead of time in water and then frying them to a crisp when it is serving time is a goodw way to plan ahead. Simply cook the potato chunks in boiling water until tender, but not falling apart, about 8 minutes. Drain them and reserve them until ready to serve. At service time heat 2 cups of olive oil to 350°F and then crisp the potatoes in the oil for about 6 minutes. Drain, salt, and serve.

# Brava Sauce

Like most Spanish tapas, this spicy tomato sauce has extra-virgin olive oil in it. It is more flavorful than virgin or pure olive oil. Paprika is used here because it is easy to find, but if you can find the Spanish smoked paprika, pimentón, your sauce will taste even more authentic.

1. Heat the extra-virgin olive oil in a saucepan on low. Add the tomato purée, sugar, paprika, cayenne pepper, and bay leaf.

2. Raise the temperature to medium and cook the sauce for about 10 minutes. It will reduce and turn darker during this time. Remove the pan from the heat.

3. Finish the sauce by stirring in the sherry vinegar and salt.

4. Serve warm with fried potatoes.

**SERVES 4**

*2 tablespoons extra-virgin olive oil*
*1½ cups tomato purée*
*1 teaspoon sugar*
*½ teaspoon paprika*
*Pinch cayenne pepper*
*1 bay leaf*
*1 teaspoon sherry vinegar*
*Salt to taste*

# Traditional Aioli

Aioli is a simple Spanish garlic sauce with origins in Catalonia. Made with a mortar and pestle with lots of garlic, it is laborious but worth it.

1. Put the salt in the bottom of the mortar and then add the garlic cloves. Pound the garlic into a mush, and then a paste, with the pestle.

2. Add the lemon juice (squeeze your own for best flavor) and pound it into the garlic paste. Add the egg yolk and pound it into the garlic.

3. Add the olive oil drop by drop to the garlic paste while pounding with the pestle until it emulsifies; keep adding the oil steadily, drop by drop, whisking with a wire whip until all of the oil is incorporated. Add water if it gets too thick.

**MAKES 1½ CUPS**

*Large pinch of kosher salt*
*4 cloves of garlic, peeled*
*1 teaspoon freshly squeezed lemon juice*
*1 pasteurized raw egg yolk*
*1½ cups extra-virgin olive oil*
*1 tablespoon water*

# Mushrooms in Sherry Garlic Sauce

**SERVES 4**

1 pound button mushrooms

2 garlic cloves, minced

3 tablespoons extra-virgin olive oil

¼ cup dry white wine

2 tablespoons dry sherry

1 teaspoon salt

½ teaspoon pepper

1 tablespoon chopped fresh parsley

Serve these morsels with toothpicks alongside for easy noshing, and a basket of bread for sopping up the juices when the mushrooms are gone. Mushrooms are a favorite of the Basques and Catalans.

1. Wipe the mushrooms clean with a damp towel to remove any dirt or debris. Set aside.

2. Sauté the garlic in the olive oil over medium heat for a few minutes, then add the mushrooms and sauté for another minute or two over medium-high.

3. Add the white wine and sherry, reduce the heat to medium-low, and simmer until the liquid reduces by half (5 to 10 minutes).

4. Season the mushrooms with salt and pepper, then remove the pan from the heat.

5. Put the mushrooms in a serving dish and sprinkle them with the parsley.

# Potato Omelet

This egg and potato dish is a tapas staple, usually
appearing as *tortilla de patatas* on tapas café menus.

**SERVES 4**

*2 medium baking potatoes,
peeled*
*¼ cup extra-virgin olive oil*
*1 small onion, peeled*
*5 tablespoons pure olive oil,
divided use*
*6 eggs*
*1½ teaspoons salt*

1. Preheat oven to 400°F. Slice the potatoes into ¼-inch slices and then roughly quarter the slices. Toss the potatoes with the extra-virgin olive oil and then scatter them in one even layer on a baking sheet lined with foil. Roast the potatoes in the oven until crisp, about 15 to 20 minutes. Set aside.

2. Thinly slice the onion and sauté it in 2 tablespoons pure olive oil until cooked, about 5 minutes. Set aside.

3. Whisk the eggs in a bowl to break them up and bring together the whites and yolks into one solid color; avoid whipping too much air into them. Sprinkle the potatoes with salt and then add them and the sautéed onions to the eggs. Stir to combine.

4. Heat 3 tablespoons pure olive oil in a 6-inch nonstick sauté pan over medium heat. Add the egg mixture to the pan and cook for 1 minute. Lower the heat and continue cooking for about 2 to 3 minutes. When the eggs look like they've set, place a plate over the pan and flip the omelet onto it. Return the pan to the heat and slide the omelet, uncooked side down, from the plate into the pan. Cook for a minute then slide it onto a clean plate.

5. Cut the omelet into wedges and serve hot.

## Manchego and Membrillo . . . . . . . . . . . . . . . . . . . . . . .

The delightful combination of Manchego (cheese) and membrillo (quince paste) is a Spanish classic that can be enjoyed as an appetizer, dessert, or snack anytime. Manchego is a hard sheep's milk cheese from the region of La Mancha (of Don Quixote fame). Membrillo is available in canned form or you can make your own. (You'll find a recipe for it in Chapter 6 on page 68.)

# Sizzling Garlic Shrimp

**SERVES 4**

1 pound medium-large shrimp, thawed if frozen

4 tablespoons extra-virgin olive oil

4 to 6 cloves of garlic, peeled

1 whole dried cayenne pepper

Salt to taste

You may substitute sliced or minced garlic for a bolder garlic taste in this recipe. Also, if a whole dried cayenne pepper is unavailable, substitute a pinch of dried, crushed red pepper (the kind that goes on pizza).

1. Peel and discard the shells from the shrimp. Cut a slit down the back of each shrimp with a sharp paring knife and remove the mud vein. Rinse the shrimp and set aside in a bowl over another bowl of ice.

2. Heat the olive oil over medium-high in a large sauté pan, add the garlic cloves, and cook a minute or two to flavor the oil.

3. Add the shrimp to the pan and sauté for about 2 minutes. Toss the shrimp, either by shaking the pan or with metal tongs, to turn them over.

4. Add the cayenne pepper and continue cooking the shrimp and garlic for 2 to 3 minutes.

5. Transfer the contents of the pan to a serving dish, sprinkle salt over the shrimp, and serve hot.

# Stewed Chorizo

Chorizo is a semihard sausage much like kielbasa, which you
can substitute if you wish, although chorizo is spicier.

1. Cut the sausage into slices, about ½-inch thick.

2. Sauté the sausage slices in olive oil over medium heat for 5 minutes.

3. Add the white wine, sherry, and thyme and bring to a boil. Turn the
heat down and simmer for 25 minutes. Serve hot.

**SERVES 4**

*2 ounces chorizo sausage*
*1 tablespoon extra-virgin olive oil*
*1 cup dry white wine*
*1 tablespoon sherry*
*1 sprig fresh thyme*

# Basque Olive Pinchos

Pinchos are the Basque style of serving tapas on a toothpick. This is a version of the most
famous of the pinchos, "Gilda," which was named after the 1940s Rita Hayworth film.

1. Toss the olive oil and sherry vinegar with the stuffed olives in a bowl
and set aside at room temperature.

2. Cut the piquillo peppers each into four pieces. Cut the cheese into
8 cubes or pieces.

3. Affix each olive with a toothpick to a cube of cheese with a piece of
pepper between them. Repeat and serve them on a little plate.

**SERVES 4**

*1 tablespoon extra-virgin olive oil*
*1 teaspoon sherry vinegar*
*8 extra-large anchovy-stuffed
green olives*
*2 piquillo peppers*
*4 ounces Idiazabal cheese (or any
semihard cheese)*

# Marinated Olives

**SERVES 4**

4 tablespoons extra-virgin
    olive oil
1 teaspoon grated lemon zest
1 tablespoon sherry vinegar
½ pound green olives, unpitted

Toss pitted nicoise olives with the marinated ones before serving.
Serve at room temperature with roasted almonds and cheese.

1. Mix olive oil, lemon zest, and sherry vinegar together in a crock (a stoneware dish similar to a ramekin) or bowl that will accommodate ½ pound of olives.

2. You may cut a slit on the olives for better penetration of the marinade if you wish. Toss the olives in the marinade to coat.

3. Cover and let olives marinate in the refrigerator for 1 to 7 days.

## Caper Berries . . . . . . . . . . . . . . . . . . . . . . .

Capers are the unripened buds of the caper shrub, and caper berries are the grown fruit of the same shrub. Both are harvested by hand, sun-dried, and then pickled variously in vinegar, brine, wine, or salt. They have a flavor similar to green olives and make a great addition to the relish tray. Sometimes the larger caper berries are used to garnish martinis, instead of olives.

# Stuffed Piquillo Peppers

You will probably need to locate a gourmet food store for these unique, cone-shaped peppers. The small, sweet, red peppers from the Navarre region of Spain are roasted over a wood fire, peeled, and canned in their own juices. If you can't find them, you can substitute roasted red bell peppers and roll them around the filling.

**SERVES 4**

½ cup soft, mild goat cheese

¼ cup softened cream cheese

½ cup cooked crabmeat

1 tablespoon chopped fresh parsley

Salt to taste

12 piquillo peppers, roasted and canned from Spain

1 lemon wedge

1 tablespoon extra-virgin olive oil

1. In a mixing bowl, combine the goat cheese and cream cheese with a wooden spoon until well blended.

2. Add the crabmeat to the cheeses and stir it in gently. Stir in the parsley and season with salt to taste. Set filling aside.

3. Drain the peppers of excess juices. Spoon filling into each pepper, dividing it equally among the peppers, and place the stuffed peppers in a casserole dish. Refrigerate it at this point if serving later.

4. Preheat the oven to 350°F. Bring the stuffed peppers to room temperature if they have been refrigerated.

5. Squeeze the lemon over the peppers and drizzle them with the olive oil. Bake for 10 to 15 minutes until heated through. Serve warm.

# Andalusian Almond Meatballs

Spain's fortified wine, sherry, is made in the Andalusian municipality of Jerez, located in the province of Cadiz. This recipe incorporates the nutty Andalusian spirit into the sauce for almond-studded meatballs.

**SERVES 4**

⅛ pound ground beef

⅛ pound ground pork sausage

2 tablespoons breadcrumbs

¼ cup finely chopped almonds

1 garlic clove, pressed

1 egg, beaten

1 teaspoon salt

½ cup all-purpose flour

4 tablespoons extra-virgin olive oil

2 tablespoons sherry

¼ cup heavy cream

Toasted sliced almonds for garnish

1. In a mixing bowl, combine the ground beef, ground pork sausage, breadcrumbs, almonds, garlic, egg, and salt and combine the mixture well with your hands.

2. Form the mixture into small (1-inch) meatballs. Toss the meatballs with the flour and set them aside.

3. Heat the olive oil in a large sauté pan and then fry the meatballs in it, turning to cook all sides. Remove the meatballs and set aside.

4. Deglaze the pan with the sherry and stir over medium heat with a wooden spoon, scraping up the browned bits left from the meatballs. Add the cream and stir to combine. Return the meatballs to the pan and simmer 5 minutes. Season the sauce with salt if necessary.

5. Spoon the meatballs onto a serving dish and pour the sauce over them. Scatter the toasted almonds over the meatballs and serve hot.

## Aging Sherry . . . . . . . . . . . . . . . . . . . . . . . . . .

The fortified wine of Jerez, Spain, is aged in wooden wine barrels employing a method called the *solera* system. The wine is first fortified with a percentage of brandy (varying from 15 percent to 17.5 percent, depending on the type of finished sherry it will become) after fermentation. Then the fortified new wine is aged in a series of up to nine oak casks. When the last cask in the series is bottled, it is not completely emptied. Part of the previous cask is transferred to the last cask with the oldest wine, and so on, up to the first cask. The new wine is added to the first barrels and the aging process continues.

# Shrimp Paella

Paella originated in Valencia as a laborers' lunch in the fields. It was cooked outdoors over a fire with local ingredients at hand. The original included land snails, but this recipe calls for shrimp, which makes it more enticing.

1. Preheat oven to 400°F.

2. Heat the olive oil in a paella pan (or 13-inch sauté pan) and sauté the shrimp over high heat for 1 minute. Remove and reserve the shrimp. Keep the pan with the olive oil on the heat.

3. Add the tomato purée and minced onion to the pan and stir for a minute. Add the garlic and turn the heat to low for several minutes. Add the clam juice, chicken broth, and salt to the pan, turn the heat to high and bring to a boil.

4. Sprinkle the rice evenly over the liquid in the pan and then cook 5 minutes, stirring often with a wooden paddle or spoon. Scatter the shrimp and peas on top of the rice and put the pan in the oven for 15 minutes.

5. Remove paella pan from the oven, cover with foil, and let rest in a warm place undisturbed for 5 to 10 minutes. Serve hot.

**SERVES 4**

2 tablespoons extra-virgin olive oil
12 large shrimp in the shell, frozen
¼ cup tomato purée
1 tablespoon minced onion
1 garlic clove, peeled and minced
1 cup bottled clam juice
2½ cups chicken broth
1 teaspoon salt
1½ cups Spanish bomba rice (short grain), or arborio
½ cup frozen peas

# Saffron Rice

This vibrant yellow rice is a perfect mini-side to go with small plates.

**MAKES 1½ CUPS COOKED**

1 cup water
¼ teaspoon salt
Pinch saffron threads
½ tablespoon extra-virgin
    olive oil
½ cup long-grain rice

1. Combine the water, salt, saffron, and olive oil in a saucepan, then stir in the rice.

2. Bring the mixture to a boil, reduce heat to medium-low, and cover with a lid.

3. Simmer for 20 minutes. Do not lift the lid before that! Remove from heat and serve hot.

## Jamon Serrano . . . . . . . . . . . . . . . . . . . . . . . . . .

No tapas spread is complete without a plate of thinly sliced dry-cured Spanish ham. Similar to Italy's proscuitto, *jamon serrano* translates to "mountain ham" in English, which refers to the higher elevation where the hams are cured in drying sheds. Serrano ham is served raw (uncooked, but cured) in thin slices, and its salty flavor is a perfect match for fruits and cheeses. It is perhaps the original tapa ("lid"), which was draped over a glass of wine, with or without bread, to serve as an insect barrier to the drink.

# Chicken Croquetas

Croquetas, or fritters, are a staple on every tapas menu I've ever seen. These are cooked in extra-virgin olive oil, Spain's favorite cooking medium.

**MAKES 20**

1 clove
¼ small onion
1 bay leaf
2 cups whole milk
4 tablespoons salted butter
¾ cup all-purpose flour
Pinch ground white pepper
Pinch nutmeg, freshly grated if
    possible
¼ cup finely diced carrots
6 ounces cooked chicken meat
¼ cup finely diced pickles
½ cup all-purpose flour
1 extra-large egg, beaten
½ teaspoon salt
¾ cup fine dry breadcrumbs
2 cups extra-virgin olive oil

1. Poke the clove into the quarter onion and place the onion and the bay leaf in a saucepan with the milk. Heat the milk over medium-high to scalding (not quite boiling) and then remove it from the heat. Let steep for 15 minutes, then remove and discard the onion and bay leaf.

2. Meanwhile, melt the butter in another saucepan, add ¾ cup of flour, and cook over medium heat for a few minutes, stirring with a wooden spoon. This will make a stiff roux. Gradually add the hot milk to the roux on the heat and whisk with a wire whip for 3 to 5 minutes to smooth out lumps. The roux will absorb the milk as it cooks and become a very thick béchamel sauce, which will be the base for the croquetas.

3. Remove the béchamel from the heat and stir in the white pepper, nutmeg, and carrots. Set aside. Pulse the cooked chicken meat in a food processor until it is finely ground. Then stir the chicken and pickles into the béchamel. Spread the mixture out onto a plastic-lined baking sheet, cover the top directly with plastic wrap and refrigerate it until it is cold. This may take an hour or two.

4. Arrange a production line for coating the croquetas by putting the ½ cup flour on a plate, the beaten egg mixed with ½ teaspoon salt in a bowl, and the breadcrumbs on a plate. When the chicken filling has cooled, remove the plastic from the top and cut the filling into twenty equal portions. Roll each portion into a cylinder, then roll it in the flour, dip it in the egg, and roll it in the breadcrumbs. Place it on a tray and repeat with the rest of the filling.

5. Put the olive oil in a deep pot or deep fryer and heat it to 375°F. Fry the croquetas in four to five batches for a minute or two, until they are golden brown. Drain on paper towels and serve hot.

# Red Sangria

In Spain this traditional wine punch is served in the hot summers as a refreshing chilled beverage. It can be served in a punch bowl for festive occasions or simply in a large pitcher that can be pulled out of the refrigerator at your whim.

1. Combine the red wine, brandy, lemon juice, orange juice, and sugar in a pitcher. Stir well and add sufficient ice to chill the mixture without all melting.

2. Slice the lemon and orange into ¼-inch-thick slices and add them to the pitcher.

3. Cut the apple in quarters, remove the core, and cut each quarter into slices and add them to the pitcher.

4. Add the raspberries to the pitcher.

5. Pour a glass for each person and be sure to include a piece of each fruit in each serving.

## Shades of Sherry. . . . . . . . . . . . . . . . . . . . . . . .

Fino, Manzanilla, amontillado, oloroso, cream—these are all different types of the Spanish fortified wine known as sherry. Varying in color, depth of flavor, and degree of dryness or sweetness, the different types of sherries provide a versatile drink that can be served as both an aperitif before a meal or as a dessert wine. Dry sherries are usually served chilled, while the sweeter ones are served at cellar temperature. Finos are dry and light; Manzanillas are dry, delicate, and slightly salty; amontillados are nutty, slightly sweet, and darker than finos; and olorosos are sweet and darker still. Cream sherry is another name for the sweet oloroso type.

# White Sangria

The original wine cooler, this sangria made with white wine instead of
red is lighter and perhaps more refreshing than the red version.

1. Combine the white wine, brandy, lemon juice, lime juice, orange juice, and sugar in a pitcher. Stir well and add sufficient ice to chill the mixture without all melting.

2. Cut the green grapes in half and add them to the pitcher.

3. Slice the orange, lemon, and lime into ¼-inch-thick slices and add them to the pitcher.

4. Cut the peach in half, remove the pit, and cut each half into wedges and add them to the pitcher.

5. Pour a glass for each person and be sure to include a piece of each fruit in each serving.

**SERVES 4**

3 cups dry, light white table wine
½ cup brandy (optional)
¼ cup freshly squeezed lemon juice
¼ cup freshly squeezed lime juice
¼ cup freshly squeezed orange juice
¼ cup sugar (or more to taste)
1 cup seedless green grapes
1 orange
1 lemon
1 lime
1 peach

# Spreads, Dips, and Sauces

# Catalonian Honey Garlic Mayonnaise

**MAKES 1 CUP**

1 clove of garlic, peeled and
    pressed
1 pasteurized raw egg
1 teaspoon lemon juice
1 cup extra-virgin olive oil
Salt to taste
4 tablespoons honey

This sweet version of aioli has a unique flavor that goes well with a
Spanish surf and turf of shrimp and lamb. Any flavor of honey you like,
such as orange blossom, blackberry, or lavender, can be used.

1. Put the pressed garlic, egg, and lemon juice in the bowl of a food processor fitted with the metal blade and pulse briefly to combine.

2. Turn the machine on and slowly pour the olive oil in a thin stream through the feed tube in the top until all of it is incorporated and emulsified. Add salt to taste.

3. Put the aioli in a bowl and stir the honey in by hand with a whisk.

# Middle Eastern Chickpea Purée

**MAKES 2 CUPS**

6 cloves garlic, peeled
½ teaspoon salt
1 can chickpeas
⅓ cup tahini
2 tablespoons lemon juice
2 tablespoons olive oil
½ teaspoon ground cumin

Also known as hummus, chickpea (or garbanzo bean) purée is a versatile condiment that
can be used as a dip or spread with anything from vegetables to breads to meats.

1. Purée the garlic and salt in a food processor. Add the chickpeas and purée to a paste.

2. Add the remaining ingredients and process until smooth, scraping down the sides of the bowl.

3. Transfer the finished purée into a bowl and serve with pita bread wedges.

### What Is Tahini? . . . . . . . . . . . . . . . . . . . . . . . .
Tahini is a paste made from ground sesame seeds that is used in Middle Eastern cuisine. It has a
nutty, malty flavor that pairs well with chick peas in the ubiquitous meze dish, hummus.

# Mexican Avocado Dip

Better known as guacamole, this pure and simple version of avocado dip is the best way to enjoy the avocado in all its naked glory. Stir in a little tomato salsa for more depth.

1. Cut soft-ripe avocadoes in half, remove seed and scoop out the flesh into a bowl. Mash it up with a potato masher. Stir in garlic.

2. Cut firm-ripe avocados in half, remove seed and scoop out the flesh, dice it and combine with lemon juice. Add to mashed avocado and mix together.

3. Season to taste with salt.

**MAKES 2 CUPS**

*2 soft-ripe avocados*
*1 clove garlic, minced*
*2 firm-ripe avocados*
*¼ cup lemon juice*
*Salt to taste*

# Tex-Mex Tomato Salsa

Tomato salsa can be served simply with tortilla chips for dippers, or it can be used as a relish on tacos, eggs, soups, and more.

1. Dice the tomatoes and red onion and combine in a large bowl. Cut the jalapeño pepper in half, remove the seeds, and then dice the flesh. Add to the bowl.

2. Mince the garlic clove, chop the cilantro, and add them to the bowl.

3. Add the lime juice, tomato juice, olive oil, chili powder, and a pinch of salt. Stir well, taste, and add more salt if needed.

**MAKES 3 CUPS**

*4 ripe tomatoes, seeded*
*¼ small red onion*
*1 jalapeño pepper*
*1 clove garlic, peeled*
*¼ bunch cilantro*
*1 tablespoon lime juice*
*1 tablespoon tomato juice*
*1 teaspoon olive oil*
*¼ teaspoon chili powder*
*Salt to taste*

# Sicilian Eggplant Relish

Serve cold or room temperature with toasts, crackers, or bread.

**MAKES ABOUT 2 CUPS**

1 eggplant (1 pound)
1 teaspoon kosher salt
4 to 6 stalks of celery
¼ large onion
¼ cup green olives
2 tablespoons olive oil
1½ cups canned diced tomatoes
1 tablespoon capers
3 tablespoons red wine vinegar
2 teaspoons sugar
1 tablespoon tomato paste
Salt and pepper to taste

1. Cut the eggplant in cubes and put them in a colander in the sink or over a larger bowl. Sprinkle them with salt and let them drain for 15 to 60 minutes.

2. Dice the celery and onion, and chop the green olives.

3. Sauté the celery and onion in 1 tablespoon of olive oil for 15 minutes over medium heat in a 6-quart pot. Transfer them to a bowl and reserve.

4. Sauté the eggplant in the pot for 10 minutes in the remaining olive oil. Return the sautéed celery and onions to the pot and add the remaining ingredients. Simmer for 20 minutes, stirring occasionally.

5. Taste and add salt and pepper to your taste. Refrigerate.

# Greek Yogurt Cucumber Sauce

In Greek this cool, refreshing sauce is known as *tzatziki*. In America we serve it with stuffed grape leaves and gyro sandwiches.

**MAKES 2 CUPS**

3 cups plain yogurt
1 to 2 small cucumbers, peeled
2 cloves garlic, peeled
1 tablespoon olive oil
1½ teaspoons red wine vinegar
¼ teaspoon salt
¼ teaspoon white pepper

1. Drain the yogurt in a coffee filter or cheesecloth-lined colander set over a larger bowl overnight in the refrigerator to make it thicker.

2. Grate the cucumbers and drain them for about 1 hour. Squeeze the excess water from them with your hands.

3. Put the garlic through a garlic press and then add it to the thickened yogurt along with the cucumbers, olive oil, vinegar, salt, and pepper.

4. Mix well; cover and refrigerate for several hours to let the flavors come together.

5. Serve with stuffed grape leaves, pita bread, or skewered lamb.

# Niçoise Olive Spread

This pungent black olive spread, also known by the name of tapenade, is easy to make ahead of time and have around to serve with crackers at a moment's notice.

1. Chop the olives, capers, and anchovy coarsely.

2. Mix the olives, capers, anchovies, lemon juice, olive oil, and pepper well.

3. Spread on bread and refrigerate any leftover spread.

**MAKES 1 CUP**

*40 pitted Niçoise olives*
*¼ cup capers*
*1 anchovy filet*
*1 teaspoon fresh lemon juice*
*2 teaspoons olive oil*
*Fresh cracked black pepper*

# Ponzu Dipping Sauce

This is a good dunk for tempura-cooked vegetables like asparagus, tempura shrimp, steamed dumplings, and fried wontons.

1. Heat soy sauce and sugar together in a saucepan until sugar dissolves.

2. Remove from heat and stir in lemon and lime juices. Let cool.

3. Stir in the green onions and serve at room temperature.

**MAKES 1 CUP**

*1 cup light soy sauce*
*¼ cup sugar*
*1 tablespoon lemon juice*
*1 tablespoon lime juice*
*2 tablespoons sliced green onion*

## Soy Sauce . . . . . . . . . . . . . . . . . . . . . . .

This popular condiment is made by brewing fermented soy beans, resulting in a brown liquid. It is usually a dark brown, thin, salty sauce, but some versions are lighter and some are syrupy and black.

# Mediterranean Warm Olive Oil Dip

**SERVES 8**

3 cloves garlic

6 anchovy filets, oil packed

½ cup extra-virgin olive oil

½ cup unsalted butter (1 stick)

Pepper to taste

Salt to taste

12 celery sticks

8 Belgian endive leaves

1 fennel bulb, sliced

12 zucchini spears

12 carrot sticks

8 bell pepper slices

1 cooked artichoke, leaves
    separated and chilled

4 green onions, trimmed

8 radishes

1 cup cauliflower florets

*Bagna Cauda* is the name for this fondue of olive oil and butter from Italy. My research shows that a version from France uses only olive oil and not butter. Both serve as a "warm bath" to dip raw vegetables into. A fondue pot is the perfect serving vessel.

1. Mince the garlic and chop the anchovies.

2. Heat the olive oil in a saucepan on medium-low and add the garlic and anchovies to it. Cook until the garlic is tender and the anchovies are melted. (Yes, they melt!)

3. Cut the butter into chunks and whisk them into the pan so they melt and blend in with the mixture. Season to taste with pepper and salt, remembering that the anchovies will already lend saltiness.

4. Transfer the dip to a fondue pot to keep it warm.

5. Arrange the celery sticks, endive, fennel slices, zucchini spears, carrot sticks, pepper slices, artichoke leaves, green onions, radishes, and cauliflower florets on a platter and serve with the warm dip.

# Mango Chutney

Sweet and spicy, this condiment is the ultimate cross between pickles and preserves.

**MAKES 1 TO 2 CUPS**

¾ cup sugar
¾ cup white wine vinegar
2 mangoes
1 garlic clove, peeled
¼ small green pepper
½ small onion
2 tablespoons grated fresh ginger
½ teaspoon white pepper
¼ teaspoon ground cinnamon
⅛ teaspoon ground cumin
Pinch ground cloves

1. Combine the sugar and vinegar in a nonreactive (stainless steel or Pyrex) saucepan and heat over low until sugar dissolves.

2. Peel and dice the mangoes, mince the garlic, and chop the green pepper and onion.

3. Add them to the pan along with the ginger, white pepper, cinnamon, cumin, and cloves.

4. Turn the heat up and simmer, stirring occasionally, for 30 minutes.

5. Remove from heat and refrigerate in a covered container.

## Coconut Curry Sauce . . . . . . . . . . . . . . . . . . .

Here is a good sauce to serve with Indian food. Heat 1 chopped shallot, 1 can coconut milk (unsweetened), 1 teaspoon curry powder, and ½ cup chicken broth to a boil. Add ¼ cup diced apple and ¼ cup diced banana, turn down the heat, and simmer until apples are tender. Purée in a blender, return to pot, reduce until thickened, and season with salt and white pepper.

# Greek Eggplant Spread

**MAKES 1 CUP**

1 medium eggplant (1 pound)
1 clove garlic, peeled and pressed
1 tablespoon plain yogurt
1 tablespoon lemon juice
3 tablespoons extra-virgin
   olive oil
½ teaspoon salt
¼ teaspoon pepper
2 tablespoons chopped fresh
   parsley
½ teaspoon dried oregano

*Melitzanosalata* is the Greek name for this creamy eggplant
spread. Serve with pita bread triangles and olives.

1. Preheat the oven to 400°F.

2. Prick the eggplant all over the skin with a fork and then bake it on a
   sheet pan for about 45 minutes, until it is soft. Let cool and then scoop
   the insides into a food processor. Discard the skin.

3. Purée the eggplant and then add the garlic, yogurt, lemon juice, olive
   oil, and seasonings. Pulse the food processor to combine everything.

4. Transfer the mixture to a bowl and refrigerate several hours to let the
   flavors mingle.

# North African Chili Sauce

**MAKES 1 CUP**

15 dried chili peppers
1 tablespoon chopped roasted
   red bell pepper
8 cloves garlic, peeled
½ cup extra-virgin olive oil
½ teaspoon ground coriander
½ teaspoon ground cumin
1 teaspoon salt

The hot pepper sauce known as *harissa* in Morocco and Tunisia is used as a condiment with
falafel and meats. This version cuts the heat, but only slightly, with red bell pepper.

1. Discard the stems from the chili peppers and soak the peppers in
   warm water until they are soft. Drain them and put them in a food
   processor with the remaining ingredients.

2. Process to a smooth consistency and refrigerate.

# Chinese Dipping Sauce

Use this sauce for dipping dim sum, potstickers, or eggrolls. You can also toss it with cooked spaghetti noodles for a cold noodle salad.

Combine all ingredients and serve with dumplings, egg rolls, spring rolls, etcetera.

## Another Dipping Sauce . . . . . . . . . . . . . . . . . . . . . . . .
To make a quick dipping sauce, mix equal parts of honey, Dijon mustard, and barbecue sauce together. Add a squeeze of ketchup for dipping French fries.

**MAKES ABOUT ¾ CUP**

*3 tablespoons soy sauce*
*3 tablespoons rice vinegar*
*1 tablespoon water*
*1 tablespoon lime juice*
*1 tablespoon sugar*
*1 tablespoon peeled fresh ginger, grated*
*¼ teaspoon chili oil*
*¼ teaspoon sesame oil*

# Indonesian Peanut Sauce

*Satay*: whether it's chicken, beef, pork, or shrimp, this is the sauce to serve with it for dipping.

1. Heat the peanut butter and water in a sauce pan over low heat, whisking to smooth out the peanut butter.

2. Add the chili pepper, garlic, brown sugar, ginger, and lemon juice and continue to cook over low heat for a few minutes, stirring to prevent scorching.

3. Stir in the soy sauce and remove from heat.

4. Stir in the chopped peanuts.

5. Serve with a variety of things such as skewered shrimp, chicken, beef, or pork.

**MAKES 1 CUP**

*½ cup smooth peanut butter*
*½ cup water*
*1 tablespoon minced red chili pepper (jalapeño or serrano)*
*2 garlic cloves, minced*
*2 teaspoons brown sugar*
*1 teaspoon grated fresh ginger*
*2 teaspoons lemon juice*
*1 tablespoon soy sauce*
*2 tablespoons chopped peanuts*

# Hoisin Dipping Sauce

Make this sauce for dipping Vegetable Spring Rolls
(page 212) or Chinese Onion Cakes (page 203).

(page 212) or Chinese Onion Cakes (page 203).

**MAKES ABOUT ¾ CUP**

5 tablespoons hoisin sauce

2 tablespoons soy sauce

3 tablespoons plum sauce

2 tablespoons oyster sauce

2 tablespoons honey

1 tablespoon dry sherry

1 tablespoon peanut oil

1 tablespoon peeled fresh ginger, grated

1 tablespoon minced garlic

1 teaspoon Chinese chili sauce

½ teaspoon five-spice powder

Combine all ingredients in a bowl and serve at room temperature.

## Asian Ingredients . . . . . . . . . . . . . . . . . . . .
Try to find an Asian market to purchase condiments and seasonings such as hoisin sauce, five-spice powder, and oyster sauce. They are often less expensive than if you were to buy them in a regular supermarket in the international foods section.

# Potsticker Dipping Sauce

This sauce was originally created for potstickers,
but you can use it for dipping any dim sum.

**MAKES ½ CUP**

¼ cup soy sauce

1 tablespoon sesame oil

2 tablespoons rice vinegar

5 jalapeño slices

1 tablespoon sliced green onions

½ teaspoon minced ginger

1 tablespoon peanut oil

½ teaspoon minced garlic

Combine all ingredients and serve at room temperature.

# Greek Taramosalata

This is a thick, creamy spread/dip with a hauntingly delicious
flavor. Serve as a spread or dip for bread or raw vegetables.

1. Cut the bread and onion into chunks. Juice the lemons and discard
   them.

2. Put all the ingredients in a food processor and blend until smooth.

## Substitutions for Tarama . . . . . . . . . . . . . . . . . . . . . . . .
If you can't find tarama or aren't sure about what it will taste like, you may try crabmeat or tuna
in its place to make a familiar-tasting seafood spread before you attempt the real thing.

**MAKES 2 CUPS**

*5 slices white bread, crusts
  removed*
*½ yellow onion*
*2 lemons*
*4 ounces tarama (cured carp or
  cod roe)*
*1 cup olive oil*
*1 cup mashed potatoes*

# American Vegetable Dip

Serve with crudités for dipping. Some good ones are zucchini sticks,
fennel slices, cauliflower and broccoli florets, carrot and celery sticks,
Belgian endive leaves, cherry tomatoes, and green onions.

1. Whisk together the mayonnaise and sour cream until smooth.

2. Add remaining ingredients and combine well.

3. Season with salt and pepper.

**MAKES 2 CUPS**

*1 cup mayonnaise*
*1 cup sour cream*
*1 teaspoon lemon juice*
*Pinch sugar*
*¼ teaspoon onion powder*
*¼ teaspoon garlic powder*
*½ teaspoon chopped oregano*
*½ teaspoon chopped dill*
*½ teaspoon chopped chives*
*½ teaspoon chopped thyme*
*1 teaspoon chopped parsley*
*½ teaspoon chopped tarragon*
*Salt and pepper to taste*

# French Red Bell Pepper Mayonnaise

**MAKES 1 CUP**

½ cup roasted red bell peppers
½ cup stale bread cubes
1 clove of garlic, peeled and
    pressed
1 pasteurized raw egg
1 teaspoon lemon juice
1 cup extra-virgin olive oil
Salt to taste

This is a version of rouille, the red pepper garlic mayonnaise served with fish soup in Provence. It is also a great dip for boiled new potatoes, grilled asparagus, or steamed artichokes, in addition to being a zingy spread for crostini and sandwiches.

1. Purée the roasted red bell peppers in a food processor with the bread. Transfer to a bowl and set aside.

2. Put the pressed garlic, egg, and lemon juice in the food processor and pulse briefly to combine.

3. Turn the machine on and slowly pour the olive oil in a thin stream through the feed tube in the top until all of it is incorporated and emulsified. Add salt to taste.

4. Transfer the mixture to the bowl with the peppers and stir well to combine.

5. Serve with boiled, fried, or roasted potatoes and toast.

## Roasting Peppers. . . . . . . . . . . . . . . . . . . . . . .

Put whole red bell peppers on a gas burner turned to medium heat and let them cook, crackle, and pop, turning with tongs until the skin is blackened and charred on all sides. Pick up peppers with tongs and put in a bowl, cover with plastic wrap, and let steam for 10 minutes. Remove peppers from the bowl, cut in half, and remove the seeds. Lay the peppers flat on a cutting board and scrape the charred skin off with a paring knife.

# Fruit Dip

This simple dip is delicious served with fresh strawberries, blueberries, and blackberries for dipping. If you make it ahead, refrigerate and let soften at room temperature a bit before serving.

1. Whip the cream cheese with an electric mixer to lighten it up and get it fluffy. Scrape down the sides of the bowl.

2. Add the marshmallow crème and combine thoroughly.

3. Transfer the dip to a serving bowl and serve.

**SERVES 6**

8 ounces cream cheese, softened
1 cup marshmallow crème

# Apricot Dipping Sauce

**MAKES 1 CUP**

½ cup apricot jam
1 teaspoon Dijon mustard
1 tablespoon lemon juice
1 tablespoon soy sauce
2 tablespoons ginger ale
1 teaspoon minced ginger
1 tablespoon toasted sesame
   seeds

Serve this dipping sauce with Shrimp Cigars (page 224) and other dim sum snacks.

1. Combine all ingredients in a food processor and purée.

2. Transfer sauce to a serving dish and sprinkle the sesame seeds on top.

## Plum Dipping Sauce . . . . . . . . . . . . . . . . . . . . . . . .
Make the Apricot Dipping Sauce, but add diced plums and chopped cilantro to it for a chunky sauce to serve with pork or poultry.

# Bread Basket

# Spanish Tomato Toast

Tomato toast is just one of the canapé-style tapas you'll
find in Spain. There is even chocolate toast!

**SERVES 6 TO 8**

1 slim loaf of crusty bread
2 garlic cloves, peeled
2 Roma tomatoes
¼ cup extra-virgin olive oil
1 tablespoon kosher salt

1. Preheat oven to 350°F. Slice the bread into ¼-inch-thick rounds and lay
   them out on a cookie sheet. Toast them in the oven for about 5 minutes.
   Turn them over and toast the other side. Remove from oven and set
   aside.

2. Rub the garlic on each piece of toast. Cut the tomatoes in half and rub
   the cut sides on each toast.

3. Drizzle toasts with olive oil and sprinkle with salt.

# Basque Tuna Toast

Of course you can use any tuna you like for these toasts,
including the lemon-flavored kind now available.

**SERVES 6 TO 8**

1 slim loaf of crusty bread
½ cup Traditional Aioli (page 11)
1 can high-quality canned tuna,
    preferably packed in oil from
    Spain
2 tablespoons chopped fresh
    parsley

1. Preheat oven to 350°F. Slice the bread into ¼-inch-thick rounds and lay
   them out on a cookie sheet. Toast them in the oven for about 5 minutes.
   Turn them over and toast the other side. Remove from oven and set
   aside.

2. Spread ½ teaspoon of aioli on each toast.

3. Place a chunk of tuna on the aioli and sprinkle with parsley.

# Italian Pizzettas

This recipe is enough for two pizzettas, each serving three as a component in a tapas selection.

1. Combine yeast with the warm water, sugar, and ¼ cup flour. Let sit 10 minutes. Add olive oil, cool water, salt, and ½ cup flour and combine with a wooden spoon. Add remaining flour and mix to form dough.

2. Knead dough on a floured board for 5 minutes, adding flour as needed to prevent sticking.

3. Let dough rise covered in an oiled bowl for 1 hour in a warm place. Punch down dough and divide in half. Roll the halves into balls and let rise, covered, for 1 hour.

4. Preheat oven to 475°F. Roll or stretch the dough into 6-inch circles on a lightly floured surface. Place the circles onto a cornmeal-dusted baking sheet.

5. Spread the tomato sauce over the surface of the dough using a ladle or spoon. Leave a 1-inch border. Dot the tomato sauce with chopped garlic, then scatter the cheese evenly over it. Bake for about 15 minutes, sprinkle oregano on top, cut into wedges, and serve.

**SERVES 6**

½ package yeast
3 tablespoons warm water
¼ teaspoon sugar
1¼ cups flour, plus more for kneading
1 tablespoon olive oil
¼ cup cool water
¾ teaspoon salt
1 tablespoon cornmeal
½ cup tomato sauce
1 tablespoon chopped garlic
2 cups mozzarella cheese, diced
1 teaspoon fresh oregano, chopped

# French Onion Pizza

This French pizza, known as *pissaladière*, is heaped with buttery cooked onions and studded with salty Niçoise olives and anchovies.

**SERVES 6**

½ package yeast

3 tablespoons warm water

¼ teaspoon sugar

1¼ cups flour, plus more for kneading

1 tablespoon olive oil

¼ cup cool water

¾ teaspoon salt

3 tablespoons butter

3 large onions, peeled

Pinch kosher salt

Fresh ground black pepper to taste

2 fresh thyme sprigs

½ cup pitted Niçoise olives

¼ cup grated Parmesan cheese

1. Combine yeast with the warm water, sugar, and ¼ cup flour. Let sit 10 minutes. Add olive oil, cool water, salt, and ½ cup flour and combine with a wooden spoon. Add remaining flour and mix to form dough.

2. Knead dough on a floured board for 5 minutes, adding flour as needed to prevent sticking.

3. Let dough rise covered in an oiled bowl for 1 hour in a warm place. Punch down dough and roll it into a tight ball and let rise, covered, for 1 hour.

4. Meanwhile, melt the butter in a large skillet. Cut the onion into thin slices and cook them slowly in the butter over medium-low heat until they are tender, about 15 minutes. Add the salt and pepper, sprinkle the fresh thyme leaves on the onions, and set aside.

5. Preheat oven to 450°F. Roll or stretch the dough into a 12-inch round on a lightly floured surface. Place the dough onto a cornmeal-dusted baking sheet and let rest 15 minutes.

6. Spread the cooked onions over the dough round and arrange the olives evenly around. Sprinkle the Parmesan cheese over the top and bake for 15 minutes, until crisp. Cut into squares to serve.

## "Raisin" to Be . . . . . . . . . . . . . . . . . . . . . . . . . . . . .

Plump raisins in warm water and Marsala or sherry, then poke them into pizza or foccacia dough before baking to make a delicious treat.

# Italian Focaccia Bread

Focaccia can be split horizontally and used to make sandwiches, topped with tomato sauce and other things and baked as a pizza, sliced into sticks to use as dippers, or cubed and toasted for croutons.

**MAKES 8 SANDWICH-SIZE SQUARES**

*2 packets yeast*
*1 teaspoon honey*
*2½ cups warm water*
*2 pounds flour*
*3 tablespoons olive oil*
*1 tablespoon salt*
*Olive oil for pan and top of dough*
*Coarse salt for top of dough*

1. Combine yeast, honey, and warm water in a stand-mixer mixing bowl and let it sit for 5 minutes.

2. Add 1 pound flour, 3 tablespoons olive oil, and salt; mix for 2 minutes, then let sit for 10 minutes.

3. Add remaining pound of flour, mix with dough hook for 5 minutes, then let dough rise covered in an oiled bowl for 1 hour in a warm place.

4. Punch down dough, then stretch and press it out onto a well-oiled 11" × 18" sheet pan. Cover and let rise in a warm place for 1 hour.

5. Preheat oven to 400°F. Uncover dough, drizzle with olive oil, poke holes all over the dough with your fingertips, sprinkle with salt, and bake for 25 minutes. Cool on a rack.

# Chapati Flatbread

**MAKES 6**

½ cup all-purpose flour
1 cup whole wheat flour
¾ cup warm water
4 tablespoons ghee or clarified butter

This flatbread is unleavened bread, which means it has no yeast, baking powder, baking soda, or other leavening agents in it. It is sometimes called "fry bread."

1. Make the dough by combining the flours together, then make a well in the center.

2. Add the warm water to the well and mix the flour into it until it comes together. Knead for 5 minutes to make a smooth dough. Divide the dough into 6 pieces and roll them into balls.

3. Dust the balls with flour and pat them out into 6-inch circles.

4. Heat a griddle or large skillet to high and melt the ghee or butter on it.

5. Cook the dough circles in the ghee for about 15 seconds per side. They will puff up in the middle and brown in little spots. Serve warm brushed with more ghee.

## Ghee . . . . . . . . . . . . . . . . . . . . . . . . . . . .

*Ghee* is clarified brown butter, a form of clarified butter that has been used for centuries in Indian cooking. Brown butter, or *beurre noisette* from French cuisine, is whole butter that has been melted and then the solids on the bottom browned.

# Catalan Flatbreads

This flatbread is made into thin strips instead of rounds,
and they are eaten like open-faced sandwich boats.

1. Combine yeast with the warm water, sugar, and ¼ cup flour. Let sit 10 minutes. Add olive oil, cool water, salt, and ½ cup flour and combine with a wooden spoon. Add remaining flour and mix to form dough.

2. Knead dough on a floured board for 5 minutes, adding flour as needed to prevent sticking.

3. Let dough rise, covered, in an oiled bowl for 1 hour in a warm place. Punch down dough and divide into six pieces. Roll the pieces into balls and let rise, covered, for 1 hour.

4. Meanwhile, cut the onion into thin slices and gently sauté in the butter over medium-low heat until they are tender, 10 to 15 minutes. Salt them and set aside.

5. Preheat oven to 350°F. Roll out the dough into 10-inch-long by 2-inch-wide strips on a lightly floured surface. Place the strips onto a cornmeal-dusted baking sheet. Poke the strips with a fork all over.

6. Spread the sautéed onions over the dough strips and sprinkle the thyme over them. Put two anchovies and several olives on each flatbread and bake for 10 to 15 minutes, until crisp.

**SERVES 6**

½ package yeast
3 tablespoons warm water
¼ teaspoon sugar
1¼ cups flour, plus more for kneading
1 tablespoon olive oil
¾ teaspoon salt
¼ cup cool water
1 small sweet onion, peeled
2 tablespoons butter
Pinch of kosher salt
1 teaspoon dried thyme
12 anchovy filets, oil-packed
½ cup pitted Spanish black olives

# Tuscan Mushroom Crostini

These earthy toasts are a great addition to any tapas spread.
They are also a great starter for an Italian-style meal.

**SERVES 6 TO 8**

1 baguette of crusty Italian bread
2 garlic cloves, peeled
¼ cup extra-virgin olive oil
1 tablespoon kosher salt
1 recipe Mushrooms in Sherry
  Garlic Sauce (page 12)
¼ cup chopped chives

1. Preheat oven to 350°F. Slice the bread into ¼-inch-thick rounds and lay them out on a cookie sheet. Toast them in the oven for about 5 minutes. Turn them over and toast the other side. Remove from oven and set aside.

2. Rub the garlic on each piece of toast, drizzle them with olive oil, and sprinkle with salt.

3. Slice the mushrooms and top the toasts with them. Sprinkle with chives and serve warm.

# French Crêpes

A good way to eat crêpes is brushed with melted butter, sprinkled with sugar,
drizzled with liqueur, folded in quarters, and eaten with your fingers. Crêpes also
make perfect wrappers for various savory fillings such as asparagus or chicken.

**MAKES ABOUT 16**

2 tablespoons unsalted butter
½ cup milk
½ cup water
2 eggs
½ cup flour
¼ teaspoon salt
Canola oil for frying crêpes

1. Melt the butter and put all the ingredients into blender. Blend 30 seconds. Scrape down the blender sides with a rubber spatula and then blend again for 30 seconds. Refrigerate for 1 hour.

2. Remix the chilled crêpe batter in blender for a few seconds before frying.

3. Fry the crêpes in a hot 6-inch nonstick pan brushed with oil, turning once. They don't take but a minute or two. Stack the finished crêpes between waxed paper.

# Provençal Leek Croutons

Cut the leek lengthwise and rinse out any dirt or sand. Discard the dark green
outer leaves and use only the tender white and light green parts of the leek.

**SERVES 6 TO 8**

1 baguette of French bread
¼ cup extra-virgin olive oil
1 tablespoon kosher salt
1 large leek, cleaned and diced
¼ cup butter
2 tablespoons dry white wine
Freshly ground black peppercorns

1. Preheat oven to 350°F. Slice the baguette into ¼-inch-thick rounds and
   lay them out on a cookie sheet. Toast them in the oven for about 5 minutes. Turn them over and toast the other side. Remove from oven and
   set aside. Drizzle each piece of toast with olive oil and sprinkle with
   salt. Set aside.

2. Sauté the leeks in butter over medium heat until cooked and tender,
   about 15 minutes. Add the white wine and cook another minute or two
   to reduce the liquid.

3. Spoon a little of the warm leek mixture onto each toast and grind a
   little black pepper on top of the leeks. Serve warm.

## Cheese Croutons. . . . . . . . . . . . . . . . . . . . . . . . . . .

Slice French bread into 1- to 2-inch-thick slices. Lay them out on a baking pan, brush them with
olive oil, and toast them in the oven on both sides. Top each toast with shredded Swiss cheese
and return to oven until brown and bubbly. Float these in French Onion Soup (page 99) for the
finishing touch.

# English Stilton Scones

SERVES 6

1½ cups flour

3 tablespoons sugar, plus more for sprinkling

½ teaspoon salt

1⅛ teaspoons baking powder

3 ounces cold, unsalted butter, cut in pieces

2 eggs

⅔ cup cream

½ teaspoon cayenne pepper sauce

¾ cup crumbled Stilton blue cheese

1 egg white

2 tablespoons chopped walnuts

These scones can be frozen before baking and then baked later from frozen for about 45 minutes.

1. Preheat oven to 400°F. Line a baking pan with parchment paper or spray lightly with oil.

2. Combine flour, sugar, salt, baking powder, and butter in a food processor with a metal blade. Process until mixture resembles cornmeal.

3. In a large bowl, combine eggs, cream, and cayenne pepper sauce using a whisk. Stir in cheese with a spatula or wooden spoon.

4. Add dry ingredients to the wet and fold in with spatula. Drop mixture into rounds on a prepared baking sheet.

5. Brush the scones with egg white and sprinkle them with walnuts. Bake for 15 minutes.

# Mexican Corn Tortillas

Tortillas are unleavened flatbreads that are made from
cornmeal or flour. This recipe is the cornmeal version.

**MAKES 6**

*1 cup cornmeal* (masa harina)
*½ teaspoon salt*
*½ cup warm water*

1. Mix the cornmeal and salt together, then add the water little by little with a wooden spoon until it becomes a stiff dough. Divide dough in half and then each half into thirds.

2. Roll each piece of dough into a ball and then flatten it to a circle, about 6 inches.

3. Heat a dry griddle or cast-iron skillet over medium-high and cook the tortillas one at a time in it. Cook for 2 minutes on the first side and then 1 minute on the second side. Serve warm.

## Tortilla Trick . . . . . . . . . . . . . . . . . . . . . . . . . .

Sometimes soft tacos get a little too juicy and they fall apart while you are eating them, so try using two corn tortillas for one taco to help prevent this problem. It also makes a more filling taco.

# Middle Eastern Pita Bread

The infamous flatbread that allows you to make a sandwich in a pocket
or an instant pizza is also used to make triangular crisps for dipping.

**MAKES 6**

½ packet yeast
¾ cup warm water
1½ teaspoons olive oil
½ teaspoon salt
1¾ cups flour

1. Combine yeast with the warm water and stir. Add olive oil and salt and mix again. Add 1¼ cups flour and combine with a wooden spoon. Add another ¼ cup flour and mix with hands to form dough.

2. Knead dough on a floured board for 10 minutes, adding the remaining flour as needed to prevent sticking. (Use more flour if necessary to prevent sticking.)

3. Let dough rise covered in an oiled bowl for 1½ hours in a warm place. Punch down dough and divide it into six pieces. Roll them into balls with your hands, cover, and let rest 5 minutes.

4. Roll the balls into 6-inch flat rounds on a floured board, cover, and let rest again for 15 minutes this time.

5. Preheat the oven to 500°F and place 2 pitas on a baking sheet pan. Bake for 5 to 10 minutes. Remove the pan from the oven and take the baked pitas off and put 2 more on the hot pan. Bake them in the oven for 3 to 5 minutes (the preheated pan will make the baking time less. Repeat with the remaining 2 rounds.

## Toast Names. . . . . . . . . . . . . . . . . . . . . . . . . .

There are a variety of names for snacks on toasted pieces of bread; crostini, crôutes, bruschetta, and croutons to name a few.

# Côte d'Azure Salt Cod Croutons

Salt cod purée, known as *brandade* in France, is a luxurious spread for
toasts, and a great filling for stuffed Spanish piquillo peppers.

**SERVES 6 TO 8**

1 baguette of French bread
¼ cup extra-virgin olive oil
1 tablespoon kosher salt
½ pound salt cod, soaked for 24
    hours, water changed 4 times
1 garlic clove, peeled
⅓ cup milk
¼ cup olive oil
1 tablespoon lemon juice
Pinch nutmeg
1 teaspoon black pepper
Salt to taste

1. Preheat oven to 350°F. Slice the baguette into ¼-inch-thick rounds and lay them out on a cookie sheet. Toast them in the oven for about 5 minutes. Turn them over and toast the other side. Remove from oven and set aside.

2. Drizzle each piece of toast with olive oil and sprinkle with salt. Set aside.

3. Put the soaked and drained salt cod into a pot with water to cover. Bring the water to a simmer and poach for 10 minutes. Drain and take out any bones or skin.

4. Put the poached cod in a food processor with the garlic. Pulse a few times, then add the milk and oil through the feed tube with the machine running to make a thick purée. Stop adding the liquid if it starts to get too loose. You want a spread consistency.

5. Add the lemon juice, nutmeg, and pepper and pulse to combine. Taste and add salt if necessary.

6. Transfer the spread to an earthenware bowl and keep it warm in the oven until time to serve. Serve by spreading on the croutons.

# Italian Eggplant Bruschetta

Rustic toasts with eggplant purée are a good accompaniment
to salad or soup, as well as part of a tapas spread.

**SERVES 6 TO 8**

*1 baguette Italian bread*
*½ cup olive oil*
*6 cloves garlic, peeled*
*1 medium eggplant*
*2 tablespoons red wine vinegar*
*1 teaspoon salt*
*Extra-virgin olive oil*
*½ cup shaved Parmesan cheese*
*¼ cup fresh basil, chopped*

1. Preheat oven to 350°F. Slice the baguette into ¼-inch-thick rounds and lay them out on a cookie sheet. Brush both sides with olive oil then toast them in the oven for about 5 minutes. Turn them over and toast the other side. Remove from oven, rub one side of each toast with garlic clove, set aside.

2. Prick eggplant all over with a fork, bake in the oven directly on top rack with foil underneath on bottom rack for about 1 hour, until tender. Remove from oven and let cool enough to handle. Use oven mitt to hold eggplant if necessary and scoop out the flesh into a bowl. Discard skin and stem.

3. Mince 3 to 4 cloves of garlic and add to cooked eggplant along with ¼ cup olive oil, red wine vinegar, and salt. Mix thoroughly. Adjust consistency with more olive oil and seasoning with salt as necessary.

4. Spread each toast with the eggplant mixture and drizzle with extra-virgin olive oil. Top each toast with a shaved Parmesan curl and a sprinkle of basil.

# French Bread Pizza

Fast and easy, this satisfies anyone who needs more than
"light hors d'oeuvres" with their happy hour.

1. Preheat oven to 400°F.

2. Slice the loaf of bread in half vertically, then in half again horizontally. You will have four pieces. Set them all with the crust-side down on a baking sheet.

3. Divide the tomato sauce evenly among the bread pieces, covering all the cut bread on the top. Sprinkle half of the cheese evenly divided among the four pieces.

4. Slice the zucchini into thin rounds, mince the shallot, and slice the sun-dried tomatoes into ribbons. Divide the zucchini, shallot, sun-dried tomatoes, and olives evenly among the pieces.

5. Sprinkle the thyme and remaining cheese over the top and bake for 15 minutes or until hot and bubbly. Cut each piece into 2-inch pieces for finger food or serve whole as an open-face sandwich.

## Pizza Possibilities . . . . . . . . . . . . . . . . . . . . . .
Use the same idea with pita bread, English muffins, hamburger and hot dog buns, croissants, and flour tortillas as with French Bread Pizza to make quick and easy pizzas.

**SERVES 4**

1 loaf French bread
1 cup tomato sauce
1 cup shredded provolone cheese
1 small zucchini
1 shallot, peeled
¼ cup sun-dried tomatoes, oil packed
¼ cup Niçoise olives
1 teaspoon chopped fresh thyme

# Cheese Course

# Spanish Cheese Plate

This is a balanced tasting of two Spanish cheeses with various noshes to accompany them.

**SERVES 4**

4 ounces Manchego cheese

4 ounces Cabrales blue cheese

4 pinquillo red peppers

¼ cup Marcona almonds

2 ounces membrillo (quince paste)

8 slices bread

1. Slice the Manchego and Cabrales cheeses and place them on a platter.

2. Arrange the peppers, almonds, and quince paste on the platter.

3. Place the bread in a basket and serve with the cheese plate.

# Italian Cheese Flight

This is a slice of Italy, cheese-style. The contrasting flavors run from nutty to salty to creamy to clean and chewy.

**SERVES 4**

3 ounces Parmigiano-Reggiano cheese

3 ounces ricotta salata cheese

3 ounces Gorgonzola blue cheese

3 ounces Fontina cheese

8 mozzarella boconcini cheeses

1. Crumble the Parmigiano-Reggiano and place it on a platter.

2. Put the ricotta salata, Gorgonzola, and Fontina on the platter in their whole pieces. Arrange the mozzarella boconcini around the other cheeses.

3. Serve with a knife and serving fork.

### Cheese Flight or Cheese Plate? . . . . . . . . . . . . . . . . .
In this book a cheese flight is a plate with a variety of about five different cheeses. They are meant to be tasted and compared, like a wine tasting. A cheese plate will have only two cheeses but will be accompanied by various complementary snacks, such as fruits, nuts, bread, and olives.

# Belgian Cheese Croquettes

These cheese fritters can be kept warm in a 250°F oven after they have been fried.

1. Poke the clove into the quarter onion and place the onion and the bay leaf in a saucepan with the milk. Heat the milk over medium-high to scalding (not quite boiling) and then remove it from the heat. Let steep for 15 minutes, then remove and discard the onion and bay leaf.

2. Meanwhile, melt the butter in another saucepan, add ½ cup of flour, and cook over medium heat for a few minutes, stirring with a wooden spoon. This will make a roux. Gradually add the hot milk to the roux on the heat and whisk with a wire whip for 1 minute to smooth out lumps. The roux will absorb the milk as it cooks and become a very thick béchamel sauce.

3. Remove the béchamel from the heat and stir in the white pepper, nutmeg, and cheeses with a wooden spoon. Beat in the egg yolk with a wooden spoon. Spread the mixture onto a plastic-lined baking sheet, cover the top surface directly with plastic wrap, and refrigerate it overnight.

4. Arrange a production line for coating the croquettes by putting the ½ cup flour on a plate, the egg white in a bowl, and the breadcrumbs on a plate. Add ¼ teaspoon salt and 1 teaspoon vegetable oil to the egg white and whisk until it is frothy.

5. Remove the plastic from the top of the croquette filling and cut the filling into 36 equal portions. Roll each portion into a ball and then roll it in the flour, dip it in the egg whites, and roll it in the breadcrumbs. Place it on a tray and repeat with the remaining portions. Refrigerate until you are ready to fry them.

6. Put 2 cups vegetable oil in a deep pot or deep fryer and heat it to 375°F. Fry the croquettes in small batches for about 3 minutes, until they are golden brown. Drain on paper towels and serve hot.

**MAKES 36**

1 clove
¼ small onion
1 bay leaf
¾ cup whole milk
3 tablespoons salted butter
½ cup all-purpose flour
Pinch ground white pepper
Pinch nutmeg, freshly grated if possible
1¾ cups shredded Gruyere cheese
1 cup grated Parmesan cheese
1 egg yolk
½ cup all-purpose flour
1 egg white
¼ teaspoon salt
1 teaspoon vegetable oil
1 cup dry breadcrumbs
2 cups vegetable oil

# Greek Cheese Plate

Soft, tangy feta is paired with salty mizithra and
accompanied by the Greek classics: olives, figs, and pita bread.

**SERVES 4**

4 ounces feta cheese
4 ounces mizithra cheese
12 Kalamata olives
4 fresh figs
1 walnut-size chunk of
honeycomb
4 rounds of pita bread

1. Cut the feta cheese into cubes and crumble the mizithra cheese into bite-size chunks. Place the cheeses on a platter.

2. Arrange the Kalamata olives, figs, and honeycomb on the platter.

3. Cut the pita bread into wedges and serve with the cheese plate.

# Italian Cheese Plate

Pecorino Romano is a hard sheep's-milk cheese and
provolone is a semihard cow's-milk cheese.

**SERVES 4**

4 ounces Pecorino Romano
cheese
4 ounces smoked provolone
cheese
4 sun-dried tomatoes, oil packed
4 pepperoncini peppers
8 prunes
¼ cup walnuts
4 (4-inch) squares of focaccia
bread

1. Crumble the Pecorino Romano into bite-size chunks and cut the provolone into cubes. Put the cheeses onto a platter.

2. Arrange the sun-dried tomatoes, pepperoncini peppers, prunes, and walnuts on the platter.

3. Cut the focaccia into sticks and put in a basket to serve with the cheese plate.

### Italian Wine . . . . . . . . . . . . . . . . . . . . . . . . . . .
Barolo, Barbaresco, and Chianti are three Italian red wines to drink with the Italian Cheese Plate.
Italian liqueurs to enjoy are Sambuca (anise), Frangelico (hazelnut), and Amaretto (almond).

# Cuban Quesadilla

The Cuban flavors of black bean and lime juice are combined
and translated into a classic Tex-Mex appetizer.

**SERVES 4**

¼ cup cooked black beans
2 tablespoons lime juice
1 tablespoon sour cream
4 (12-inch) flour tortillas
1 banana
½ cup grated queso blanco
    (cheese)
1 teaspoon vegetable oil

1. Mash the black beans and stir the lime juice and sour cream into them.

2. Spread two tortillas with the black bean mixture.

3. Peel and cut the banana into slices and place them on top of the black beans.

4. Sprinkle the cheese on the bananas and black beans and place the tortillas on top to make two "sandwiches."

5. Heat the vegetable oil in a large skillet and cook each sandwich for 1 to 2 minutes per side, until cheese is melted and tortillas are crisp and browned. Cut into wedges and serve hot.

# Mexi-Cali Pepper Jack Fondue

The dip known as chili con queso gets a bump up on
the heat scale with spicy pepper jack cheese.

**SERVES 6**

⅓ cup cream
3 ounces cream cheese, chunked
8 ounces pepper jack cheese,
    shredded
½ cup canned green chilies,
    chopped

1. Heat the cream in a pan. Stir in the cream cheese piece by piece until it all melts.

2. Add jack cheese over low heat and stir until creamy and melted.

3. Stir in green chilies, remove from heat, and spoon into ramekins or cups to serve.

# Classic Swiss Cheese Fondue

Gruyere and Emmenthal cheeses are the best Swiss cheeses to use in this fondue. If you don't have kirsch (cherry liqueur) substitute brandy.

**SERVES 8 TO 10**

1 clove garlic, peeled and pressed

1 tablespoon butter

1 cup dry white wine

¼ cup kirsch

2 pounds Swiss cheese, shredded

2 tablespoons flour

1 loaf crusty bread, torn or cut into bite-size pieces

1. Sauté garlic in butter for 3 minutes, add wine and kirsch, and reduce at a simmer for about 15 minutes. Turn heat to medium-low.

2. Toss the shredded cheese with flour, then whisk it into the hot wine mixture a handful at a time until it is all melted. Remove from heat.

3. Pour into a fondue pot, set over heat source, and serve with bamboo skewers and bread pieces.

### Substitutions. . . . . . . . . . . . . . . . . . . . . . . . . . . . . . .
Juice may be used instead of wine and cherry liqueur for a cheese fondue without alcohol. Juices to try are apple, white grape, ruby red grapefruit, and pear.

# Euro-Scandinavian Cheese Flight

Here is a tasting of nutty and creamy Northern European cheeses, including the creamy combination of Gorgonzola and Camembert: Cambozola.

**SERVES 4**

3 ounces Dutch Gouda

3 ounces Danish dill Havarti

3 ounces Swiss Gruyere

3 ounces Norwegian Jarlsberg

1 (4-ounce) wedge German Cambozola

1. Cut the Gouda and dill Havarti into cubes and put them on a platter.

2. Slice the Gruyere and Jarlsberg and arrange the slices on the platter.

3. Place the wedge of Cambozola on the platter and serve with a knife and serving fork.

### Aquavit . . . . . . . . . . . . . . . . . . . . . . . . . . . . . . . . . .
Serve the Scandinavian liqueur aquavit with this cheese flight. It is a clear liqueur made from rye and caraway. Serve chilled.

# Baked French Brie

Creamy Brie cheese is stuffed with sun-dried tomatoes, basil, and almonds and wrapped in puff pastry for this warm appetizer.

1. Preheat oven to 400°F.

2. Lightly flour puff pastry, and roll out until it is a bit thinner.

3. Cut the Brie in half horizontally and set the bottom half in the center of the pastry. Scatter the sun-dried tomatoes, basil, and almonds on the Brie bottom. Cover with the top half of the Brie.

4. Wrap the pastry up and around the Brie and seal the edges by pressing with your fingers. Cut off extra pastry and seal in those spots too.

5. Place pastry-wrapped Brie on a baking sheet, seam side down. Brush the pastry with the egg yolk mixed with the water. Bake 15 to 20 minutes until golden.

6. Serve warm with a knife and pie server.

**SERVES 12**

1 sheet puff pastry, thawed
1 wheel of baby Brie cheese (about 14 ounces)
¼ cup chopped sun-dried tomatoes, oil packed
2 tablespoons chopped basil
¼ cup sliced almonds
1 egg yolk
2 tablespoons water

# English Cheese Plate

**SERVES 4**

4 ounces Stilton blue cheese

4 ounces sharp Cheddar cheese

1 apple

1 pear

¼ cup walnuts

1 tablespoon candied ginger, diced

4 graham crackers

The king of English cheeses, Stilton, is paired with the original Cheddar here
for a cheese plate made for dessert accompanied by port wine.

1. Place the whole pieces of Stilton and Cheddar on a platter.

2. Slice the apple and pear and arrange them with the walnuts and candied ginger on the platter.

3. Serve the cheese plate with graham crackers and a cheese planer and knife.

# Greek Flaming Cheese

**SERVES 2**

1 (½-inch-thick) slice Kasseri cheese

Pepper to taste

Salt to taste

¼ cup flour

1 teaspoon olive oil

1 teaspoon butter

1 ounce brandy

1 lemon wedge

Pita wedges, warmed

Flaming cheese, known as saganaki, is served in Greek restaurants in America tableside.

1. Sprinkle the salt and pepper on both sides of the Kasseri cheese.

2. Put the flour on a plate and dredge the cheese in it on all sides.

3. Melt the butter with the olive oil in a sauté pan over medium heat.

4. Fry the cheese for about 2 minutes on each side. Remove from heat and pour the brandy over the top. Ignite the brandy carefully with a match, let it flame, and then douse the flame with a squeeze of lemon wedge.

5. Serve immediately with warm pita wedges.

# French Cheese Flight

Goat cheese, blue cheese, mild cheese, herbed cheese, and rind-cured soft cheese comprise this selection of French cheeses.

**SERVES 4**

*1 crotin chevre (goat cheese)*
*3 ounces Bleu de Bresse cheese*
*3 ounces Port Salut cheese*
*1 round Boursin herbed cheese spread*
*3 ounces Camembert cheese*
*8 strawberries*
*¼ cup green grapes*

1. Place the chevre, Bleu de Bresse, and Boursin whole on a platter with canapé spreaders.

2. Cut the Port Salut and Camembert into slices and arrange them on the platter.

3. Scatter the strawberries and green grapes around the platter and serve.

# North American Cheese Flight

United States cheeses from Oregon, California, and Iowa are served with Canadian and Mexican cheeses for a taste of North America.

**SERVES 4**

*3 ounces Tillamook Cheddar cheese*
*3 ounces Vella Dry Jack cheese*
*3 ounces Maytag Blue cheese*
*3 ounces Canadian White Cheddar cheese*
*3 ounces Mexican Cojita cheese*

1. Slice the Tillamook and Canadian cheddars and arrange them on a platter.

2. Crumble the Maytag Blue and Cojita cheeses and arrange them on the platter.

3. Place the whole piece of Vella Dry Jack on the platter and serve with a cheese planer and serving fork.

## Cheese Definition . . . . . . . . . . . . . . . . . . . .
Dry Jack is aged Monterey Jack cheese that has been rubbed with a combination of cocoa, oil, and pepper. The texture is hard, similar to fine Parmesan.

# Danish Savory Cheesecake

**SERVES 12**

½ cup flour

3 ounces melted butter

½ cup ground almonds

¼ cup grated Parmesan cheese

18 ounces cream cheese, softened

2 tablespoons cornstarch

3 eggs

1½ cups sour cream

6 ounces Danish Blue cheese, crumbled

½ cup dried apricots, chopped

1 teaspoon chopped fresh sage (optional)

The delicious combination of blue cheese and apricots makes this savory cheesecake an interesting selection for a tapas table.

1. Preheat oven to 350°F. In a bowl, combine flour, melted butter, almonds, and Parmesan cheese with a rubber spatula. Press mixture into the bottom of a springform pan that has been sprayed with oil. Bake for 10 minutes. Remove from oven and set aside.

2. With an electric mixer beat the cream cheese until fluffy. Add the cornstarch and beat it into the cream cheese.

3. Beat in the eggs one at a time, scraping down the bowl after each one. Stir in the sour cream.

4. Fold in the blue cheese, apricots, and sage. Pour the mixture into the springform pan and bake for 1 hour.

5. Remove from oven and cool at room temperature, then chill completely overnight.

6. Remove the ring of the springform pan and cut the cheesecake into wedges. Serve a wedge on a plate with crackers for each person or present the whole cheesecake with crackers on the side for a buffet.

# French Cheese Plate

Creamy Brie and salty Roquefort cheeses are matched
with classic French fruits, nuts, and olives.

1. Place the whole pieces of cheese on a platter.

2. Slice the pear and arrange it with the raspberries, nuts, and olives on the platter.

3. Slice the baguette and serve it with the cheese plate. Provide a cheese knife and serving fork.

**SERVES 4**

*4 ounces Brie cheese*
*4 ounces Roquefort blue cheese*
*1 French butter pear*
*Handful of raspberries*
*¼ cup toasted hazelnuts*
*¼ cup toasted almonds*
*12 Picholine olives*
*¼ cup Niçoise olives*
*1 baguette French bread*

# American Cheese Plate

American fruits and nuts are matched with two delicious American
cheeses and maple syrup butter for this star-spangled cheese plate.

1. Slice the Vermont Cheddar and place it on a platter with the whole piece of Maytag Blue.

2. Slice the apple and arrange it on the platter with the dried cherries and pecans.

3. Mix the maple syrup and butter together, put it in a small dish, and place it on the platter. Serve crackers with the cheese plate.

**SERVES 4**

*4 ounces Vermont Cheddar
cheese*
*4 ounces Maytag Blue cheese*
*1 apple*
*¼ cup dried cherries*
*¼ cup toasted pecans*
*1 tablespoon maple syrup*
*2 tablespoons soft butter*
*14 crackers*

## Artisanal Cheeses . . . . . . . . . . . . . . . . . . . . . . . . . .

America is home to many fine small-production cheeses. Here are a few to look for: Maytag Blue, Bellwether Farms Pepato, Cypress Grove Humboldt Fog, Cowgirl Creamery Mt. Tam, Grafton Village Cheddar, Laura Chenel Chevre, and Vella Dry Jack.

# English Savory Cheesecake

Dried pears and candied ginger stud this savory Stilton
cheesecake. Serve with port wine or cider.

**SERVES 12**

½ cup flour

3 ounces melted butter

½ cup ground walnuts

¼ cup graham cracker crumbs

18 ounces cream cheese, softened

2 tablespoons cornstarch

3 eggs

1½ cups sour cream

6 ounces Stilton blue cheese,
    crumbled

½ cup dried pears, chopped

1 tablespoon chopped candied
    ginger

1. Preheat oven to 350°F. In a bowl, combine flour, melted butter, walnuts, and graham cracker crumbs with a rubber spatula. Press mixture into the bottom of a springform pan that has been sprayed with oil. Bake for 10 minutes. Remove from oven and set aside.

2. With an electric mixer beat the cream cheese until fluffy. Add the cornstarch and beat it into the cream cheese.

3. Beat in the eggs one at a time, scraping down the bowl after each one. Stir in the sour cream.

4. Fold in the blue cheese, pears, and candied ginger. Pour the mixture into the springform pan and bake for 1 hour.

5. Remove from oven and cool at room temperature and then chill completely overnight.

6. Remove the ring of the springform pan and cut the cheesecake into wedges. Serve a wedge on a plate with crackers for each person or present the whole cheesecake with crackers on the side for a buffet.

# Nuts and Fruits

# Spanish Quince Paste

**SERVES 8**

5 ripe quinces
2 teaspoons lemon juice
4½ cups sugar
1½ teaspoons dry pectin
½ cup sugar (after curing)

Membrillo, as it is known in Spain, is easy to make, but requires patience to wait for it to cure—it takes twenty days. The result is beautiful, deep pinkish-orange ambrosia. The perfect accompaniment is Manchego cheese.

1. Peel the quinces, cut them into quarters, and then cut the core out of each quarter. Bring quinces and 5 cups water to a simmer in a large pot. Simmer about 1 hour, until quinces are tender when pierced with the tip of a knife.

2. Purée the quinces in a food processor after draining the water from them and then put them in a clean pot. Add the lemon juice and sugar to the pot, stir, and bring to a boil.

3. Reduce the heat and simmer about 1 hour, then remove from heat and add the pectin in by stirring.

4. In a loaf pan lined with parchment paper, pour the confiture and smooth out the top. Let cool, then cover loosely with parchment paper and let dry and cure for 10 days in a dark, cool, dry place.

5. Turn the quince paste out of the loaf pan after 10 days and wrap it loosely with parchment paper. Let it cure again for 10 days, then coat it with ½ cup sugar. Cut into slices to serve.

## Quince Paste by Any Other Name . . . . . . . . . . . . . . .
Quince paste is also enjoyed in Italy, where it goes by *cotognata*, and France, where it is known as *cotignac*. Oven drying is an option if you want to speed up the curing and drying process.

# Spanish Saffron-Poached Pears

Juicy pears are candied in syrup scented with saffron,
cinnamon, and lemon in this sophisticated fruit dish.

1. Rub the lemon juice on the pears.

2. In a sauce pan, combine the water, wine, and sugar and heat over low to dissolve the sugar. Add the lemon peel, cinnamon stick, and saffron and simmer for 5 minutes.

3. Add the pear halves to the simmering liquid and place a piece of parchment paper over the surface of the liquid. Poke a few slits in the paper to let steam escape.

4. Simmer the pears for 20 to 25 minutes, until tender. (Poke them with a paring knife to test for tenderness.)

5. Remove from heat and let pears cool in poaching liquid. Refrigerate in liquid until ready to serve.

**SERVES 4**

4 ripe pears, peeled, halved and cored
2 tablespoons lemon juice
2 cups water
¼ cup white wine
½ cup sugar
1 strip lemon peel
1 cinnamon stick
¼ teaspoon saffron

# Mexican Caramel Apple Wedges

**SERVES 6**

1 pound caramels, unwrapped
¼ cup canned goat milk
2 cups chopped pecans
3 red apples
1 yellow apple
1 green ripe apple (Granny Smith)

*Cajeta* is a Mexican goat-milk caramel sauce.
This is a simplified version of cajeta used as a dip.

1. Melt the caramels and goat-milk over low heat.

2. Toast the pecans in the oven for 12 minutes at 350°F.

3. Cut the apples into quarters, cut out the cores, and cut the quarters into slices for dipping.

4. Arrange the slices of apples on a platter with the toasted pecans in a bowl and the melted caramel in a warm earthenware bowl.

5. Dip an apple wedge into the caramel and then the pecans.

## Carnival Apples . . . . . . . . . . . . . . . . . . . . . . . . .

Make caramel apple wedges like caramel apples that are served at carnivals. Dip the apple wedges in caramel and nuts and then refrigerate them to set the caramel. Serve the predipped apple wedges with popcorn and other carnival treats.

# Cuban Tropical Fruit Plate

Exotic and flavorful describe this fruit salad composed of eight different tropical fruits, shredded coconut, and a touch of rum.

1. Toss all the fruits together gently in a large bowl.

2. Chill fruit salad before serving.

3. Serve the salad on individual plates or in one large bowl.

**SERVES 6**

*1 sliced guava*
*½ cup passionfruit seeds*
*1 carambola (starfruit), sliced*
*1 banana, peeled and cut into rounds*
*½ cup tangerine segments*
*½ papaya, sliced*
*½ cup fresh pineapple chunks*
*½ cup peeled, diced mango*
*¼ cup shredded coconut*
*1 tablespoon dark rum*

# Middle Eastern Almond-Stuffed Dates

These treats are good for dessert, after dessert with coffee, with tea, and even alone as a snack. They are also a simple, sweet, and divine accompaniment to Parmesan cheese.

1. Cut a slit on one side of each date and remove the pit. Replace it with an almond.

2. Place the powdered sugar in a bowl.

3. Roll the dates in the powdered sugar.

**SERVES 6**

*12 Medjool dates*
*½ cup whole almonds*
*1 cup powdered sugar*

Marzipan and Mascarpone . . . . . . . . . . . . . . . . . . . . . . .
Another delicious filling for dates is marzipan, a sugary confection made with almond paste. Mascarpone cheese (Italian cream cheese) is also a less-sweet alternative for stuffing dates.

# Mediterranean Mascarpone-Filled Figs

**SERVES 8**

½ cup toasted almonds

1 tablespoon almond paste

½ cup mascarpone or cream cheese

8 fresh purple mission figs

Creamy clouds of almond mascarpone float in fig "flowers" in this appetizer or dessert.

1. Chop the almonds in a food processor until finely chopped. Add the almond paste and mascarpone cheese and process until well mixed.

2. Cut the tips off the figs and then cut an X down through the top of each fig. Spread the wings of the figs apart to accommodate the filling.

3. Spoon a tablespoon of the almond mixture into each fig. Serve immediately.

### Figgy Fillings . . . . . . . . . . . . . . . . . . . . . . . . .
Other things to fill figs with are pecan cream cheese, chocolate mousse, walnuts, and mint and prosciutto mascarpone cheese.

# Pacific Rim Pickled Peaches

**MAKES 4**

4 peaches

1 star anise

1 cup rice vinegar

2 cups water

⅓ cup sugar

1½ teaspoons salt

These piquant peaches will last six months if refrigerated.
Serve them chilled as a relish with roast duck or pork.

1. Wash and dry the peaches, keep them whole.

2. Put the star anise in the bottom of a jar large enough to fit 4 peaches and 3 cups of liquid. Put the vinegar, water, sugar, and salt in the jar and stir.

3. When the sugar has dissolved, stir again, then add the peaches. Cover with a lid tightly and refrigerate at least 3 days.

# American Spiced Apple Rings

These aren't the spiced apples dyed with red food coloring that come in jars. These poached apples have a subtle scent of orange, cinnamon, and rosemary.

1. Cut the apples into rings and rub the lemon juice on the apple rings.

2. In a sauce pan, combine the water, cider, and sugar and heat over low to dissolve the sugar. Add the orange peel, cinnamon sticks, and rosemary and simmer for 5 minutes.

3. Add the apple rings to the simmering liquid and place a piece of parchment paper over the surface of the liquid. Poke a few slits in the paper to let steam escape.

4. Simmer the apple slices on low for 20 to 25 minutes, until tender. (Poke them with a paring knife to test for tenderness.)

5. Remove from heat and let apple rings cool in poaching syrup. Refrigerate in syrup until ready to serve.

**SERVES 4**

4 apples, peeled and cored whole
2 tablespoons lemon juice
1¼ cups water
1 cup apple cider
½ cup sugar
1 strip orange peel
3 cinnamon sticks
1 sprig fresh rosemary

# Spanish Clementines and Blood Oranges

Clementines are a type of mandarin orange that was developed in
Spain. They are seedless, easy to peel, and sweet.

**SERVES 4**

2 blood oranges
1 teaspoon rose water
¼ cup pomegranate seeds
2 clementines or mandarin
    oranges

1. Slice the tops and bottoms off the blood oranges and set them on one of the cut surfaces.

2. With a sharp knife, cut the peel and pith off the oranges in downward strips around each orange to reveal the flesh. Cut the oranges into thin slices across the width, making round wheel slices. Remove any seeds.

3. Arrange the orange slices on four plates and sprinkle the rose water over them. Sprinkle the pomegranate seeds over the slices.

4. Peel the clementines and separate them into individual sections. Scatter the sections onto the blood oranges, dividing them among the four plates.

## Spain's Tangerine. . . . . . . . . . . . . . . . . . . . . . . . . .

Clementines are tiny, seedless oranges that were developed first in Spain. They are similar to mandarin oranges and tangerines. They are grown in California now too, but the climate in Spain is perfect for these gems. Clementines are very easy to peel.

# American Brined Pumpkin Seeds

You need to scrape your own pumpkin out for the seeds
in this recipe. A small pie pumpkin is perfect.

**SERVES 4**

1 cup raw pumpkin seeds
1 cup water
2 tablespoons kosher salt

1. Rinse the pumpkin seeds and dry them overnight on paper towels.

2. Create a brine by mixing the salt with the water until it dissolves.

3. Soak the pumpkin seeds in the brine overnight.

4. Drain, but don't rinse, the pumpkin seeds and dry them on paper towels overnight.

5. Preheat oven to 250°F. Spread the pumpkin seeds in a single layer on a baking sheet. Bake for 1 hour.

# Spanish Sweet and Spicy Almonds

Almonds grow everywhere in Spain, so you will definitely find them on tapas menus.

**SERVES 4**

2 tablespoons extra-virgin
    olive oil
1 teaspoon salt
1 teaspoon pimentón or paprika
¼ teaspoon cayenne pepper
¼ cup honey
1 cup whole almonds, skin on

1. Preheat oven to 350°F.

2. Combine the olive oil, salt, pimentón, cayenne pepper, and honey in a bowl with a fork. Add the almonds and stir to coat.

3. Pour the coated almonds onto a baking sheet lined with nonstick foil and separate them into individual nuts with a fork.

4. Bake for 10 minutes, stir the nuts around, and bake another 5 minutes. Let cool on the foil and then break them into individual nuts and store them in a tin with a tight-fitting lid.

## Extra Spice . . . . . . . . . . . . . . . . . . . . . . . . . . . .

Toss the sweet and spicy almonds with a mixture of equal parts sugar and salt and a big pinch of cayenne pepper and cinnamon while they are still warm. Then let them cool. They will have a frosty coating of spicy crystals when they harden.

# Rosemary Walnuts

SERVES 4

1 tablespoon olive oil
1 tablespoon chopped fresh
    rosemary
1 teaspoon black pepper
¼ cup honey
Pinch kosher salt
1 cup walnut halves

Serve these fragrant nuts alone, or mix them with other
flavored or roasted nuts to make "mixed nuts."

1.  Preheat oven to 350°F.

2.  Combine the olive oil, rosemary, pepper, honey, and salt in a bowl with
    a fork. Add the walnuts and stir to coat.

3.  Pour the coated walnuts onto a baking sheet lined with nonstick foil
    and separate them into individual nuts with a fork.

4.  Bake for 10 minutes, stir the nuts around, and bake another 5 minutes.
    Let cool on the foil and then break them into individual nuts and store
    them in a tin with a tight-fitting lid.

# Asian Honey Ginger Peanuts

SERVES 4

2 tablespoons heavy cream
1 tablespoon grated fresh ginger
1 teaspoon soy sauce
¼ cup honey
2 cups shelled peanuts, roasted
    but unsalted
Pinch kosher salt

These peanuts are good to nibble alone, and they are also good in a salad made of shredded
cabbage, chicken, and cold (spaghetti) noodles with sesame seeds and peanut dressing.

1.  Preheat oven to 350°F.

2.  Combine the cream, ginger, soy sauce, and honey in a bowl with a fork.
    Add the peanuts and stir to coat.

3.  Pour the coated peanuts onto a baking sheet lined with nonstick foil
    and separate them into individual nuts with a fork.

4.  Bake for 10 minutes, stir the nuts around, and bake another 5 minutes.
    Sprinkle nuts with salt, break them into individual nuts, and let cool on
    the foil. Store in a tin with a tight-fitting lid.

# Louisiana Praline Pecans

These sweet tidbits are made from whole individual (shelled)
pecans with a rum praline coating on each one.

**SERVES 4**

1 tablespoon heavy cream
1 tablespoon dark rum
¼ teaspoon Tabasco sauce
1 cup pecan halves
¼ cup brown sugar

1. Preheat oven to 350°F.

2. Combine the cream, rum, and Tabasco in a bowl. Add the pecans
   and stir to coat. Add the brown sugar and toss with a fork to coat the
   pecans.

3. Pour the coated pecans onto a baking sheet lined with nonstick foil
   and separate them into individual nuts with a fork.

4. Bake for 10 minutes, stir the nuts around, and bake another 5 minutes.
   Let cool on the foil and then store in a tin with a tight-fitting lid.

## Rum and Sugar . . . . . . . . . . . . . . . . . . . . . . . . . . . .

Most anywhere sugarcane grows rum is made, because rum is made from sugarcane. This
includes the Caribbean. Jamaican rum is dark and slightly sweet, and Puerto Rican rum is lighter
and drier. Whether the rum is dark, gold, white, or spiced, it is usually 80 proof, which means it is
40 percent alcohol. The exception is 151 rum, which is 75.5 percent alcohol. Beware!

# Persian Almonds

**SERVES 4**

*2 tablespoons heavy cream*
*½ teaspoon ground coriander*
*1 teaspoon rose water*
*¼ cup honey*
*1 cup whole blanched almonds*
*(no skins)*

Rose water and coriander scent these almonds.
Almonds are (botanically speaking) in the rose family.

1. Preheat oven to 350°F.

2. Combine the cream, coriander, rose water, and honey in a bowl with a fork. Add the almonds and stir to coat.

3. Pour the coated almonds onto a baking sheet lined with nonstick foil and separate them into individual nuts with a fork.

4. Bake for 10 minutes, stir the nuts around, and bake another 5 minutes. Let cool on the foil. Break up into individual nuts and then store them in a tin with a tight-fitting lid.

## Blanching and Skinning Almonds . . . . . . . . . . . . . . . .

To blanch and skin whole almonds with skin on, boil for 1 minute. Drain and cool for a few minutes. Slip the skins off by pinching the almonds between your thumb and forefinger. The skins will slip right off and the almonds will pop out.

# Indian Pistachios

Fragrant and elegant, orange-flower pistachios are like a
crunchy version of the candy Turkish Delight.

**SERVES 4**

2 tablespoons heavy cream
1 teaspoon grated orange zest
1 teaspoon orange flower water
¼ cup honey
2 cups shelled pistachios

1. Preheat oven to 350°F.

2. Combine the cream, orange zest, orange-flower water, and honey in a bowl with a fork. Add the pistachios and stir to coat.

3. Pour the coated pistachios onto a baking sheet lined with nonstick foil and separate them into individual nuts with a fork.

4. Bake for 10 minutes, stir the nuts around, and bake another 5 minutes. Let cool on the foil and then break them into individual nuts and store them in a tin with a tight-fitting lid.

# Salads

# Moroccan Blood Orange and Red Onion Salad

Oranges and onions are a classic combination that is served
as a salad along with *tagines* (stews) in Moroccan cuisine.

**SERVES 4**

3 blood oranges
1 small red onion, peeled
2 tablespoons olive oil
2 teaspoons lemon juice
Salt and pepper to taste
1 tablespoon chopped fresh
   parsley

1. Cut the top and bottom off the oranges and stand them up on their cut
   ends. With a serrated paring knife, cut away the rind in top-to-bottom
   strips. Remove as much white pith as you can.

2. Turn the oranges on their sides and cut crosswise into slices. Arrange
   the orange slices on a plate.

3. Cut slices from the onion crosswise and scatter them across the orange
   slices.

4. Put the olive oil, lemon juice, salt, pepper, and parsley in a jar with a
   lid and shake the ingredients together.

5. Pour the vinaigrette over the oranges and onions and serve at room
   temperature or chilled.

# Italian Antipasto Salad

This is a family-style salad, to be served on a large platter and
shared at the table on individual smaller plates.

1. Toss the salad greens with the Italian dressing and place them in the middle of a platter.

2. Arrange the olives, peppers, and artichoke hearts around the salad greens.

3. Roll each slice of salami into a tight roll and place them around the platter.

4. Cut the provolone cheese into cubes and scatter them over the platter.

5. Serve with small plates and salad tongs.

## Wilted Spinach Salad . . . . . . . . . . . . . . . . . . . . . .

Mix together ¼ cup cider vinegar, 2 tablespoons hot bacon fat, ½ cup olive oil, a pinch of sugar, 1 teaspoon minced onion, and salt and pepper to taste. Toss warm dressing with spinach and crumbled bacon. Top with chopped hard-boiled egg and sliced mushrooms.

**SERVES 4**

1 cup mixed salad greens
¼ cup Italian dressing
¼ cup black olives
¼ cup pepperoncini peppers
¼ cup sliced roasted red bell
    peppers
¼ cup artichoke hearts,
    quartered
8 to 12 slices salami
4 ounces provolone cheese

# Provençal Vegetable Salad

**SERVES 4**

¼ cup diced onion

2 tablespoons diced red bell pepper

2 tablespoons diced green bell pepper

2 cloves minced garlic

¼ cup olive oil

1 cup diced eggplant

½ cup diced zucchini

¼ cup diced tomatoes, fresh or canned

1 tablespoon fresh thyme, chopped

Salt to taste

Pepper to taste

Eggplant, zucchini, red onions, bell peppers, tomatoes, and garlic
are cooked with herbs and olive oil to make this vibrant salad.

1. Sauté the onion, peppers, and minced garlic in olive oil for 5 minutes.

2. Add the eggplant and zucchini, toss to coat with oil, then add the fresh tomatoes and thyme.

3. Cover and simmer for 30 minutes, stirring occasionally.

4. Season with salt and pepper and chill.

5. Serve chilled or at room temperature.

# Greek Tomato Salad

This is Greek salad without the lettuce and with more
tomatoes. Try Greek olive oil for authentic flavor.

1. Make a dressing by mixing together oregano, oil, and vinegar, then
   season to taste with salt and pepper.

2. Slice the tomatoes and arrange them on a platter. Slice the red onion
   thinly and scatter over the tomato slices.

3. Peel and seed the cucumber and cut it into thin slices and scatter the
   slices over the red onion.

4. Pour the dressing over the vegetables on the platter. Crumble the feta
   cheese and scatter the olives over the salad.

5. Serve with side plates and serving utensils.

## Niçoise Salad . . . . . . . . . . . . . . . . . . . . . . . . . . . . .

Niçoise salad is a composed salad that makes good tapas eating. It consists of tuna, tiny green
beans, boiled new potatoes, hard-boiled eggs, anchovies, tomatoes, and Niçoise olives. It is
named after Nice, the area where the olives come from.

**SERVES 4**

1 teaspoon dried oregano
½ cup olive oil
3 tablespoons red wine vinegar
Salt to taste
Pepper to taste
2 beefsteak tomatoes
¼ red onion
½ cucumber
2 ounces feta cheese
¼ cup Kalamata olives

# Valencia Oranges with Orange-Flower Water

SERVES 2

*2 Valencia oranges*
*1 teaspoon orange-flower water*
*2 tablespoons chopped pistachios*

Oranges are given an exotic treatment with fragrant orange-blossom essence and pistachios.

1. Slice the tops and bottoms off the Valencia oranges and set them on one of the cut surfaces.

2. With a sharp knife, cut the peel and pith off the oranges in downward strips around each orange to reveal the flesh. Cut the oranges into thin slices across the width, making round wheel slices. Remove any seeds.

3. Arrange the orange slices on a plate and sprinkle the orange-flower water over them. Scatter the pistachios over the slices.

## Knock-Knock . . . . . . . . . . . . . . . . . . . . . . . . . . . .

Valencia oranges are sweet oranges that are often employed in juice making. Seville oranges are bitter oranges and are used to make marmalade and liqueurs. Navel oranges are sweet oranges that have no seeds.

# European Celery Root Slaw

This crunchy salad is a good accompaniment with pâté and
cheese, roast chicken, or as part of a salad sampler.

**SERVES 4**

½ pound celery root
¼ cup minced shallots
¼ cup olive oil
2 tablespoons lemon juice
1 teaspoon grated lemon zest
1 teaspoon Dijon mustard
Salt and pepper to taste
2 tablespoons chopped chives

1. Peel the celery root and cut it into ¼-inch-thick slices. Stack the slices a few at a time and cut them into julienne strips. Place the strips in a large bowl.

2. Put the shallots, olive oil, lemon juice, lemon zest, mustard, salt, pepper, and chives in a jar with a lid and shake to combine.

3. Pour the dressing over the celery root and toss to combine. Cover and refrigerate for at least 1 hour.

# American Carrot Salad

The contrasting colors of carrots and green onions and the flavors of
lemon and mustard make this a bright salad, both in color and flavor.

**SERVES 4**

½ cup salad oil
2 tablespoons honey mustard
1 tablespoon lemon juice
Salt to taste
Pepper to taste
4 medium carrots
2 green onions

1. In a blender, combine salad oil, honey mustard, and lemon juice and blend until smooth. Add salt and pepper to your taste, then set aside.

2. Peel and shred the carrots and put them in a mixing bowl.

3. Slice the green onions and toss them with the shredded carrots.

4. Pour the dressing over the carrot-onion mixture and toss well to combine.

5. Refrigerate overnight to let the flavors develop.

# Belgian Endive with Apples and Blue Cheese

**SERVES 4**

2 Belgian endives
1 apple
2 tablespoons olive oil
1 teaspoon minced shallot
1 teaspoon lemon juice
Salt and pepper to taste
2 ounces Danish blue cheese

This is an elegant and simple salad. You can accessorize it
with chopped candied or toasted walnuts if you desire.

1. Slice the endives across the width into 1-inch pieces, discarding the core end.

2. Core the apple and slice it into ¼-inch slices. Stack the slices and cut into julienne strips.

3. Combine the olive oil, shallot, lemon juice, salt, and pepper in a small jar, put the lid on and shake vigorously.

4. Toss the endive and apple together in a large bowl, add the dressing, and toss to coat.

5. Divide the salad among four plates and crumble the blue cheese over each serving.

## Endless Endive Ideas . . . . . . . . . . . . . . . . . . . . . .
You can also make this salad with whole endive leaves, or julienne them lengthwise into long, delicate sticks. Serve the endive leaves whole as hors d'oeuvres with a bit of blue cheese and diced apple on one end, or use the leaves as tender scoops for vegetable dip on a crudités platter.

# Avocado and Mango Salad

This combination of avocado, mango, and lime can go with anything from tacos to grilled fish.

1. Cut the avocados in half and remove the pits. Cut the avocado, still in the skin, into long thin strips. Scoop them out of the skin with a large spoon. Fan the strips out on a serving plate.

2. Peel the mango skin with a knife, then cut the sides off of the pit.

3. Cut the mango into cubes and scatter them over the avocados.

4. Whisk the shallot, olive oil, lime juice, salt, and pepper together in a bowl.

5. Drizzle the mixture over the salad and serve.

**SERVES 4**

*2 avocados*
*1 mango*
*1 tablespoon minced shallot*
*¼ cup olive oil*
*1 tablespoon lime juice*
*Salt and pepper to taste*

# Italian Caesar Artichokes

This salad made with tender artichoke hearts and fresh Caesar dressing can be served alone or atop a bed of romaine lettuce.

1. Put the egg yolk, lemon juice, garlic, anchovy paste, mustard, and Worcestershire sauce in a blender and blend briefly.

2. With the blender on, slowly pour the olive oil through the hole in the lid of the blender.

3. Add the Parmesan cheese and blend. Taste and add pepper and salt as necessary.

4. Cut the artichoke hearts in quarters and toss them with the Caesar dressing.

5. Divide the salad among four small plates to serve.

**SERVES 4**

*1 pasteurized egg yolk*
*1½ teaspoons lemon juice*
*1 teaspoon minced garlic*
*2 teaspoons anchovy paste*
*1 teaspoon Dijon mustard*
*Dash of Worcestershire sauce*
*½ cup olive oil*
*1 tablespoon grated Parmesan cheese*
*Pepper to taste*
*Salt to taste*
*1 cup artichoke hearts*

# Mediterranean Shaved Fennel

**SERVES 4**

½ cup olive oil

2 tablespoons lemon juice

1 teaspoon grated lemon zest

1 tablespoon minced shallot

1 tablespoon chopped fresh
    oregano

1 teaspoon fennel seeds

Salt to taste

Pepper to taste

2 fennel bulbs

Fennel has a light licorice flavor and a celerylike crunch, making it a perfect side for grilled fish.

1. Combine olive oil, lemon juice, lemon zest, shallot, oregano, and fennel seeds in a blender and blend until smooth. Add salt and pepper to taste.

2. Slice the fennel bulbs very thin and toss them in a bowl with the vinaigrette.

3. Refrigerate for an hour and serve chilled.

# American Fruit Salad

**SERVES 4**

½ cup cubed cantaloupe

½ cup cubed honeydew melon

½ cup cubed watermelon

½ cup red grapes

½ cup quartered strawberries

This classic fruit salad is the perfect accompaniment with breakfast, granola and yogurt, eggs, brunch dishes, sandwiches, and lunches.

1. Toss all the fruits together gently in a large bowl.

2. Chill fruit salad before serving.

3. Serve the salad family-style or divide it among four small plates.

### Pink Grapefruit Salad. . . . . . . . . . . . . . . . . .
A refreshing salad combination is pink grapefruit and avocado. Simply arrange slices of avocado and sections of peeled pink grapefruit in a pinwheel pattern on a salad plate and drizzle with grapefruit juice and a splash of olive oil. Sprinkle it with toasted coconut before serving.

# Soups and Stews

# Spanish Gazpacho

**SERVES 4**

*3 large red tomatoes*

*½ yellow bell pepper*

*¼ red bell pepper*

*¼ green bell pepper*

*1 sweet onion*

*1 cucumber*

*1 garlic clove, peeled*

*¼ cup sherry vinegar*

*¼ cup extra-virgin olive oil*

*¾ cup tomato juice*

*¼ cup bread cubes*

*¼ teaspoon pimentón or paprika*

*Pinch cayenne*

*Salt and pepper to taste*

*1 avocado, pitted, peeled, and diced*

*1 tablespoon lemon juice*

*4 green onions, trimmed but whole*

This is the traditional cold tomato soup from sunny Spain. Add diced tomatoes, bell peppers, and cucumbers before serving for a chunkier version.

1. Chop the tomatoes and place them in a blender.

2. Chop the peppers, onion, and cucumber and add them to the blender.

3. Add the remaining ingredients up to salt and pepper, to the blender and purée until smooth and there are no large chunks.

4. Pour into a serving pitcher and chill.

5. Serve chilled, garnished with avocados tossed in lemon juice and green onions.

### Gazpacho Shrimp Cocktail . . . . . . . . . . . . . . . . . . .
Try serving shrimp cocktail with gazpacho instead of red cocktail sauce. Take six jumbo prawns or shrimp and hook them over the lip of an oversized martini glass filled with chilled gazpacho.

# Zarzuela

This is a Spanish fish stew, similar to bouillabaisse in
Southern France and Cioppino in California.

1. In a large pot, sweat the onion and garlic in olive oil for 3 minutes. Stir
   in the tomato purée, add the tomatoes, and cook until soft. Add the
   brandy and cook until dry. Add the white wine and reduce by half.

2. Add the clam juice, chicken broth, pepper, pimentón, and parsley.
   Cook until the liquid has reduced by a third. Remove parsley from the
   broth and season it with salt to taste.

3. Bring the bouillon to a simmer, cut the fish into large chunks, and add
   them to it. Cut the lobster tail through the shell into 1-inch pieces. Add
   the lobster, shrimp, mussels, and clams to the pot. Cook until the mussels and clams open.

4. Stir in the Aioli-Romesco and serve hot with toasted bread slices.

Aioli-Romesco . . . . . . . . . . . . . . . . . . . . . . . .
Combine 2 garlic cloves, 1 egg yolk, 1 roasted red bell pepper, 1 tablespoon lemon juice, ¼ teaspoon smoked paprika (pimentón), 2 tablespoons almonds, and 2 thin slices of bread in a food
processor. Process until smooth and then pour in ½ cup olive oil in a stream with the machine
running. Season with salt and pepper to taste.

**SERVES 8**

1 medium onion, diced
5 garlic cloves
2 tablespoons olive oil
¼ cup tomato purée
2 large tomatoes, diced
3 tablespoons brandy
1 cup dry white wine
2 cups clam juice
2 cups chicken broth
1 teaspoon black pepper
1 teaspoon pimentón or paprika
5 parsley sprigs
Salt to taste
1 pound halibut
1 pound red snapper
1 pound cod
1 (1-pound) lobster tail
8 shrimp in the shell, deveined
1 cup mussels in the shell,
   scrubbed clean and
   debearded
1 cup clams in the shell, scrubbed
   clean
¾ cup Aioli-Romesco
1 loaf crusty bread

# Tomato Bisque

SERVES 4

¾ cup chopped onion
1 tablespoon olive oil
1 tablespoon butter
2 cups peeled and chopped
    tomatoes
3 cups chicken broth
½ cup cream
1 tablespoon cognac
Salt and pepper to taste
2 tablespoons chopped fresh
    chives

This creamy soup is perfect for sipping in small coffee mugs or demitasse cups, perhaps with a stick of grilled cheddar cheese panini.

1. Sauté onions in oil and butter until tender.

2. Add tomatoes and sauté 2 minutes.

3. Add chicken broth and simmer for 25 minutes.

4. Purée soup in a blender and return to the pan. Add cream and cognac over low heat, stir and season with salt and pepper.

5. Serve hot with a sprinkle of chives.

# French Chilled Potato Soup

SERVES 4

3 potatoes, peeled and diced
1 leek (white part only), diced
2 cups water
1 cup cream
Salt and pepper to taste
Fresh chives, chopped

Serve this soup, also known as vichyssoise, in tall, thin shot glasses for a tapas tasting.

1. Boil potatoes and leeks in water until tender, about 25 minutes.

2. Purée in blender, add cream, salt, and pepper, and blend well.

3. Chill thoroughly before serving. To serve, thin out with more cream if necessary, and garnish with chopped chives.

## Vichyssoise . . . . . . . . . . . . . . . . . . . . . . . .

Chef Louis Diat's creation of chilled potato leek soup was inspired by the soup his mother made him for breakfast as a child in France. Diat invented this classic while working at the Ritz-Carlton Hotel in New York.

# American Squash Soup

Fried whole sage leaves make an interesting garnish for this soup. Simply panfry fresh sage leaves in butter or olive oil for a minute and drain on a paper towel.

1. In a soup pot, sauté onions and sage in olive oil until translucent.

2. Add chicken broth and squash.

3. Bring to a boil, then simmer until squash is cooked, 45 minutes.

4. Purée soup in a blender until smooth, then season with salt and pepper.

5. Serve hot with croutons and bacon crumbles sprinkled on top of the soup.

½ cup chopped onion
1 tablespoon fresh sage, chopped
2 tablespoons olive oil
4 cups chicken broth
2 cups butternut squash, peeled and chopped
Salt to taste
Pepper to taste
½ cup croutons
¼ cup bacon crumbles

# Cioppino

SERVES 8

1 medium onion, diced

5 garlic cloves

2 tablespoons olive oil

¼ cup tomato sauce

2 large tomatoes, diced

3 tablespoons Marsala

1 cup red wine

2 cups clam juice

2 cups chicken broth

1 teaspoon black pepper

1 teaspoon oregano

5 parsley sprigs

Salt to taste

1 pound halibut

1 pound scallops

1 pound squid, cut into rings and tentacles

2 Dungeness crabs, legs and claws

8 shrimp in the shell, deveined

1 cup mussels in the shell, scrubbed clean and debearded

1 cup clams in the shell, scrubbed clean

This is an Italian fisherman's stew that originated at San Francisco's Fisherman's Wharf. Sourdough bread is all you need to serve with it.

1. In a large pot, sweat the onion and garlic in olive oil for 3 minutes. Stir in the tomato sauce, add the tomatoes, and cook until soft. Add the Marsala and cook until dry. Add the red wine and reduce by half.

2. Add the clam juice, chicken broth, pepper, oregano, and parsley. Cook until the liquid has reduced by a third. Remove parsley from the broth and season it with salt to taste.

3. Bring the bouillon to a simmer, cut the halibut into large chunks, and add them to it. Add the scallops, squid, Dungeness crabs, shrimp, mussels, and clams to the pot. Cook until the mussels and clams open.

4. Discard any unopened clams or mussels.

5. Serve hot in large bowls and be sure to add a little of each fish, shellfish, and squid to each serving.

# Bouillabaisse

This fish soup comes from sunny Provence in the south of France. It is traditionally served in two parts: the broth and the fish separately.

1. In a large pot, sweat the onion, celery, carrot, fennel, and garlic in olive oil for 3 minutes. Stir in the tomato paste and coat all of the vegetables. Add the tomatoes and cook until soft. Add the Pernod and cook until dry. Add the white wine and reduce by half.

2. Add the clam juice, chicken broth, water, peppercorns, cayenne pepper, orange peel, bay leaf, thyme sprigs, saffron, and parsley. Cook until the liquid has reduced by a third. Remove bay leaf, thyme sprigs, and parsley from the broth and season it with salt to taste.

3. Bring the bouillon to a simmer and add each filet of fish individually based on its thickness (thickest filets first). Cut the lobster tail through the shell into 1-inch pieces. Add the lobster, shrimp, mussels, and clams to the broth. Cook until the mussels and clams open.

4. Serve hot with potato rouille spread on toasted baguette slices.

Potato Rouille . . . . . . . . . . . . . . . . . . . . . . . .
Combine 2 garlic cloves, 1 egg yolk, 1 roasted red bell pepper, 1 tablespoon lemon juice, ¼ teaspoon cayenne pepper, and ¾ cup cooked potato in a food processor. Process until smooth and then pour in ½ cup olive oil in a stream with the machine running. Season with salt and pepper to taste.

**SERVES 8**

½ medium onion, diced
2 celery stalks, diced
1 carrot, diced
½ fennel bulb, diced
5 garlic cloves
2 tablespoons olive oil
1 tablespoon tomato paste
2 large tomatoes, diced
3 tablespoons Pernod
1 cup white wine
2 cups clam juice
2 cups chicken broth
2 cups water
1 teaspoon freshly ground black peppercorns
1 teaspoon cayenne pepper
1 teaspoon grated orange peel
1 bay leaf
2 sprigs of thyme
1 pinch saffron
5 parsley sprigs
Salt to taste
1 pound sole filets
2 pounds red-snapper filets
1 pound sea-bass filets
1 (1-pound) lobster tail
8 shrimp in the shell, deveined
1 cup mussels in the shell, scrubbed clean
1 cup clams in the shell, scrubbed clean
Potato rouille
1 baguette

# Tex-Mex Tortilla Soup

A staple of Tex-Mex and Southwestern cuisine, corn tortillas are sliced and simmered like noodles in a clean, bright broth accented with lime juice.

**SERVES 6**

1 small onion, diced

2 tablespoons olive oil

½ cup diced green chilies (canned)

1 cup diced, peeled tomatoes

4 cups chicken broth

2 cups chopped, cooked chicken meat

3 corn tortillas, cut in ¼-inch strips

1 teaspoon ground cumin

2 limes

Salt and pepper to taste

Cayenne-pepper sauce

¼ cup chopped cilantro

2 avocadoes, diced

1 cup crushed tortilla chips

1 cup shredded Monterey Jack cheese

1. In a soup pot, sauté the onion in olive oil until translucent. Add green chilies, tomatoes, and chicken broth.

2. Bring to a boil, add chicken meat, tortilla strips, and cumin, and simmer for 15 minutes. Remove from heat.

3. Cut one lime in half and add the juice to the soup pot. Cut the other lime in wedges to serve with each bowl.

4. Season the soup with salt, pepper, cayenne-pepper sauce, and cilantro.

5. Put diced avocado in soup bowls, ladle soup into bowls, garnish with cheese and tortilla chips, and serve with lime wedges.

## Variations on a Theme . . . . . . . . . . . . . . . . . . . . .

I have observed that there are basically three different styles of tortilla soup and countless variations within them. In Tex-Mex cuisine it is often a clear brothy soup; in the Southwestern cuisine of Arizona and New Mexico it often has a Native American influence with blue corn tortillas; and in California it is often a purée with fresh corn in it.

# French Onion Soup

This is a classic soup deep in the heart of comfort-food territory, especially on a rainy day.

**SERVES 4**

*1 large onion*
*1 tablespoon butter*
*1 tablespoon olive oil*
*¼ cup white wine*
*1 tablespoon brandy*
*2 cups chicken broth*
*2 cups beef broth*
*½ teaspoon dried thyme*
*Pepper to taste*
*Salt to taste*
*½ cup bread-cube croutons*
*½ cup shredded Swiss cheese*

1. Slice the onion and sweat in the butter and olive oil until caramelized. Cook a little longer to a rich mahogany color.

2. Deglaze the pan with the onions still in it with the wine and brandy, scraping up all the browned bits and cooking to make a reduction of caramelized onions.

3. Add chicken and beef broth and stir to combine into a soup consistency. Add thyme, salt, and pepper and simmer for 45 minutes.

4. Ladle the soup into individual crocks and top each with croutons and Swiss cheese.

# Miso Soup

This simple soup of miso broth with chunks of tofu and bits of green onion in it is perfect before sushi.

**SERVES 4**

*3 cups water*
*4 tablespoons miso*
*½ cup cubed tofu*
*1 sliced green onion*

1. Boil the water and combine it with the miso.

2. Divide the tofu among four bowls. Pour the miso broth into the bowls and garnish with the green onion.

3. Serve hot.

# Caribbean Curried Banana Soup

**SERVES 4**

2 cups chicken broth

1 ripe banana

1 large potato

1 Granny Smith apple

1 celery heart

1 sweet onion

1 cup cream

1 tablespoon dark rum

1 teaspoon curry powder

1 teaspoon salt

½ cup banana chips

2 tablespoons chopped fresh
   chives

This velvety soup has a variety of unlikely components that
combine to make a complex and satisfying flavor.

1. Put the chicken broth in a soup pot.

2. Peel the banana and potato, chop them, and put them in the soup pot.
   Core the apple, chop it and add it to the soup pot. Chop the celery
   heart and onion and add them to the soup pot.

3. Bring the soup to a boil and then lower the heat and simmer for 10 to
   15 minutes. Add the cream, rum, curry powder, and salt.

4. Put the hot soup in a blender and purée.

5. Serve the soup hot garnished with banana chips and chives.

## Chill It . . . . . . . . . . . . . . . . . . . . . . . . .

This soup is very good served chilled too. Let it cool to room temperature and refrigerate it. After
it is chilled, whisk in a little extra cream and pour it into tea cups. Sprinkle chives on top and
serve.

# Irish Pub Shepherd's Pie

You can use frozen hash browns for the shredded potatoes in this recipe for ease of preparation.

1. Preheat oven to 375°F.

2. Brown the ground beef, remove from pan and set aside. Sauté the onion, carrots, and celery in the vegetable oil for five minutes over medium. Add the mushrooms and cook 5 more minutes, then add the meat back to the pan.

3. Sprinkle the meat mixture with flour, stir, then add the beef broth and Worcestershire sauce. Simmer until thickened, stir in the cream and peas, and season with salt and pepper. Pour the stew into a casserole dish.

4. Mix the shredded potatoes, mayonnaise, and cheese together in a bowl and then spread the mixture over the stew.

5. Sprinkle the potatoes with paprika and bake for 30 minutes.

## Substitution . . . . . . . . . . . . . . . . . . . . . . . . . . . . . .
Mashed potatoes are the usual top "crust" for shepherd's pie, and you may use them instead of the shredded potatoes in this recipe. Mashed sweet potatoes are another option.

**SERVES 4**

1 pound ground beef
1 small onion, diced
2 carrots, peeled and diced
1 celery stalk, sliced
2 tablespoons vegetable oil
½ cup chopped mushrooms
2 tablespoons flour
1¼ cups beef broth
1 tablespoon Worcestershire sauce
¼ cup heavy cream
½ cup peas, fresh or frozen
Salt and pepper to taste
2 cups shredded potatoes
¼ cup mayonnaise
1 cup shredded cheddar cheese
Pinch paprika

# Italian Minestrone

**SERVES 6**

½ cup chopped onion

½ cup chopped carrots

¼ cup chopped celery

2 tablespoons olive oil

2 cloves garlic, minced

¼ cup chopped spinach

32 ounces chicken broth

2 cups chopped zucchini

1 cup chopped, peeled tomatoes

1 cup cooked white beans

½ cup broken spaghetti

Salt and pepper to taste

½ cup grated parmesan cheese

Serve this Italian-style vegetable soup with antipasto dishes
and bread for a light supper or as part of a tapas selection.

1. Sauté the onions, carrots, and celery in the olive oil 15 minutes.

2. Add garlic and spinach and cook until spinach is wilted.

3. Add chicken broth, zucchini, tomatoes, and white beans and bring to a boil.

4. Simmer for 15 minutes. Add the spaghetti and simmer 15 minutes longer, then season with salt and pepper.

5. Serve hot with Parmesan cheese sprinkled on top.

# Thai Coconut Chicken Soup

**SERVES 4**

1 can unsweetened coconut milk

1 teaspoon red curry paste

4 cups chicken broth

1 tablespoon lemon juice

1 tablespoon lemongrass, minced
very fine

2 raw chicken breasts, thinly
sliced

2 minced shallots

1 teaspoon grated fresh ginger
root

1 teaspoon fish sauce

¼ cup chopped cilantro

1 sliced Serrano chili pepper

½ cup sliced mushrooms

This gem of a soup sparkles with the bright flavors of lemongrass,
cilantro, ginger, and red curry paste in a coconut-milk broth.

1. Combine everything in a saucepan and bring to a boil.

2. Lower the heat and simmer for 20 minutes.

3. Serve piping hot.

# Cuban Black Bean Soup

Yummy and hearty, a big bowl of this soup is perfect solo for lunch, or served in smaller cups as part of a tapas-style meal.

1. Sauté onion and garlic in olive oil, add potatoes and chicken broth, and simmer for 30 minutes.

2. Add black beans and cumin and simmer 45 minutes.

3. Purée ⅓ of the soup in a blender and return it to the pot.

4. Stir in the lime juice, salt, cayenne-pepper sauce, and cilantro.

5. Serve with a garnish of Banana Salsa and sour cream.

## Banana Salsa . . . . . . . . . . . . . . . . . . . . .

Mix together 1 cup diced banana, 1 tablespoon diced jalapeño pepper, 1 tablespoon diced red bell pepper, ½ teaspoon olive oil, 1 teaspoon lemon juice, and 1 teaspoon minced cilantro. Season with salt and pepper if you think it needs it and serve immediately with black bean soup.

**SERVES 6**

¼ cup onion, diced
1 clove garlic, minced
2 tablespoons olive oil
1 large potato, peeled and diced
32 ounces chicken broth
2 cups cooked black beans
½ teaspoon ground cumin
1 tablespoon lime juice
2 teaspoons salt
5 drops cayenne-pepper sauce
2 tablespoons chopped fresh cilantro
1 cup banana salsa
⅓ cup sour cream

# Potatoes

# Spanish Fried Potatoes with Herbed Aioli

This is a necessity for a tapas party, as it is on almost every tapas bar and café menu.

**SERVES 4**

1 pound russet potatoes
2 cups extra-virgin olive oil
Salt to taste
½ cup Traditional Aioli (page 11)
2 tablespoons chopped fresh
    parsley
1 tablespoon chopped chives

1. Peel the potatoes and cut them into 1-inch chunks. If you won't be frying them right away, save them in water so they don't turn brown. Be sure to drain and blot them dry before frying so they won't splatter.

2. Heat the olive oil in a deep, heavy-bottom pot or a deep fryer to 275°F. Check with a candy thermometer for correct temperature.

3. Carefully lower the potato chunks (blotted dry) into the olive oil with a slotted spoon and poach them for about 10 minutes. This is to precook them, so they shouldn't turn golden in color yet. Drain the poached potatoes on paper towels and set aside.

4. Raise the temperature of the olive oil to 350°F. Carefully lower the poached potatoes into the olive oil again and fry them until they are crisp and golden brown. Drain the potatoes and sprinkle them with salt.

5. Mix the parsley and chives into the aioli and serve with the potatoes.

# British Chips

These potatoes are half of the famous duo "fish and chips." Serve with malt vinegar.

**SERVES 4**

2 pounds russet potatoes

3 cups vegetable oil

kosher salt

1. Peel the potatoes and cut them into 1-inch-wide, ½-inch-thick planks. If you won't be frying them right away, save them in water so they don't turn brown. Be sure to drain and blot them dry before frying so they won't splatter.

2. Heat the oil in a deep, heavy-bottom pot or a deep fryer to 325°F. Check with a candy thermometer for correct temperature.

3. Carefully lower 1 cup of the potato sticks (blotted dry) into the oil with a slotted spoon and poach them for about 8 minutes. This is to precook them, so they shouldn't turn golden in color yet. Drain the poached potatoes on paper towels and set aside. They can be kept at room temperature for several hours before the final frying.

4. Raise the temperature of the oil to 375°F. Carefully lower the poached potatoes into the oil again and fry them until they are crisp and golden brown, 1 to 2 minutes. Drain the fries and sprinkle them with salt.

## Deep-Fried Stuff . . . . . . . . . . . . . . . . . . . . . . .

The same establishments in Britain that make fish and chips have also started making deep-fried candy bars in recent years. State fairs in the United States have jumped on the bandwagon, offering deep-fried things like Twinkies, egg rolls, and even Coke.

# Belgian French Fries

SERVES 4

2 pounds russet potatoes
3 cups vegetable oil
Kosher salt

Known as *frietjes* in Belgium and *pommes frites* in France, these are the original "french fries."

1. Peel the potatoes and cut them into ½-inch-wide sticks. If you won't be frying them right away, save them in water so they don't turn brown. Be sure to drain and blot them dry before frying so they won't splatter.

2. Heat the oil in a deep, heavy-bottom pot or a deep fryer to 325°F. Check with a candy thermometer for correct temperature.

3. Carefully lower 1 cup of the potato sticks (blotted dry) into the oil with a slotted spoon and poach them for about 5 minutes. This is to precook them, so they shouldn't turn golden in color yet. Drain the poached potatoes on paper towels and set aside. They can be kept at room temperature for several hours before the final frying.

4. Raise the temperature of the oil to 375°F. Carefully lower the poached potatoes into the oil again and fry them until they are crisp and golden brown, 1 to 2 minutes. Drain the fries and sprinkle them with salt.

# Spanish Potato Fritters

*These fritters can be made and fried ahead of time and frozen.*
*Reheat in a 325°F oven for 15 to 20 minutes.*

**MAKES 20**

1 clove
¼ small onion
1 bay leaf
2 cups whole milk
4 tablespoons salted butter
¾ cup all-purpose flour
Pinch ground white pepper
Pinch nutmeg, freshly grated if
    possible
1 cup cooked potatoes, hand
    mashed or put through a ricer
½ cup all-purpose flour
1 extra-large egg, beaten
½ teaspoon salt
¾ cup fine dry breadcrumbs
2 cups extra-virgin olive oil

1. Poke the clove into the quarter onion and place the onion and the bay leaf in a saucepan with the milk. Heat the milk over medium-high to scalding (not quite boiling) and then remove it from the heat. Let steep for 15 minutes, then remove and discard the onion and bay leaf.

2. Meanwhile, melt the butter in another saucepan, add ¾ cup of flour, and cook over medium heat for a few minutes, stirring with a wooden spoon. This will make a roux. Gradually add the hot milk to the roux on the heat and whisk with a wire whip for about 5 minutes to smooth out lumps. The roux will absorb the milk as it cooks and become a very thick béchamel sauce.

3. Remove the béchamel from the heat and stir in the potatoes, white pepper, and nutmeg. Spread the mixture out onto a plastic-lined baking sheet, cover the top directly with plastic wrap, and refrigerate it until it is cool. This may take an hour or two.

4. Arrange a production line for coating the fritters by putting the ½ cup flour on a plate, the beaten egg mixed with ½ teaspoon salt in a bowl, and the breadcrumbs on a plate. When the filling has cooled, remove the plastic from the top and divide the filling into twenty equal portions. Roll each portion into an egg shape, then roll it in the flour, dip it in the egg, and roll it in the breadcrumbs. Place it on a tray and repeat with the rest of the filling.

5. Put the olive oil in a deep pot or deep fryer and heat it to 375°F. Fry the fritters in four or five batches for a minute or two, until they are golden brown. Drain on paper towels and serve hot.

## Spud Add-Ons
You can add spinach to these to make them "Florentine," or shredded cheddar cheese and crumbled bacon to make them "baked potato-y," and so on.

# Indian Potato Turnovers

Samosas, the Indian triangular or pyramid pastries, are the inspiration for these turnovers.

**SERVES 4**

*3 cups water*

*¼ teaspoon turmeric*

*1 cup diced frozen potatoes*

*1 sheet puff pastry, thawed in the refrigerator*

*1 egg, beaten with 1 teaspoon water*

*¼ cup frozen peas*

*1 teaspoon paprika*

*¼ teaspoon curry powder*

*¼ teaspoon cumin*

*¼ teaspoon coriander*

*½ teaspoon salt*

*¼ teaspoon lemon pepper*

1. Preheat the oven to 400°F.

2. Bring the water to a simmer and add the turmeric. Blanch the potatoes in the liquid for 3 minutes and strain them. Lay them out to cool.

3. Roll the puff pastry into an 11" × 11" square on a floured surface. Cut the square into four smaller squares. Paint the beaten egg on the pastry squares.

4. Put ¼ cup of the cooled potatoes in the middle of each square. Put 1 tablespoon frozen peas on top, then sprinkle the paprika, curry powder, cumin, coriander, salt, and lemon pepper over the vegetables.

5. Fold each square over to make a triangle to encase the filling. Press down on the outer edges with your fingers or a fork to seal.

6. Brush the egg on the turnovers and bake for 10 minutes. Turn the oven down to 350°F and continue baking for about 10 to 15 minutes longer.

# American Tavern Potato Skins

You know what kind of cheese this is if you're a "whiz" kid. It's the right cheese for the job.

1. Preheat oven to 350°F.

2. Cut the potatoes into wedges with 1 to 2 inches of skin on them. Toss them with the melted butter then the flour and arrange them on a baking sheet in one layer. Bake for 20 minutes and remove from the oven.

3. Scoop the extra potato flesh out of the skins and save it for another use.

4. Heat the peanut oil in a deep fryer, heavy pot, or wok to 375°F. Fry the potato skins in the oil in batches for 1 to 2 minutes. Drain on paper towels and arrange on plates skin-side down.

5. Fill the potato boats with melted cheese and bacon crumbles. Sprinkle with green onions, and top with sour cream.

## American Cheese . . . . . . . . . . . . . . . . . . . . . . . .
Some people turn their noses up at American cheese, but where would the cheeseburger be without it? What's more, pasteurized processed "cheese food" is actually more nutritious than other true cheeses because it has whey added back to it to make it meltable.

---

**SERVES 6**

4 russet potatoes
¼ cup butter, melted
½ cup flour
2 to 3 cups peanut oil
½ cup American cheese spread in a jar, melted
½ cup bacon crumbles
¼ cup sliced green onions
½ cup sour cream

# Spanish Potato-Stick Tortilla

**SERVES 4**

1 small onion, peeled

5 tablespoons pure olive oil, divided use

6 eggs

2 cups fried potato sticks

This is made with the crunchy fried potato sticks that are available canned in the snack and chip section of the supermarket.

1. Thinly slice the onion and sauté it in 2 tablespoons olive oil until cooked, about 5 minutes. Set aside.

2. Whisk the eggs in a bowl to break them up and bring together the whites and yolks into one solid color, but avoid whipping too much air into them. Add the potato sticks and the sautéed onions to the eggs. Stir to combine.

3. Heat 3 tablespoons olive oil in a 6-inch, nonstick sauté pan over medium heat. Add the egg mixture to the pan and cook for 1 minute. Lower the heat and continue cooking for about 2 to 3 minutes. When the eggs look like they've set, place a plate over the pan and flip the omelet onto it. Return the pan to the heat and slide the omelet, uncooked-side down, from the plate into the pan. Cook for 1 minute, then slide it onto a clean plate.

4. Cut the tortilla into wedges and serve hot.

# Latkes

These crispy potato pancakes traditionally served at Hanukkah are also
delicious in a brunch tapas spread, along with Florentine bagels.

1. Peel the potatoes and grate them. Put the grated potatoes in a bowl
   and fill with water to rinse.

2. Beat the egg in another bowl and add the onion, salt, pepper, and
   parsley to it.

3. Squeeze the water out of the shredded potatoes in handfuls and put
   them in the bowl with the egg. Sprinkle the flour over the potatoes,
   then mix everything together.

4. Heat the olive oil in a large skillet over medium-high and scoop latkes
   into it. Flatten the latkes and cook until brown and crisp on both sides,
   2 to 3 minutes per side.

5. Serve hot with applesauce and sour cream.

## Homemade Applesauce. . . . . . . . . . . . . . . . . . . .

It's easy to make your own applesauce. Peel, core, and cut three apples (one Golden delicious, one
Fuji, and one Gala) into chunks. Cook them in a saucepan over medium heat with 2 tablespoons
sugar, a cinnamon stick, and ¼ cup apple juice until they are fully cooked. Remove the cinnamon
stick and put the mixture through a food mill. Voila!

**MAKES 6**

½ pound potatoes
1 egg
2 tablespoons chopped yellow
 onion
½ teaspoon kosher salt
Pinch pepper
1 teaspoon chopped fresh parsley
1½ tablespoons flour
¼ cup olive oil
½ cup applesauce
½ cup sour cream

# American New-Potato Cups

This is an elegant tapa, perfect for special celebrations like New Year's Eve and Valentine's Day.

**SERVES 4**

8 red-skinned new potatoes
½ cup butter, melted
¼ cup sour cream
2 tablespoons chopped fresh
    chives
4 tablespoons salmon roe

1. Preheat oven to 350°F. Wash potatoes and bake until tender, about 30 minutes. Remove from oven and let cool slightly so you can handle them.

2. Cut each potato in half and scoop out a hole in the center of each half with a melon baller to make a cup. Discard the part you have scooped out or save it for another use.

3. Cut a tiny slice off the bottom of each potato half (so it won't roll around) and place the halves on a baking sheet.

4. Brush each potato cup with butter and bake until crispy, about 5 minutes. Let cool to room temperature.

5. Top each potato cup with a teaspoon of sour cream and a dollop of roe and garnish with chives.

# Warm Potato Salad

Serve this warm salad with a cold potato salad for contrast, or as a side to a fish entrée.

1. Cut the potatoes into chunks, leaving the skin on.

2. Put the potatoes in salted water and bring to a boil. Cook for 8 minutes, drain, and put in a large mixing bowl.

3. Dice the bacon and cook it in a skillet over medium heat until crisp. Remove the bacon crumbles and add them to the potatoes in the bowl.

4. Mix the lemon juice, oil, and pepper into the skillet with the bacon fat. Pour the bacon dressing over the potatoes and bacon.

5. Add the onion and tarragon and toss to coat the potatoes. Serve warm.

## Purple Potatoes . . . . . . . . . . . . . . . . . . . . . .

Try making potato salads with purple potatoes for an interesting look. Just cook them in the same way, or steam or roast them as in the recipe above. They come in a variety of purples and blues now so you can enjoy the indigo/violet end of the spectrum in your potato salad!

**SERVES 4**

1 pound red potatoes
1 teaspoon salt
5 slices bacon
¼ cup sliced sweet onion
1 tablespoon chopped fresh tarragon
¼ cup lemon juice
2 tablespoons walnut or olive oil
Pepper to taste

# Tempura Sweet Potatoes

SERVES 4

¾ cup beer
¾ cup flour
¾ teaspoon salt
2 cups vegetable oil
1 sweet potato, peeled and
   sliced thin

Serve these frittered slices with soy sauce or Ponzu Dipping Sauce (page 29) for dipping, along with Miso Soup (page 99) and sushi rolls.

1. Whisk beer into flour until smooth, then stir in salt.

2. Heat oil to 375°F in a deep fryer or large pot.

3. Dip sweet potato slices individually in batter, let excess drip off, then drop carefully into the hot oil.

4. Cook about 3 minutes, then remove from oil with a slotted spoon, chopsticks, or tongs.

5. Drain on paper towels or brown paper and serve immediately.

# American Potato Salad

SERVES 4

2 medium potatoes, peeled,
   cubed, and boiled
¾ cup mayonnaise
½ cup sour cream
1 tablespoon pickle relish
1 tablespoon chopped pimentos
½ teaspoon salt
2 tablespoons chopped fresh
   parsley
½ cup onion, diced

This good old picnic and BBQ fare is a good accompaniment to finger sandwiches and barbecued riblets for a tapas-style party meal.

1. Let the cooked potatoes cool to room temperature.

2. Add the remaining ingredients to the potatoes and mix to combine.

3. Chill in the refrigerator at least 1 hour before serving. Add more mayonnaise if it gets too dry before serving.

# Spanish Olive Oil Mashed Potatoes

Traditional mashed spuds go Iberian with the addition of extra-virgin olive oil instead of the customary butter. Sprinkle with pimentón for additional Spanish flavor.

**SERVES 4**

3 large potatoes, about 3 pounds
2 teaspoons kosher salt,
    divided use
2 ounces extra-virgin olive oil
⅓ cup milk
½ teaspoon white pepper

1. Peel potatoes and cut them into 2-inch uniform pieces.

2. Put potato pieces in a pot with cold water and 1 teaspoon salt to cover.

3. Turn heat to medium-high and bring potatoes and water to a boil. Then turn down to simmer and cook until the potatoes can be easily pierced with a fork, about 15 minutes.

4. Drain potatoes in a colander and let the steam dissipate for 5 minutes.

5. Put cooked potatoes in a bowl and mash with a potato masher or an electric mixer. Add olive oil and milk and mix to a creamy consistency. Season with salt and white pepper.

## Finger Mashed Potatoes . . . . . . . . . . . . . . . . . . . .

Combine 2 cups of mashed potatoes with two beaten eggs and pipe them from a pastry bag with a star tip into rosettes on a parchment-lined sheet pan. Brown the rosettes for 15 minutes in a 350°F oven and serve hot with sour cream to dip them in.

# Sweet Potato Salad

**SERVES 4**

1 large sweet potato, peeled,
    cubed, and steamed
¼ cup extra-virgin olive oil
2 tablespoons tarragon vinegar
1 tablespoon Dijon mustard
1 teaspoon honey
½ teaspoon salt
1 tablespoon chopped fresh
    tarragon
½ cup red onion, diced

This potato salad is a change of pace from the usual style of white potatoes and mayonnaise.

1. Let the steamed sweet potato cubes cool to room temperature.

2. Combine the olive oil, vinegar, mustard, honey, salt, and tarragon in a bowl with a whisk.

3. Add the sweet potato cubes and diced red onion to the bowl and toss to coat. Serve at room temperature.

### Sweeter Potatoes . . . . . . . . . . . . . . . . . . . . . . . .
Try roasting the sweet potatoes instead of steaming them. The natural sugars in the sweet potatoes will caramelize and brown to make a sweeter salad that can be served warm as a different kind of side dish for beef, turkey, or fish.

# Eggs

# Spanish Eggs Benedict

**SERVES 4**

*2 English muffins*

*1 avocado, peeled, pitted, and sliced*

*2 pieces chorizo sausage, 3 inches long*

*4 eggs*

*1 teaspoon distilled white vinegar*

*½ cup Chipotle Hollandaise Sauce (page 121)*

*1 tablespoon chopped cilantro*

*4 pinches pimentón or paprika*

Double the recipe and serve a whole English muffin
with two eggs for a full breakfast or brunch entrée.

1. Split English muffins, put on plate, cover, and keep in a warm oven until ready to use.

2. Poach eggs in simmering water with a teaspoon of distilled white vinegar until the eggs hold their shape, but still have runny yolk centers. Remove poached eggs from simmering liquid with a slotted spoon and lay them on several layers of paper towel. Trim any straggling pieces of egg white from the poached eggs.

3. Cut the chorizo sausages in half lengthwise and brown in a skillet.

4. On each muffin half put several slices of avocado, chorizo sausage, and then a poached egg. Spoon or pour hollandaise sauce to cover each egg. Top each egg with a sprinkle of pimentón and chopped cilantro. Serve immediately on four small plates.

# Chipotle Hollandaise Sauce

Put this sauce in a thermos to keep it warm while you prepare the food it will be served with.

1. Whisk egg yolks and water in a stainless steel or glass bowl over simmering water and cook until mixture thickens to ribbon stage.

2. Slowly pour melted butter into yolks, drop by drop at first, whisking constantly to form an emulsion. Pour the butter in a thin stream after the emulsion gets started and the sauce starts to thicken; continue whisking.

3. Remove bowl from heat and whisk in the lemon juice and chipotle pepper purée.

4. Season sauce with salt and white pepper to taste.

## Chipotle Peppers. . . . . . . . . . . . . . . . . . . . . . . . .
Chipotle peppers are red ripe jalapeños that have been smoked. They are available canned in adobo sauce. Purée the chipotles and adobo sauce in a food processor or blender.

4 egg yolks
1 tablespoon cold water
8 ounces butter, melted
1 tablespoon lemon juice
2 tablespoons chipotle pepper purée
Salt to taste
White pepper to taste

# Italian Noodle Fritatta

SERVES 4

1 small onion, peeled
2 tablespoons olive oil
6 eggs
½ teaspoon kosher salt
¼ teaspoon pepper
1 tablespoon chopped fresh
    parsley
1 cup cooked spaghetti, cold or
    room temperature

This is like a puffy omelet with cooked spaghetti in it. Usually frittatas are made with potatoes instead of noodles.

1. Thinly slice the onion and sauté it in 2 tablespoons olive oil in a 6-inch nonstick sauté pan over medium heat.

2. Whisk the eggs in a bowl to break them up and bring together the whites and yolks into one solid color, but avoid whipping too much air into them. Stir in the salt, pepper, and parsley.

3. Add the eggs to the pan with the onions and cook for 1 minute. Add the spaghetti, lower the heat to medium, and continue cooking for about 2 to 3 minutes.

4. When the eggs look like they've set, place a plate over the pan and flip the fritatta onto it. Return the pan to the heat and slide the fritatta, uncooked-side down, from the plate into the pan. Cook for a minute or two, then slide it onto a clean plate.

5. Cut the fritatta into wedges and serve hot.

# British Scotch Eggs

Often made with sausage, this has a slightly different flavor
and the coating is not raw meat like the sausage version.

**MAKES 8**

8 ounces sliced ham
1 teaspoon Worcestershire sauce
1 teaspoon Dijon mustard
¼ teaspoon cinnamon
Pinch ground allspice
Pinch nutmeg
¼ teaspoon pepper
2½ cups breadcrumbs
2 raw eggs, beaten
6 hard-boiled eggs, peeled
½ cup bacon fat
½ cup vegetable oil

1. Mince the ham in a food processor until ground fine. Transfer it to a large bowl.

2. Add the Worcestershire sauce, mustard, cinnamon, allspice, nutmeg, pepper, breadcrumbs, and ¾ of the beaten eggs to the ham and mix it all together.

3. Dip the hard-boiled eggs into the remaining beaten egg. Mold the mixture around each hard-boiled egg with your hands to encase it.

4. Heat the bacon fat and vegetable oil in a deep pot over medium-high heat. Add the eggs and brown them on all sides. Turn down the heat if they brown too fast.

5. Drain them on paper towels and gently cut them into quarters to serve.

## Scotch Quail Eggs . . . . . . . . . . . . . . . . . . . . . . . .
Boil quail eggs for about 5 minutes, let cool, then peel. Substitute them for the hard-boiled eggs in the British Scotch Eggs recipe. Serve them whole or cut in half.

# American Pickled Eggs

MAKES 6

6 hard-boiled eggs, peeled
½ cup beet juice
½ cup water
1 cup white vinegar
1 teaspoon minced onion
¼ teaspoon dill seed
Pinch sugar
⅛ teaspoon celery seed
Pinch kosher salt

After a week of pickling, the bright color from the beets penetrates through the white and into the edge of the yolk, making an apricot transition from magenta to yellow.

1. Pack the eggs into a pint jar.

2. In a saucepan, heat the beet juice, water, vinegar, onion, dill seed, sugar, and celery seed over medium-low heat until simmering.

3. Pour the pickling liquid into the jar over the eggs up to ½ inch from the top.

4. Screw the lid on and let cool to room temperature, then refrigerate for 1 week.

5. Cut eggs into halves and sprinkle with kosher salt to serve.

# French Brie Omelets

When serving this tapas-style, either cut it into slices or
serve it with a knife and serving utensil.

**SERVES 1 TO 4**

*2 eggs*
*½ teaspoon water*
*Pinch kosher salt*
*Pinch pepper*
*1 teaspoon chopped fresh
    tarragon*
*1 tablespoon butter*
*1 slice ham, cut in small squares*
*1 ounce brie, cut into pieces*
*1 teaspoon chopped fresh chives*

1. Break eggs into a small, metal bowl and whisk with the water, salt, and pepper. Add the tarragon and whisk to combine.

2. Melt the butter in a nonstick 6-inch sauté pan over medium-high heat. Sauté the ham in it briefly, then add the egg mixture.

3. Cook the omelet about 3 minutes, until it looks set, then flip it over (with the aid of a heat-resistant spatula if necessary) and cook 1 more minute.

4. Place the brie pieces on top of the omelet, fold the omelet over in half, and leave in the pan with the heat on low for 30 seconds to melt the brie.

5. Turn onto a plate and sprinkle with chives. Serve immediately.

## Classic Omelet.　.　.　.　.　.　.　.　.　.　.　.　.　.　.　.　.　.　.　.　.

The classic French omelet is made without filling. It is not folded in half, but in thirds to make the shape of a cigar. A simple garnish of chives is all it needs.

# American Deviled Eggs

SERVES 4

4 eggs
3 tablespoons mayonnaise
½ teaspoon yellow mustard
¼ teaspoon onion powder
2 shakes celery salt
¼ teaspoon dill weed
3 drops Tabasco sauce
Pinch white pepper
Paprika

This is a favorite in the South and Midwest of the United States. It should be everywhere.

1. Put eggs in cold water and bring to a boil. Cover with lid, turn off heat, and set timer for 15 minutes.

2. Run cold water in pan and let eggs cool off in cold water for 10 minutes.

3. Peel eggs and cut in half. Scoop yolks out into bowl. Mash yolks with fork and mix them with all ingredients except paprika.

4. Fill whites with spoonful of yolk mixture. Cover and chill.

5. To serve, sprinkle paprika on yolks.

# Spanish Stuffed Eggs

Make these ahead and refrigerate for several hours for a chilled
tapa to serve with a combination of hot and cold tapas.

1. Put the eggs in a saucepan and cover them with water. Bring water to a boil, turn to simmer, and set the timer for 15 minutes. When done, pour out the hot water and replace with cold water. Change water several times until it is no longer warm. Drain.

2. Crack and peel eggs carefully so they are smooth and pretty. Cut peeled eggs in half, carefully remove yolks, and set aside white halves. Put yolks in a bowl and mash with a fork.

3. Add mayonnaise, onion, tomato paste, garlic powder, salt, pepper, olive oil, and pimentón to the yolk mixture and mix together with fork to a smooth paste.

4. Scoop about 1 tablespoon of the yolk filling into each white.

5. Wrap each stuffed egg with a piece of Serrano ham and serve.

## Tapeo Rituals . . . . . . . . . . . . . . . . . . . . . . .
The art of eating tapas involves standing and pecking at food, instead of sitting down at table to eat; and conversation during the pecking is an important part of the ritual.

**SERVES 8**

8 eggs
¼ cup mayonnaise
1 tablespoon grated onion
1 teaspoon tomato paste
Pinch garlic powder
1 teaspoon salt
½ teaspoon pepper
1 teaspoon extra-virgin olive oil
½ teaspoon pimentón or paprika
8 thin slices Serrano ham, cut
   in half

# Japanese Sushi Omelet

MAKES 1

*3 eggs*
*1 tablespoon sugar*
*½ teaspoon salt*
*¼ cup dashi or water*
*1 tablespoon rice wine*
*1 teaspoon vegetable oil*

This is the kind of omelet used to make tamago nigiri sushi. A square Japanese omelet pan is traditionally used to make this tasty sweet egg mixture.

1. Beat the eggs with the sugar, salt, water, and rice wine in a bowl.

2. Heat the oil in a nonstick 6-inch sauté pan over medium-high heat.

3. Pour half of the egg mixture into the hot pan and swirl it around to coat the pan. Lower the heat to medium and cook until the edges are sizzling and the center is set.

4. Flip the omelet out onto a cutting board and return the pan to the heat. Add the rest of the egg mixture to the pan.

5. Roll the cooked omelet like a cigar and put it in the end of the pan farthest away from you, on top of the egg batter. Cook the omelet until the edges are again sizzling and the center is set. Remove from heat and roll the first omelet up into the second one and lay the roll on a cutting board. Let cool to room temperature.

6. Cut the omelet into a rectangle by cutting off the rounded ends. Wrap in plastic and chill. To serve, cut the rectangle into ½-inch-thick slices and use in sushi making.

# Classic French Quiche

Use Spanish Serrano ham for authentic tapas or try smoked salmon for a brunch tapas menu.

1. Preheat oven to 375°F.

2. Sauté onions in olive oil and butter until tender. Spread them on the bottom of the prebaked pastry shell. Sprinkle cheese on top of onions, then the ham.

3. Combine eggs, cream, nutmeg, salt, and peppers. Stir in chives.

4. Pour egg mixture over the ingredients in the tart shell, gently pressing down on anything that floats to the top to keep it submerged.

5. Bake for 30 minutes, until set. Serve warm or chill, slice, and reheat. Cut into twelve slices and serve two per plate.

## Twice Baked . . . . . . . . . . . . . . . . . . . . . . . . . .
To prebake a pie crust, line a pie pan with pie dough, put coffee filters over the dough, and fill with dried beans or pie weights. Bake at 350°F until set, about 25 minutes. Remove beans and coffee filters and bake crust about 10 more minutes, until crust is fully baked.

**SERVES 6**

1 cup sliced onions
1 tablespoon olive oil
1 tablespoon butter
1 cup shredded Gruyere cheese
½ cup sliced ham, chopped
3 eggs
1½ cups cream
1/16 teaspoon nutmeg
½ teaspoon salt
Pinch cayenne pepper
¼ teaspoon white pepper
2 tablespoons chopped chives
1 pie crust, prebaked in a 9-inch tart pan with removable bottom

# Spanish Poached Eggs with Serrano Ham

**SERVES 6**

1 bunch fresh asparagus
2 tablespoons olive oil
1 teaspoon kosher salt
½ teaspoon pepper
6 eggs
8 thin slices Serrano ham

Ham and eggs hit their stride when partnered with fresh spring asparagus to enliven them.

1. Bend one asparagus stalk near the cut end until it snaps. This will find the natural breaking point of the asparagus.

2. Using the snapped asparagus as a guide, measure and cut the other stalks at the same place and discard the woody ends, saving the parts with the tips on them. Toss asparagus with oil, salt, and pepper. Grill for about 5 minutes, until tender and tips are crispy. Set aside to cool.

3. Poach the eggs in simmering water, drain with a slotted spoon, and blot the water off by resting them on a clean tea towel. Transfer the poached eggs to individual custard cups or ramekins.

4. Wrap a slice of ham around three asparagus into bundles.

5. Arrange a bundle of asparagus on individual plates with an accompanying poached egg.

# American Brunch Eggs with Fish Eggs

Fish eggs are what caviar is made from, and of course they go with hens eggs very well.

1. Toast the bread, let it cool, then spread it with soft butter. Set aside.

2. In a bowl, whisk the eggs, salt, and pepper. Melt the unsalted butter in a 6-inch nonstick sauté pan over medium heat. Add the eggs and cook, stirring now and then with a silicone spatula until you have fluffy curds. Remove from heat.

3. Spoon some of the eggs onto the buttered toast slices. Cut the toasts in half diagonally into triangles.

4. Top each triangle with a dab of sour cream and sprinkle with chives.

5. Put a spoonful of caviar on top of each triangle and serve immediately.

## Fish Eggs . . . . . . . . . . . . . . . . . . . . . .

Black caviar may be the most familiar type of fish eggs, but other fish eggs are available, such as tobiko (flying fish) and salmon roe. Tobiko are tiny, bright orange eggs used in sushi. Salmon roe is the size of a huckleberry and is translucent pale orange with a darker orange dot inside.

**SERVES 4**

*4 slices thinly sliced fine white bread*

*Butter, softened, for toast*

*4 eggs*

*Large pinch of kosher salt*

*Pinch pepper*

*1 tablespoon unsalted butter*

*1 tablespoon sour cream*

*1 teaspoon chopped fresh chives*

*4 teaspoons caviar*

# Chinese Tea Eggs

These lovely eggs look like marble because the cracked shell lets the
fragrant liquid sink in to the white in a crackled pattern.

**MAKES 8**

*8 eggs*
*3 tablespoons soy sauce*
*2 star anise*
*Pinch five-spice powder*
*2 tablespoons black tea*

1. Put the eggs in water in a sauce pan and bring to a boil. Put the lid on and simmer for 12 to 15 minutes.

2. Drain the hot water from the eggs, then crack the shells of the eggs all over, but don't peel them.

3. Put them back in the saucepan and add water to cover. Add the soy sauce, star anise, and five-spice powder. Put the tea in a tea ball or infuser and add.

4. Bring the water to a boil and then turn the heat down and simmer for 20 minutes without a lid. Let the eggs cool in the liquid to room temperature, then refrigerate for 12 hours.

5. Peel the eggs and serve them whole, cut in half, or cut in quarters.

# Mexican Egg Tostadas

Add cheese, sour cream, jalapeño peppers, olives, or any other topping
you like to these mini tostadas to tailor them to your own taste.

1. Spread some of the black beans on each chip and put them on a sheet pan and into a preheated 350°F oven. Remove when the beans have warmed, about 10 minutes.

2. Fan out two slices of avocado on each chip.

3. Spoon some scrambled eggs onto the avocados.

4. Top the eggs with salsa and garnish with cilantro.

5. Serve hot.

## Breakfast Burritos . . . . . . . . . . . . . . . . . . . .
Wrap scrambled eggs, crumbled bacon, shredded cheddar cheese, salsa, and sour cream in small flour tortillas and serve warm with Mexican Breakfast Tostadas and Spanish Eggs Benedict for a tapas brunch buffet.

**SERVES 2 TO 4**

½ cup refried black beans
12 round tortilla chips
24 thin slices of avocado
4 eggs, scrambled and warm
¼ cup salsa
12 cilantro leaves or small sprigs

# Spanish Béchamel-Coated Quail Eggs

**SERVES 8**

2 cloves

¼ onion

1 cup milk

1 sprig fresh thyme

1 bay leaf

5 tablespoons butter

6 tablespoons flour

½ cup chicken broth

Salt to taste

White pepper to taste

8 hard-boiled quail eggs, peeled

1 raw egg, beaten with 1/8 cup water

1 cup dried breadcrumbs

3 cups olive oil

Serve the eggs warm with mixed-green salad for a small plate lunch entrée, or alone as part of a selection of tapas.

1. Poke the cloves into the quarter onion. Put the milk in a sauce pan with the onion, thyme sprig, and bay leaf and heat to scalding (not quite boiling), then turn the heat off. Let steep for 15 minutes, then remove onion, thyme sprig, and bay leaf.

2. To make the béchamel sauce, melt butter in a sauce pan, add flour, and cook, stirring for a few minutes. Gradually add the hot milk and whisk to smooth out lumps. Add chicken broth, bring to a boil, then reduce heat and simmer until thickened, about 2 minutes. Stir frequently during simmering to prevent sticking and burning on the bottom.

3. Season to taste with salt and pepper and let the sauce cool to room temperature. Dip the eggs in the béchamel sauce, then place them on a plastic-lined sheet pan and place in the refrigerator for 1 hour, or up to overnight, to get firm.

4. Dip the béchamel-coated quail eggs in the beaten egg and then roll in breadcrumbs.

5. Heat the oil in a deep fryer or large heavy pot to 365°F. Fry the eggs in the oil for several minutes, then drain on paper towels.

# French Toast Pinchos

If you're not a fan of mixing sweet and meat in the same bite, substitute sliced peaches for the sausage. Older bread is best for this recipe.

1. Combine eggs, milk, cinnamon, and vanilla in a bowl using a whisk.

2. Dip the bread slices in the custard, drain the excess, and panfry in melted butter on both sides.

3. Brown the sausage links and cut in half.

4. Put one piece of sausage on one piece of French toast and insert a toothpick.

## Waffle Pinchos . . . . . . . . . . . . . . . . . . . . . .
Cut up Belgian waffles and put them on toothpicks with whipped cream cheese and sliced strawberries for another brunch pincho.

**SERVES 6**

3 eggs
¾ cup milk
Pinch cinnamon
½ teaspoon vanilla
4 slices bread, Texas-toast thickness
2 ounces butter
6 breakfast sausage links

# CHAPTER 1

# Vegetables

# Garlic Confit

These whole garlic cloves are simmered slowly in olive
oil. Eat them as a snack or use them in ratatouille.

**MAKES 1 CUP**

*1 cup garlic cloves, peeled*
*1 cup olive oil*
*1 tablespoon kosher salt*

1. Put the garlic in a saucepan and pour the olive oil over it.

2. Add the salt and bring to a simmer.

3. Simmer over low heat for 45 minutes. Let the garlic cool in the oil. Store in the refrigerator.

# Fennel Garlic Olives

My favorite olive is the French picholine, a green olive
with the pit intact, but you can use any olive you like.

**SERVES 4**

*1 teaspoon lemon zest*
*4 tablespoons olive oil*
*1 tablespoon lemon juice*
*½ pound picholine olives*
*1 teaspoon fennel seeds*
*¼ cup Garlic Confit (above)*

1. Mix lemon zest, olive oil, and lemon juice together in a crock or bowl that will accommodate ½ pound of olives.

2. Toss the olives in the marinade to coat. Add the fennel seeds and garlic and toss gently.

3. Cover and let olives marinate overnight in the refrigerator. Serve at room temperature.

**Radishes with Bread and Butter** . . . . . . . . . . . . . . . . . . .
A crisp and clean tasty vegetable tapas is fresh radishes served with sweet butter and baguette.
And a little *fleur de sel* (fancy sea salt) adds sophisticated seasoning.

# Ginger-Glazed Baby Carrots

Try this recipe with regular carrots sliced on the
diagonal instead of baby carrots for a different look.

1. Steam the carrots until they are tender but firm, about 5 minutes.

2. Sauté the steamed carrots with the ginger in the butter over medium-high heat for 2 minutes.

3. Stir in the lemon juice, orange zest, honey, and pepper and reduce the heat to medium-low.

4. Cook for a few minutes, stirring to coat the carrots with the glaze as it thickens. Season with salt and remove from heat.

5. Divide the carrots among four small plates, or serve on one plate family style.

**SERVES 4**

*1 cup baby carrots*
*2 teaspoons grated fresh ginger*
*1 tablespoon butter*
*2 teaspoons lemon juice*
*1 teaspoon orange zest*
*2 teaspoons honey*
*¼ teaspoon pepper*
*¼ teaspoon salt*

# Italian Deli Pepper Poppers

Serve these piquant peppers with caponata, Caesar artichokes,
salami, and crusty bread for an antipasto plate.

1. Cut the stems off the cherry peppers and remove the seeds.

2. Cut the prosciutto slices into thirds and wrap one piece around each cube of provolone cheese.

3. Stuff a prosciutto-wrapped cheese cube into each cherry pepper and marinate in olive oil. Refrigerate and serve with toothpicks.

**SERVES 6**

*12 pickled cherry peppers*
*4 slices prosciutto*
*12 cubes provolone cheese*
*1 cup olive oil*

# Asparagus Strudel

SERVES 4

4 sheets phyllo dough

2 tablespoons walnut oil

¼ cup ground walnuts

1 bunch asparagus

¼ cup shredded Swiss cheese

These are individual strudels that can be eaten either as finger food, or with a fork and knife on a plate.

1. Preheat oven to 350°F.

2. Lay out one sheet of phyllo dough and brush it with walnut oil. Sprinkle one quarter of the ground walnuts over the oil. Place another sheet over the walnuts and repeat with the remaining sheets. Cut the stack of phyllo sheets into six strips across the width.

3. Trim the bottoms of the asparagus about 2 inches. Place three asparagus stalks on each strip of phyllo.

4. Sprinkle the asparagus with the cheese and roll up the phyllo like a rug with the asparagus in the middle. Some asparagus will stick out the sides.

5. Place the rolls on a baking sheet, seam-sides down. Brush the tops of the rolls with walnut oil and bake 15 to 20 minutes. Serve warm.

# Orange Niçoise Olives

Niçoise olives are tiny black olives that go well with the
orange and rosemary flavors in this marinade.

1. Mix orange zest, olive oil, orange juice, and champagne vinegar together in a crock or bowl that will accommodate ½ pound of olives.

2. Toss the olives in the marinade to coat. Add the rosemary and toss again.

3. Cover and let olives marinate overnight in the refrigerator. Serve at room temperature.

## Crudités. . . . . . . . . . . . . . . . . . . . . . . . . . . .

Another great vegetable tapa is the crudités platter. Arrange various fresh veggies on a platter to serve with dips. Here are some good ones: Belgian endive leaves, carrot sticks, green onions, celery sticks, zucchini, cherry tomatoes, cucumbers, and bell peppers.

**SERVES 4**

1 teaspoon orange zest
4 tablespoons olive oil
2 teaspoons orange juice
2 teaspoons champagne vinegar
½ pound unpitted Niçoise olives
2 teaspoons chopped fresh
    rosemary

# Creamed Leeks

SERVES 4

1 tablespoon butter, softened
1 large leek
Salt and pepper to taste
½ cup cream
½ cup panko breadcrumbs
Pinch ground nutmeg

This rich gratin is a luxurious side dish to roast chicken or baked ham, and it makes a substantial tapas vegetable dish. The panko (Japanese-style) breadcrumbs add a crispy texture.

1. Preheat oven to 375°F. Butter the bottom and sides of a gratin dish.

2. Cut the dark green leaves of the leek off, then cut it almost in half lengthwise, but stop 2 to 3 inches above the root.

3. Under running water, rinse the sand and dirt out of the layers of the leek. Shake off excess water and cut the roots off.

4. Next, cut the leek into 2-inch-wide pieces across the grain. Arrange the leeks in the buttered gratin dish and season with salt and pepper. Pour the cream over the leeks and then sprinkle the breadcrumbs over them and season with nutmeg.

5. Bake 45 minutes to 1 hour, until bubbly and browned.

## Baby Leeks . . . . . . . . . . . . . . . . . . . . . . . . . . .
Baby leeks make a good tapa when they are grilled and then served cold with a Dijon mustard and pink peppercorn vinaigrette.

# Shallot Tart

This tart can be cut into smaller squares for bite-size
hors d'oeuvres. Serve warm or at room temperature.

1. Preheat oven to 400°F. Spread the soft butter over the bottom of an
   8" × 8" glass dish.

2. Slice the shallots into ¼-inch-thick slices and arrange them in the
   dish, cut-side down in one layer. Sprinkle them with salt, pepper, and
   thyme.

3. Unfold the puff pastry and cut it into a square that will fit in the dish.
   Prick the pastry all over with a fork. Put the pastry on top of the shallots
   and tuck the pastry down in the dish.

4. Bake for 15 minutes, reduce heat to 325°F, and continue baking for
   30 minutes.

5. Remove the dish from the oven and put a cookie sheet over it. Flip the
   dish over onto the cookie sheet and carefully remove it. The tart will be
   on the cookie sheet. Cut it into four squares and serve sprinkled with
   chives.

**SERVES 4**

2 tablespoons unsalted butter,
   softened
6 shallots, peeled
1 teaspoon salt
¼ teaspoon pepper
½ teaspoon dried thyme
1 sheet frozen puff pastry,
   thawed
2 tablespoons chopped fresh
   chives

# Broiled Tomatoes

Artichoke hearts and Parmesan cheese top these
tomatoes in this easy-to-make vegetable dish.

**SERVES 4**

2 small ripe tomatoes
Salt to taste
2 tablespoons chopped artichoke
  hearts
1 tablespoon panko bread
  crumbs
1 tablespoon grated Parmesan
  cheese
2 teaspoons mayonnaise
⅛ teaspoon garlic salt
Pinch fresh ground pepper

1. Cut each tomato in half through the middle horizontally. Set tomatoes with their cut-sides up in individual gratin dishes or a baking dish. Sprinkle them with salt.

2. Combine artichokes with bread crumbs, cheese, mayonnaise, garlic salt, and pepper.

3. Top each tomato half with ¼ of the breadcrumb mixture.

4. Preheat the broiler for a minute or two.

5. Broil the tomatoes for 5 minutes, until crumb topping browns, and then reduce the oven temperature to 350°F. Finish baking the tomatoes for 5 to 10 minutes.

## Peeling Tomatoes . . . . . . . . . . . . . . . . . . . . . . .

If you have an abundance of ripe tomatoes at the end of the summer and you don't want them to get rotten before you make sauce from them, you can just put them in the freezer whole. They won't be good raw, but you can use them for cooking all winter. The peels come off easily, too, without having to blanch them.

# Mint Artichokes

When choosing artichokes look for the ones that have tightly packed leaves, not leaves that are starting to open away from the center.

1. Prepare the artichokes for stuffing by cutting the stems off the bottoms first. Rub the cut lemon on all the places of the artichokes that you will cut to prevent browning. Next, cut the top inch off of each artichoke with a serrated knife and rub the lemon on the cut. Discard the cut-off part. Snip the thorny tips off the remaining leaves with kitchen scissors and rub the cut surface with the lemon.

2. Pull out the center leaves to expose the fuzzy choke in the center and then scoop out the choke with a melon baller. Squeeze lemon juice into the center of each artichoke.

3. Mix the breadcrumbs, Parmesan cheese, garlic, mint, parsley, olive oil, salt, and pepper. Spoon the stuffing into the center of each artichoke.

4. Pour the water and white wine into the bottom of a large pot. Place a steamer rack in the bottom of the pot and put the artichokes upright on the rack. Cover the pot with a tight-fitting lid and simmer for 50 minutes or until a leaf can be pulled easily from an artichoke.

5. Cut the artichokes in quarters and serve warm with melted butter and lemon wedges.

**SERVES 8**

*4 whole artichokes*
*1 lemon, cut in half*
*1¼ cups panko breadcrumbs*
*½ cup grated Parmesan cheese*
*2 cloves garlic, minced*
*¼ cup fresh mint*
*¼ cup chopped parsley*
*¼ cup olive oil*
*1 teaspoon salt*
*¼ teaspoon pepper*
*½ cup dry white wine*
*1½ cups water*
*Melted butter*
*Lemon wedges*

# Japanese Pickled Cucumbers

Serve these quick pickles with Miso Soup (page 99) and sushi,
or as a relish to cool down spicy Thai or Indian food.

*2 to 3 medium cucumbers, sliced
 ¼-inch thick*

*1 shallot, sliced ¼-inch thick*

*3 tablespoons kosher salt*

*¼ cup rice vinegar*

*2 tablespoons water*

*2 tablespoons sugar*

1. Layer cucumbers and shallot with salt in a colander set in the sink and drain for 2 to 3 hours.

2. Combine vinegar, water, and sugar in a saucepan and bring to a boil.

3. Add drained cucumbers and turn off the heat. Pour them into a glass or stainless bowl.

4. Chill the cucumbers and serve in small dishes.

## Edamame . . . . . . . . . . . . . . . . . . . . . .

Edamame, fresh soy beans, are a quick, healthy addition to a sushi tapas menu or as a part of a crudités selection. Buy them frozen and bring 6 cups of water to boil. Add 1 pound of edamame and ½ teaspoon salt. Boil for 4 to 5 minutes, drain well and serve; or chill and serve cold. To eat, just peel the pods off and eat the soy beans inside.

# Ratatouille-Stuffed Mushrooms

Ratatouille is the French term for Provençal vegetables. It makes a flavorful stuffing for these giant mushroom caps.

1. Brush the mushroom caps with the olive oil on both sides, sprinkle with the sherry vinegar, and season with salt and pepper.

2. Grill the mushroom caps on both sides, about 5 minutes per side.

3. Heat the ratatouille (Provencal Mixed Vegetables) in a sauce pan over medium-low heat, just until warmed.

4. Put ½ cup of the ratatouille on each mushroom cap, undersides up. Top each with a clove of Garlic Confit. Sprinkle the breadcrumbs and Parmesan cheese on top and drizzle with extra-virgin olive oil.

5. Heat the broiler for 1 minute, then broil mushrooms for about 2 minutes, until browned. Serve warm.

**SERVES 6**

6 portabello mushrooms
1 tablespoon olive oil
1 tablespoon sherry vinegar
Salt and pepper
3 cups Provençal Vegetable Salad (page 84)
6 cloves Garlic Confit (page 138)
¼ cup panko breadcrumbs
¼ cup grated Parmesan cheese
2 tablespoons extra-virgin olive oil

# Scandinavian Cucumber Canapés

These cool, pale green and pink canapés are a pretty way to
add vegetables to a meat-heavy tapas selection.

3 cucumbers

3 slices Norwegian smoked
    salmon

4 ounces cream cheese

1 tablespoon prepared
    horseradish

2 tablespoons chopped fresh dill

1 tablespoon lemon juice

Salt and pepper to taste

2 tablespoons lemon zest

Dill sprigs for garnish

¼ cup minced red onion

1.  Cut the cucumbers into 1-inch-thick rounds. Set them with the cut-side
    down and scoop out a hollow with a melon baller. Leave enough on
    the bottom for a base.

2.  Purée the smoked salmon, cream cheese, horseradish, dill, and lemon
    juice in a food processor. Taste and season with salt and pepper if
    necessary.

3.  Spoon a dollop of the cream cheese mousse into the hollows of the
    cucumbers. Garnish with lemon zest, dill sprigs, and red onion.

## Celery Boats. . . . . . . . . . . . . . . . . . . . . . . .

This is a tasty little vegetable tapa that borrows from Thai flavors and the American relish tray.
Fill celery stalks with peanut butter and smooth out the top. Cut the celery on the diagonal into
1-inch slices. Arrange the bites on a platter and serve.

# Peppers Brandade

This is an authentic Spanish vegetable selection that can be
served simply with cheese, sliced ham, bread, and olives.

1. Preheat the oven to 350°F.

2. Put the soaked and drained salt cod into a pot with water to cover.
   Bring the water to a simmer and poach for 10 minutes. Drain and take
   out any bones or skin.

3. Put the poached cod in a food processor with the garlic. Pulse a
   few times, then add the milk and oil through the feed tube with the
   machine running to make a thick purée. Stop adding the liquid if it
   starts to get too loose.

4. Add the lemon juice, nutmeg, and pepper and pulse to combine. Taste
   and add salt if necessary.

5. Drain the peppers of excess juices. Spoon brandade into each pepper,
   dividing it equally among the peppers, and place the stuffed peppers
   in a casserole dish.

6. Squeeze the lemon over the peppers and drizzle them with the extra-
   virgin olive oil. Bake for 10 to 15 minutes, until heated through. Serve
   warm.

**SERVES 4**

12 piquillo peppers, or other
roasted red peppers
½ pound salt cod, soaked for 24
hours, water changed 4 times
1 garlic clove, peeled
⅓ cup milk
¼ cup olive oil
1 tablespoon lemon juice
Pinch nutmeg
1 teaspoon black pepper
Salt to taste
1 lemon wedge
1 tablespoon extra-virgin olive oil

# Grilled Avocados

**SERVES 4**

*2 avocados*

*2 tablespoons olive oil*

*Salt and pepper*

*¼ cup diced red onion*

*½ cup diced tomatoes*

*1 teaspoon lemon juice*

*1 tablespoon extra-virgin olive oil*

When purchasing avocados for this recipe, choose firm-ripe ones and not the soft ones that are better for guacamole.

1. Preheat a grill pan or grill.

2. Cut the avocadoes in half, remove the pits, and scoop the flesh out with a large serving spoon in one piece. Discard the skin.

3. Rub the avocado halves with olive oil, then season with salt and pepper.

4. Place the avocado halves on the grill with the pit-side down and grill for about 1 minute. Remove and place avocado halves, pit-side up, on a serving plate or four small plates.

5. Scatter the red onions and tomatoes over the avocados and drizzle with extra-virgin olive oil and lemon juice. Serve at room temperature.

# Grains and Pasta

# Tabbouleh

Cucumbers are added to this refreshing grain salad. For a more traditional version leave out the cucumbers.

**SERVES 6**

½ cup medium bulgur wheat

1½ cups water

⅓ cup lemon juice

2 tablespoons chopped fresh mint

1 teaspoon salt

1 teaspoon pepper

¼ cup extra-virgin olive oil

1 cup chopped fresh parsley

½ cup chopped green onions

2 large tomatoes, diced

½ cup diced cucumber

1 tablespoon minced garlic

1. Soak the bulgur in the water for at least 2 hours.

2. Drain the excess water and put the bulgur in a large bowl.

3. Add the remaining ingredients to the bulgur and mix well.

4. Let sit at room temperature for 1 hour or refrigerate overnight.

5. Serve chilled or at room temperature.

### Substitution . . . . . . . . . . . . . . . . . . . . . . .
You may use couscous instead of bulgur wheat for tabbouleh. Couscous is fluffier and has finer texture than bulgur and is faster to make.

# Fruited Rice Pilaf

You may use any dried fruit, such as cherries or cranberries, in this recipe. I like the color contrast of the green onions and apricots.

**SERVES 4**

4 tablespoons butter

½ cup sliced green onions

1 cup uncooked long-grain white rice

1¾ cups chicken broth

½ teaspoon salt

¼ teaspoon white pepper

1 bay leaf

¼ cup dried currants

¼ cup dried apricots, chopped

1. Preheat oven to 350°F.

2. Melt butter in a sauce pan and sauté the green onions in it until tender.

3. Add rice and sauté for 3 to 5 minutes with the green onions.

4. Pour rice mixture into a baking dish. Add chicken broth, salt, pepper, bay leaf, currants, and apricots. Stir to incorporate.

5. Cover and bake for 45 minutes. Remove bay leaf before serving.

# Herbed Brown Rice

Brown rice takes longer than white rice to cook and it has a chewier texture due to the outer husk that is still intact.

1. Combine everything in a saucepan and bring to a boil.

2. Stir, cover, and reduce the heat to low.

3. Set timer for 45 minutes. After 45 minutes, turn off heat and let rice sit with the lid on for 10 minutes.

## Dirty Rice . . . . . . . . . . . . . . . . . . . . . . .
Dirty rice is a spicy Cajun dish from Louisiana that is often made with chicken livers or gizzards and is served as a side dish with fried chicken, collard greens, and cole slaw.

# Pearl Barley

This recipe gives you a chance to try a different kind of grain instead of rice for variety in your repertoire.

1. Place a medium-size saucepan over medium heat and add the olive oil. Add barley and sauté for 2 minutes, stirring with a wooden spoon. Add green onions and garlic, stirring constantly for an additional minute.

2. Add beef broth and water while stirring. Add salt and pepper.

3. Bring to a boil. Reduce heat to low. Cover and cook until barley is tender to the bite, about 40 to 45 minutes. Serve warm.

# Meyer Lemon Couscous

This makes a good stuffing for trout or tomatoes, in addition to a bed for stews and tagines.

**SERVES 4**

¼ cup minced sweet onion

2 tablespoons olive oil

1½ cups chicken broth

1 teaspoon fresh Meyer
    lemon juice

1 teaspoon Meyer lemon zest

¼ cup picholine olives (green),
    chopped

1 teaspoon lemon pepper

1½ teaspoons salt

1 cup couscous

1. Gently sauté sweet onion in the olive oil until the onion is translucent.

2. Add chicken broth, lemon juice, lemon zest, olives, lemon pepper, and salt.

3. Bring to a boil. Remove from heat, stir in couscous, cover, and let stand for 5 minutes to absorb the liquid.

4. Fluff couscous with a fork before serving.

# Semolina Pasta

This fresh pasta needs only a brief 3 to 5 minutes cooking time in
boiling water, instead of about 12 minutes for dried pasta.

**SERVES 2**

½ cup semolina flour

½ cup flour

½ teaspoon salt

1 egg, beaten

2 teaspoons water (more if
    necessary)

1. Combine flours and salt and make a well in the center.

2. Combine egg with water and pour into the well in the flour mixture. Gradually bring the flour into the egg with a fork to form a dough, adding drops of water if necessary.

3. When dough has been formed, knead it for 10 minutes. Wrap in plastic.

4. Let rest 45 minutes before rolling with a pasta machine or rolling pin.

## Substitution . . . . . . . . . . . . . . . . . . . . . .
You may use all flour instead of half semolina to make pasta. It will be a softer dough, which is easier to knead by hand and roll with a rolling pin if you don't have a pasta machine.

# Shellfish Paella Deluxe

This is the special-occasion paella to make if you like seafood.
Add or substitute crab, squid, scallops, or fish for variation.

1. Preheat oven to 400°F.

2. Heat the olive oil in a paella pan (or 13-inch sauté pan) and sauté the shrimp over high heat for 1 minute. Remove and reserve the shrimp. Keep the pan with the olive oil on the heat.

3. Add the tomato purée and minced onion to the pan and stir for 1 minute. Add the garlic and turn the heat to low for several minutes. Add the clam juice, chicken broth, saffron, and salt to the pan, turn the heat to high, and bring to a boil.

4. Sprinkle the rice evenly over the liquid in the pan and then cook 5 minutes, stirring often with a wooden paddle or spoon. Scatter the shrimp, clams, mussels, lobster claws, and peas on top of the rice, and put the pan in the oven for 15 minutes.

5. Remove paella pan from the oven, cover with foil, and let rest in a warm place undisturbed for 5 to 10 minutes. Serve hot.

**SERVES 4**

2 tablespoons extra-virgin olive oil
8 large shrimp in the shell, frozen
¼ cup tomato purée
1 tablespoon onion, minced
1 garlic clove, peeled and minced
1 cup bottled clam juice
2½ cups chicken broth
Pinch saffron
1 teaspoon salt
1½ cups Spanish bomba rice (short-grain), or arborio
¼ pound manila clams in the shell, brine-soaked then scrubbed clean
¼ pound mussels in the shell, scrubbed and debearded
4 lobster claws
½ cup frozen peas

# Japanese Sushi Rice

**SERVES 4**

1 cup short-grain sushi rice
2 tablespoons seasoned rice
  vinegar

Also known as sticky rice, this rice is a preparation used in
making sushi rolls, hand-formed sushi, and scattered sushi.

1. Rinse the rice in cold water several times until the water runs clear, then drain it.

2. Put it in a saucepan with 1¼ cups cold water over high heat. Bring to a boil, cover, turn heat to low, and set the timer for 20 minutes. Turn the heat off and leave the lid on 10 more minutes.

3. Turn the rice out into a large wooden or glass bowl. Sprinkle the rice vinegar over it and stir it in with a wooden spoon, making slashing motions through the rice. Fan the rice from time to time as it gets turned over. Do not refrigerate, let cool naturally. It will keep at cool room temperature for 4 to 6 hours for making sushi.

### Different Kinds of Sushi . . . . . . . . . . . . . . . . . . . . . .

Among the different kinds of sushi, a very popular one is the roll, known as *maki* in Japanese. There are inside-out rolls with rice on the outside and nori (seaweed) on the inside around the filling. *Nigiri* sushi is hand-formed "fingers" of rice with fish or Japanese omelet on top, and "battleship" sushi is an oval of rice surrounded by nori and topped with salmon roe, flying fish roe, or oysters. Other types are hand rolls, scattered sushi (in a bowl), and pressed sushi. Sashimi is just the sliced raw fish with no rice.

# Indian Basmati Rice

This fragrant rice doesn't need anything but the addition of a
few extras after the cooking time to dress it up for a party.

**SERVES 4**

1¾ cups water
Pinch kosher salt
1 cup basmati rice
Pinch saffron
¼ cup frozen peas
2 tablespoons sliced almonds

1. Bring the water to a boil. Add the salt and rice, stir, cover, and lower the heat to low. Set timer for 20 minutes. Do not remove the lid until then.

2. Turn the heat off, lift the lid, add the saffron, peas, and almonds, and replace the lid.

3. Let stand until the peas are hot, about 10 minutes. Serve immediately.

# Gullah Red Rice

This style of rice is from island communities of former Colonial rice plantations in the
Low Country in coastal South Carolina and Georgia. Gullah is the language of Sea
Islanders, a combination of Elizabethan English and many African languages. The cultural
influence is from West Africa, West Indies, Europe, and Native Americans.

**SERVES 6**

3 thick slices bacon
2 tablespoons bacon drippings
   (saved)
1 small yellow onion, chopped
1 cup long-grain white rice
1¾ cups crushed tomatoes
Salt and pepper to taste
Cayenne pepper to taste
1 cup chicken broth

1. Cook the bacon until crisp and set aside. Put the bacon drippings in a pot over medium heat, add the onion, and sauté for 2 minutes.

2. Add the rice and sauté for 5 minutes, stirring occasionally. Add the crushed tomatoes, salt, pepper, and cayenne pepper, and mix well. Pour in the broth and bring to a boil.

3. Cover with lid, reduce heat to low, and set the timer for 30 minutes. Do not lift the lid during this time. Serve the rice immediately in bowls with the bacon crumbled over the rice.

# Bento-Box Orzo Pasta

**SERVES 4**

½ cup mayonnaise

1 tablespoon sesame oil

1 teaspoon lemon zest

1 teaspoon grated fresh ginger

2 cups cooked orzo pasta, cooled

½ cup sliced celery

2 tablespoons chopped fresh
chives

This is a cold pasta salad that makes up part of a bento
box lunch-style tapas selection along with chilled
prawns and Japanese Pickled Cucumbers (page 146).

1. Mix the mayonnaise, sesame oil, lemon zest, and ginger in a large
   bowl.

2. Add the cooked pasta and celery and toss to coat. Cover and chill.

3. To serve, add the chives and fold them in.

## Edamame Ravioli. . . . . . . . . . . . . . . . . . . . . . .

Fresh ravioli can be made with wonton wrappers and cooked fresh edamame (soy beans). Just
take two wrappers and three to five edamame, shelled from their pods and skins slipped off. Coat
a wrapper with beaten egg, place the edamame in the middle and top with another wrapper.
Press the edges to seal and boil the ravioli for several minutes.

# Crusty Persian Rice

Persian rice is fragrant and full of fruits and nuts. It has a crunchy crust on the bottom, which becomes the top when the rice is inverted to a serving dish.

**SERVES 4**

2 cups basmati rice
1 tablespoon salt
½ cup melted butter
1 cup diced sweet onions
Pinch saffron
2 tablespoons almonds
1 teaspoon orange zest
½ teaspoon cinnamon
¼ teaspoon white pepper
2 tablespoons dried sour cherries
2 tablespoons golden raisins
2 tablespoons pistachios

1. Rinse the rice several times until the water runs clear, then soak it for 15 minutes. Bring 4 quarts water to a boil, add the salt, and then drain the rice and add it to the boiling water. Cook uncovered for 10 minutes, stirring every few minutes, then drain in a mesh strainer to remove extra water.

2. Put 2/3 of the melted butter in a heavy-bottom pan over medium heat and sauté the onions in it. Add the saffron and stir to distribute.

3. Add the almonds, orange zest, cinnamon, and white pepper, stir, then add the rice, cherries, and raisins. Toss the rice to distribute the fruit, pour the remaining butter over the top, cover, and cook for 40 minutes over low heat.

4. Add the pistachios and serve hot.

5. Serve with some of the crusty part from the bottom of the pot.

## The Desirable Crust . . . . . . . . . . . . . . . . . .

The golden crust that forms on the bottom of the pot when making Persian rice is so desirable it has its own name: *tah-digh*.

# Seafood

# Shrimp Croquettes

You can form these crispy shrimp fritters into smaller bite-size
croquettes to be served as part of an hors d'oeuvre selection.

**MAKES 20**

¼ small onion

1 clove

1 bay leaf

2 cups whole milk

4 tablespoons butter

¾ cup all-purpose flour

Pinch ground white pepper

Pinch nutmeg, freshly grated if
    possible

12 ounces cooked shrimp,
    chopped

½ cup all-purpose flour

1 extra-large egg, beaten

½ teaspoon salt

¾ cup fine dry breadcrumbs

2 cups peanut oil

1. Poke the clove into the quarter onion and place the onion and the bay
   leaf in a saucepan with the milk. Heat the milk over medium-high to
   scalding (not quite boiling) and then remove it from the heat. Let steep
   for 15 minutes, then remove and discard the onion and bay leaf.

2. Meanwhile, melt the butter in another saucepan, add ¾ cup of flour,
   and cook over medium heat for a few minutes, stirring with a wooden
   spoon. This will make a stiff roux. Gradually add the hot milk to the
   roux on the heat and whisk with a wire whip for 3 to 5 minutes to
   smooth out lumps. The roux will absorb the milk as it cooks and
   become a very thick béchamel sauce, which will be the base for the
   croquettes.

3. Remove the béchamel from the heat and stir in the white pepper, nutmeg,
   and chopped shrimp. Spread the mixture out onto a plastic-lined baking
   sheet, cover the top directly with plastic wrap, and refrigerate it until it is
   cold. This may take an hour or two.

4. Arrange a production line for coating the croquettes by putting the
   ½ cup flour on a plate, the beaten egg mixed with ½ teaspoon salt in
   a bowl, and the breadcrumbs on a plate. When the shrimp filling has
   cooled remove the plastic from the top and cut the filling into twenty
   equal portions. Roll each portion into a cylinder, then roll it in the flour,
   dip it in the egg, and roll it in the breadcrumbs. Place it on a tray and
   repeat with the rest of the filling.

5. Put the peanut oil in a deep pot or deep fryer and heat it to 375°F. Fry
   the croquettes in four to five batches for a minute or two, until they are
   golden brown. Drain on paper towels and serve hot.

# Mango Crab Sushi Rolls

You may use imitation crab legs for this if snow crab is unavailable, or use lump crabmeat.

1. Cut the nori in half and lay one piece on a bamboo sushi mat covered with plastic wrap. Cover the nori with sushi rice, about 1-inch thick.

2. Sprinkle 1 tablespoon toasted sesame seeds over the rice and press them in lightly. Turn the nori over so the rice side is down on the sushi mat. Position it on the bottom edge of the mat.

3. Peel the mango and cut it into strips. Place several strips on the bottom edge of the nori spanning the entire width. Place crab-leg meat above the mango in the same manner.

4. Roll the sushi mat up like a carpet, with the filling becoming the middle of the sushi roll. Use the mat as a guide and continue rolling until you have a roll with rice on the outside. Cut the roll in half and then cut the two halves into thirds. Turn the pieces cut-side up onto a plate. Repeat with the remaining ingredients to make four rolls.

5. Serve with soy sauce, wasabi paste, and pickled ginger.

## Sushi Tip . . . . . . . . . . . . . . . . . . . . . . . . . .

Believe it or not, mayonnaise is often used in sushi. It is mixed with loose crabmeat for California rolls and other rolls using crabmeat. It helps the sushi pieces stay together after the roll is cut, and it adds creaminess and flavor.

**SERVES 4**

2 sheets nori (seaweed)
1 recipe Japanese Sushi Rice (page 156)
4 tablespoons toasted sesame seeds
1 mango
Meat from 8 snow crab legs
Soy sauce
Wasabi paste
Pickled ginger

# California Rolls

**SERVES 4**

2 sheets nori (seaweed)

1 recipe Japanese Sushi Rice
  (page 156)

4 tablespoons toasted
  sesame seeds

1 avocado

8 to 12 imitation crab legs

½ cucumber, peeled and cut into
  julienne strips

Soy sauce

Wasabi paste

Pickled ginger

You may use lump crabmeat instead of imitation crab legs if
desired. Mix it with a dab of mayonnaise to hold it together.

1. Cut the nori in half and lay one piece on a bamboo sushi mat covered with plastic wrap. Cover the nori with sushi rice, about 1-inch thick.

2. Sprinkle 1 tablespoon toasted sesame seeds over the rice and press them in lightly. Turn the nori over so the rice side is down on the sushi mat. Position it on the bottom edge of the mat.

3. Peel the avocado and cut it into slices. Place several slices on the bottom edge of the nori spanning the entire width. Place the imitation crabmeat above the avocado in the same manner. Add several cucumber strips above the crab.

4. Roll up the sushi mat like a carpet, with the filling becoming the middle of the sushi roll. Use the mat as a guide and continue rolling until you have a roll with rice on the outside. Cut the roll in half and then cut the two halves into thirds. Turn the pieces cut-side up onto a plate. Repeat with the remaining ingredients to make four rolls.

5. Serve with soy sauce, wasabi paste, and pickled ginger.

# English Pub Beer-Batter Fish

Serve this classic fried fish with British Chips (page 107) and malt vinegar,
British Scotch Eggs (page 123), and brown ale for a pub-style meal.

**SERVES 4**

1½ pounds cod or other firm
    white fish
1¾ cups flour
1 teaspoon salt
½ teaspoon pepper
1½ teaspoons baking powder
6 ounces dark beer
⅓ cup milk
2 egg yolks
2 egg whites
4 cups peanut oil

1. Cut the fish into planks about 2 inches wide and 3 inches long.

2. Combine ¾ cup flour, salt, pepper, and baking powder. Gradually whisk in beer, then milk, then egg yolks.

3. Beat egg whites to stiff peaks, then fold them into the batter.

4. Dip each fish piece in flour (remaining 1 cup) then dip in batter.

5. Fry fish in batches in oil heated to 365°F in a large pot or deep fryer, immediately after dipping them in batter, for about 5 minutes. Check one to see if the fish is done before removing all of them. The fish will flake apart with a fork when done. Drain on paper towels and serve hot.

## Tartar Sauce . . . . . . . . . . . . . . . . . . . .

Tartar sauce is a good dip for fried fish. Make your own by mixing mayonnaise with lemon juice, diced pickles or pickle relish, and parsley or chives.

# Bay Shrimp Cocktail

This is served like a sundae, so use old-fashioned glass ice-cream dishes if you have them.

**SERVES 4**

1 pound cooked bay shrimp, chilled
4 tablespoons cocktail sauce
4 teaspoons grated horseradish (not creamed)
4 lemon wedges
4 parsley sprigs
½ cup oyster crackers

1. Place ¼ pound bay shrimp in four sundae glasses.

2. Spoon 1 tablespoon of cocktail sauce on top of each glass of shrimp.

3. Place 1 teaspoon of grated horseradish on top of the cocktail sauce.

4. Garnish each cocktail with a lemon wedge and a parsley sprig.

5. Serve chilled with small seafood forks and oyster crackers on the side.

# Prawn Skewers

Fill a broad vase with colorful dried calypso beans and anchor
the skewers in them for a bouquet-style presentation.

**SERVES 4**

8 bamboo skewers
2 tablespoons sherry
2 tablespoons melted butter
1 teaspoon honey
Salt and pepper to taste
8 large raw prawns, shells on

1. Soak the skewers in water. Preheat grill or grill pan.

2. Combine sherry, melted butter, honey, salt, and pepper in a bowl. Add the prawns and toss to coat.

3. Thread each prawn onto a skewer under the tail, up between the shell and meat, creating a "backbone" with the skewer.

4. Grill the prawns for about three minutes per side.

### Shell Game . . . . . . . . . . . . . . . . . . . . . . . . . . .
You may also use smaller shrimp that has been peeled on skewers, but you will need to use two parallel skewers for each serving and thread three shrimp on them. If you use only one skewer the shrimp will spin around and be hard to handle.

# Thai Shrimp Sauté

This recipe is best with 51-60-size shrimp, which means there are 51 to 60 per pound.

1. Combine ¼ cup olive oil, green onions, ginger, garlic, salt, pepper, white wine, and Thai sweet chili sauce in a large zip-top bag. Add shrimp to the bag, squeeze out all the air, and seal. Turn bag to coat shrimp. Refrigerate for 1 hour.

2. Heat a large, heavy skillet over medium-high heat. Add remaining olive oil to hot pan and swirl to coat. Remove shrimp from marinade, reserving marinade, and place in a single layer in the hot pan.

3. Cook for 1 minute, then flip the shrimp to the other side. Do not overcook the shrimp or it will become rubbery. Add the reserved marinade to the pan. Cook 1 minute, then continue cooking, if necessary, until the liquid reduces and thickens into a sauce. Serve hot.

**SERVES 4**

¼ cup olive oil, plus 2 tablespoons
2 green onions, chopped
1 tablespoon minced ginger
2 cloves garlic, sliced
1 teaspoon kosher salt
¼ teaspoon pepper
1 to 1½ pounds raw shrimp, peeled
⅓ cup white wine
1 tablespoon Thai sweet chili sauce

# Bay Scallops Gratinee

Sauvignon Blanc, Pinot Gris, or Pinot Grigio are all good wines to use in this recipe because they are light and crisp and won't overpower the delicate scallops.

1. Preheat oven to 400°F.

2. Butter a gratin dish and arrange the bay scallops in one layer over the butter. Sprinkle the white wine over the scallops and season them with salt and pepper.

3. Combine the bread crumbs, garlic, lemon zest, and parsley and sprinkle the mixture over the scallops.

4. Bake for 12 minutes. Remove from the oven and sprinkle the lemon juice over the scallops.

5. Serve immediately.

**SERVES 4**

1 tablespoon butter, softened
1 pound bay scallops
2 tablespoons white wine
Salt and pepper to taste
¼ cup panko breadcrumbs
1 garlic clove, pressed
1 teaspoon lemon zest
1 tablespoon chopped fresh parsley
1 teaspoon lemon juice

# Dungeness Crab Louis

San Francisco and Seattle both claim to be the birthplace of Crab Louis. In either case, it is a vintage recipe from the turn of the twentieth century using Pacific coast crabmeat and pink dressing.

**SERVES 4**

1 pound Dungeness crabmeat

2 hard-boiled eggs, peeled

2 Roma tomatoes

¼ cup cocktail sauce or ketchup

½ cup mayonnaise

1 tablespoon heavy cream

Dash of Tabasco sauce

1 tablespoon chopped parsley

1 tablespoon minced green bell pepper

1 tablespoon minced green onions

1 teaspoon lemon juice

2 cups shredded iceberg lettuce

1. Pick through the crabmeat to remove any cartilage, then set aside.

2. Cut the eggs and tomatoes into quarters, then set aside.

3. Mix the cocktail sauce, mayonnaise, cream, Tabasco, parsley, bell pepper, green onions, and lemon juice together to make the pink dressing.

4. Divide the lettuce among four plates. Place a mound of crabmeat on each plate of lettuce. Pour the dressing over the crabmeat.

5. Garnish each plate with two wedges of egg and two wedges of tomato.

## Remoulade Sauce . . . . . . . . . . . . . . . . . . . . . . .
Remoulade is a cold spicy French sauce that is served with fish and seafood. It is similar to tartar sauce and the pink dressing served with Dungeness Crab Louis.

# Smoked Salmon Pita Crisps

Kippered smoked salmon is firmer than lox smoked salmon because it is hot smoked. It can be broken up into chunks and doesn't need to be sliced thinly.

1. Preheat the oven to 350°F. Separate the pita rounds in half, making two rounds out of each. Cut the six resulting rounds into wedges and place them on a baking sheet.

2. Bake the pita wedges for 10 minutes, until crisp. Let cool.

3. Combine the honey, mustard, and dill.

4. Spoon a bit of the mustard mixture onto each pita crisp.

5. Top each pita crisp with a chunk of smoked salmon.

**SERVES 6**

3 rounds of pita bread
1 tablespoon honey
¼ cup Dijon mustard
1 tablespoon dill
¼ pound kippered smoked
   salmon

# Steamed Mussels

**SERVES 4**

1 shallot

1 tablespoon olive oil

2 pounds mussels, scrubbed and debearded

½ cup white wine

2 tablespoons chopped parsley

It is very important that the mussels are well scrubbed and debearded. Ask your fishmonger to do it for you.

1. Mince the shallot and sauté it in the olive oil over medium-high heat in a large pot.

2. Add the mussels all at once, then the wine, and cover with a lid.

3. Turn the heat to high and let the mussels steam for 10 minutes.

4. Remove the pot from the heat and discard any unopened mussels.

5. Transfer the mussels to four soup plates and strain the liquid. Pour the strained liquid into the bowls and sprinkle the parsley over the mussels. Serve hot.

## Steamed Clams

You may steam clams in the same manner as mussels, but they don't have "beards," so you don't have to worry about that. They do need to be scrubbed well though. Some experts suggest that clams also be soaked first to purge them of sand and grit.

# Baked Mussels

Oven-roasted mussels with lemon-scented crust are rich and delicious.
Start with the recipe for Steamed Mussels (page 170) and proceed.

**SERVES 4**

*2 dozen steamed mussels*
*¼ pound butter, softened*
*¼ cup panko breadcrumbs*
*1 clove garlic, minced*
*¼ cup ground almonds*
*1 tablespoon chopped parsley*
*1 teaspoon lemon zest*
*¼ teaspoon salt*
*⅛ teaspoon pepper*

1. Preheat the oven to broil.

2. Save two dozen mussel shell halves and loosen the mussels from them. Put each mussel in a shell half. Set aside.

3. Combine the butter, breadcrumbs, garlic, almonds, parsley, lemon zest, salt, and pepper in a food processor until smooth.

4. Spread about 1 teaspoon of the butter mixture over each mussel to cover it. Arrange the mussels in four broiler-safe dishes.

5. Broil the mussels for 3 minutes, until the crust is golden. Serve immediately.

## Moroccan Preserved Lemons . . . . . . . . . . . . . . . . .

Use preserved lemons instead of lemon zest to add a Moroccan flavor to the mussels. Make your own by cutting washed lemons into eighths almost all the way through. Leave one end intact so the lemons stay together. Pack kosher salt into the cut areas of the lemons and then pack the lemons tightly into a jar that you have already put a whole, dried cayenne pepper in. Fill up the jar with lemon juice and put a lid on. Leave at room temperature for at least 1 week. To use, scrape out the pulp and chop the rinds to use in recipes.

# Stone-Crab Claws

**SERVES 4**

*8 stone-crab claws, thawed*

*½ cup mayonnaise*

*3 tablespoons Dijon mustard*

These are simple and delicious. You may serve them with melted
butter and lemon as an alternative to the dipping sauce.

1. To thaw the frozen stone-crab claws, place in the refrigerator for 12 to 18 hours.

2. Combine the mayonnaise and Dijon mustard.

3. Crack the claws with a mallet and serve chilled with the mayonnaise mustard sauce for dipping.

## Dungeness Crab . . . . . . . . . . . . . . . . . . . . . . . .
Dungeness crab is good served with the same sauce above for dipping. The crab needs to be steamed and then chilled.

# Mini Sushi Balls

**MAKES 20**

*½ recipe Japanese Sushi Rice (page 156)*

*1 ounce smoked salmon, sliced very thin*

*½ small cucumber, sliced very thin*

*2 teaspoons wasabi paste*

*2 tablespoons sour cream*

This is a way to have little bites of sushi made up ahead of time. Just unwrap before serving.

1. Cut the smoked salmon slices into quarter-size pieces. Lay twenty 4" × 4" pieces of plastic wrap out flat on a work surface. Put 10 smoked salmon pieces in the middle of half of them and cucumber slices on the rest.

2. Rub a dab of wasabi paste on the smoked salmon and cucumber, then top them all with a teaspoon of sushi rice. Gather the plastic wrap up into a purse around the rice and twist it so the rice turns into a ball. Repeat with all and set aside.

3. To serve, unwrap the balls and place them salmon- and cucumber-sides up on a platter. Top each with a dab of sour cream.

# Shrimp Tempura Rolls

This sushi roll has crunchy, warm shrimp tempura,
which adds texture to contrast with the soft rice.

1. Whisk beer into flour until smooth, then stir in salt. Heat oil to 375°F in a deep fryer or heavy-bottom pot. Dip shrimp individually in batter, let excess drip off, then drop in hot oil. Cook battered shrimp about 3 minutes, then remove from oil. Drain on paper towels.

2. Cut the nori in half and lay one piece on a bamboo sushi mat covered with plastic wrap. Cover the nori with sushi rice, about 1 inch thick.

3. Sprinkle 1 tablespoon toasted sesame seeds over the rice and press them in lightly. Turn the nori over so the rice side is down on the sushi mat. Position it on the bottom edge of the mat.

4. Place several tempura shrimp on the bottom edge of the nori spanning the entire width. Roll the sushi mat up like a carpet, with the shrimp becoming the middle of the sushi roll. Use the mat as a guide and continue rolling until you have a roll with rice on the outside.

5. Cut the roll in half and then cut the halves into thirds. Turn the pieces cut-side up onto a plate. Repeat with the remaining ingredients to make four rolls. Serve with soy sauce, wasabi paste, and pickled ginger.

**SERVES 4**

12 large uncooked shrimp, shelled
¾ cup pilsner beer
¾ cup all-purpose flour
¾ teaspoon salt
2 cups vegetable oil
2 sheets nori (seaweed)
1 recipe Japanese Sushi Rice (page 156)
4 tablespoons toasted sesame seeds
Soy sauce
Wasabi paste
Pickled ginger

# Norwegian Savory Cheesecake

Norwegian smoked salmon and Norwegian Jarlsberg cheese are
seasoned with dill and made into a savory cheesecake.

**SERVES 12**

½ cup flour

3 ounces butter, melted

½ cup rye crisp cracker crumbs or
    pumpernickel bread crumbs

1 teaspoon black pepper

18 ounces cream cheese, softened

2 tablespoons cornstarch

3 eggs

6 ounces Jarlsberg cheese,
    shredded

1 teaspoon chopped dill

1 teaspoon lemon juice

1 teaspoon lemon zest

1½ cups sour cream

1 cup crème frâiche

½ cup thinly sliced Norwegian
    smoked salmon

2 tablespoons chopped chives

¼ cup chopped red onion

black caviar (optional)

melba toast

1. Preheat oven to 350°F. In a bowl, combine flour, melted butter, cracker
   (or bread) crumbs, and pepper with a rubber spatula. Press mixture
   into the bottom of a springform pan that has been sprayed with oil.
   Bake for 10 minutes. Remove from oven and set aside.

2. With an electric mixer beat the cream cheese until fluffy. Add the cornstarch and beat it into the cream cheese. Beat in the eggs one at a time,
   scraping down the bowl after each one. Stir in the Jarslberg cheese,
   dill, lemon juice, and lemon zest.

3. Fold in the sour cream and pour the mixture into the springform pan
   and bake for 1 hour. Remove from oven and cool at room temperature
   and then chill completely overnight.

4. Whip the crème frâiche with an electric mixer until it is stiff like
   whipped cream. Spread it over the cheesecake and return to the refrigerator for 2 hours to set.

5. Remove the ring of the springform pan and scatter the smoked salmon
   over the top. Garnish with red onion and chives. Cut the cheesecake
   into wedges.

6. Serve a wedge on a plate with a dollop of caviar and toast points for
   each person or present the whole cheesecake with caviar and melba
   toast on the side for a buffet.

# Poultry

# Thai Sweet Chili Wings

SERVES 6

½ cup all-purpose flour
½ teaspoon salt
1½ pounds chicken wings
½ cup butter, melted
1 tablespoon minced garlic
¼ cup Thai sweet chili sauce
¼ cup hot pepper sauce

Sweet and spicy chicken wings like these go well with Vegetable Spring
Rolls (page 212) and Caribbean Curried Banana Soup (page 100).

1. Preheat oven to 375°F.

2. Combine the flour and salt in a large bowl and toss the chicken wings
   in it. Shake off the excess flour and put the wings on a baking-sheet
   pan lined with nonstick foil. Repeat with another sheet pan if necessary to get all the wings on baking sheets.

3. Bake wings for 30 minutes. Remove from oven, turn the wings over
   with tongs, and bake another 15 minutes.

4. Combine butter, garlic, sweet chili sauce, and hot pepper sauce in
   a large bowl. Remove the chicken wings from the oven, toss them
   in the sauce and return them to the baking pans. Bake for another
   15 minutes.

### Drumettes. . . . . . . . . . . . . . . . . . . . . .
If you cut the tips off chicken wings and then cut the remaining wings in half at the joint, you
have tiny little drumsticks and wings. They are very cute and the perfect size for tapas.

# Oven-Fried Chicken Drumsticks

These crispy chicken drumsticks can be served hot or chilled. Cold fried chicken drumsticks make great portable picnic tapas with deviled eggs, fresh fruit, and a cheese plate.

1. Mix the buttermilk and the cayenne pepper sauce. Soak the chicken drumsticks in the buttermilk mixture overnight.

2. Preheat the oven to 350°F.

3. Combine the flour, salt, and pepper in a large bowl. Remove the drumsticks from the buttermilk and coat each piece with the flour mixture. Melt the shortening in a large skillet and heat to 360°F on a candy thermometer.

4. Place four drumsticks in the shortening and fry for about 3 minutes on each side until the coating is a light golden brown. Remove the drumsticks from the skillet and place them on a baking sheet lined with nonstick foil. Repeat with the other four drumsticks.

5. Bake the drumsticks for 1 hour.

**SERVES 8**

2 cups buttermilk
½ teaspoon cayenne pepper sauce
8 chicken drumsticks
1 cup self-rising flour
1½ teaspoons salt
1½ teaspoons black pepper
1 cup vegetable shortening (without trans fats)

# Indonesian Satay Chicken Strips

**SERVES 6**

2 tablespoons peanut butter
½ cup coconut milk
¼ teaspoon Thai red curry paste
1 teaspoon vegetable oil
12 chicken tenders
2 cups panko breadcrumbs
1 cup ground peanuts
½ cup sesame seeds
1 teaspoon onion powder
2 teaspoons salt
¼ teaspoon pepper
¼ cup butter, melted
12 bamboo skewers

Satay is usually skewered meat that is grilled and served with peanut sauce. This version borrows the flavors of Indonesia for crunchy baked chicken strips. Serve with Indonesian Peanut Sauce (page 33) for dipping.

1. Preheat oven to 350°F. Line a baking sheet with foil and set aside.

2. Mix peanut butter, coconut milk, oil, and curry paste in a bowl. Marinate the chicken tenders in this mixture for several hours in the refrigerator.

3. Combine breadcrumbs, peanuts, sesame seeds, onion powder, salt, and pepper in a bowl.

4. Coat the chicken tenders with the breadcrumb mixture. Arrange the coated chicken strips on the foil.

5. Pour the melted butter over the chicken and bake for 1 hour. Remove from the oven and let rest 5 minutes. Push the skewers into one end of each strip going ⅔ of the way up into the chicken strip. Serve hot.

## Tandoori Grill . . . . . . . . . . . . . . . . . . . . . . . . .

Tandoori chicken is an Indian dish made from chicken that is marinated in yogurt, lime juice, and spices and is traditionally cooked in a clay oven. Try making tandoori chicken drumsticks that have been marinated this way and then grill them on a hot grill for an Indian tapas party.

# Crab-Stuffed Chicken Rolls

This recipe can also be doubled to be served as an
entrée item that will accommodate six people.

1. Melt unsalted butter in a large skillet over medium heat. Add lemon zest, garlic, parsley, green onion, green bell pepper, and celery; sauté vegetables until soft. Fold in the crabmeat, salt, paprika, and peppers. Fold in the fine breadcrumbs and half-and-half. Let the filling cool.

2. Preheat oven to 350°F.

3. Flatten chicken breasts to ¼-inch thickness. Spread the cooled crab mixture on the chicken breasts and roll each one up like you would a jelly roll. Press edges to seal.

4. Dip each chicken roll in melted salted butter and roll in panko breadcrumbs. Place them in a 9" × 13" baking dish.

5. Cover and bake for 45 minutes. Uncover and bake until golden brown, about 10 more minutes. Let rest 5 minutes, then cut the chicken rolls into slices and arrange them on plates. Sprinkle with parsley and serve with lemon wedges.

## SERVES 6

2 ounces unsalted butter
1 tablespoon lemon zest
1 teaspoon minced garlic
1 tablespoon chopped parsley
2 tablespoons minced green onion
1 tablespoon minced green bell pepper
2 tablespoons minced celery
4 ounces lump crabmeat or imitation crabmeat
¼ teaspoon salt
Pinch paprika
Pinch black pepper
Pinch cayenne pepper
½ cup fine dry bread crumbs
2 tablespoons half-and-half
3 boneless, skinless chicken breasts
¼ cup melted salted butter
½ cup panko breadcrumbs
Fresh parsley, chopped, for garnish
Lemon wedges

# Chicken Scampi Bites

*Scampi* in this recipe refers to a preparation usually used for shrimp: garlic, butter, and lemon. Serve these zingy chicken bites with toothpicks, pincho-style.

**SERVES 6**

3 boneless, skinless chicken
  breasts
½ cup panko breadcrumbs
2 tablespoons chopped fresh
  parsley
½ cup Parmesan cheese
1 egg, beaten
2 ounces salted butter
1 minced garlic clove
¼ cup lemon juice

1. Preheat oven to 375°F.

2. Cut the chicken into uniform bite-size pieces.

3. Combine the breadcrumbs, parsley, and Parmesan cheese in a bowl.

4. Dip the chicken pieces in the egg, then coat with breadcrumb mixture. Place the chicken pieces in a 9" × 13" glass baking dish.

5. Melt the butter, garlic, and lemon juice in a skillet. Gently pour half of this mixture over the chicken pieces. Bake uncovered for 45 minutes. Spoon the rest of the lemon garlic butter over the chicken and serve hot.

## Chicken Biscuits . . . . . . . . . . . . . . . . . . . . . . .

Mini biscuits with crispy chicken nuggets, honey, and sliced baby dill pickles make tasty bite-size sandwiches for a tapas selection of southern food or breakfast or brunch.

# Duck Rillettes

This is a spread served on thin toasts. Port wine reduction adds color and flavor.

**SERVES 6**

2 duck legs confit, purchased
¼ cup dried cherries
1 tablespoon minced shallots
¼ cup butter, softened
Salt to taste
Pepper to taste
1 cup inexpensive port wine
1 sourdough baguette
Fresh chives, chopped

1. Shred the meat from the duck legs and put it in a bowl.

2. Chop the dried cherries and add them to the duck.

3. Sauté the shallots in butter with salt and pepper until tender. Remove from heat and add to the duck. Toss everything together well and pack it into a crock.

4. Put the port wine in a saucepan and cook it over medium-high heat to reduce it to one quarter of the original amount. Let it cool and then refrigerate it. It will be thicker, like thin syrup.

5. Cut the baguette into thin slices and toast them. Spread some of the duck rillettes on each toast, drizzle the port on top, and sprinkle with chives.

## Substitution . . . . . . . . . . . . . . . . . . . . . . . . . . . . .

If duck confit is unavailable try roast Chinese duck or roast your own duck and use the legs. Cooked chicken legs, smoked trout, or pulled pork also can be made into rillettes.

# Smoked Turkey Roll-Ups

Turkey and cranberries are a classic combination that are partnered with spicy arugula greens in this Thanksgiving-appropriate nosh.

**SERVES 4**

4 slices smoked turkey

4 tablespoons cranberry sauce

¼ cup arugula

4 sticks of string cheese

1. Lay out a slice of smoked turkey.

2. Spread 1 tablespoon cranberry sauce on the turkey.

3. Scatter a few arugula leaves on the cranberry sauce.

4. Place a stick of string cheese on the smoked turkey at one end.

5. Roll up the turkey around the string cheese. Cut in half on the diagonal or serve whole. Repeat with remaining ingredients.

## Holiday Wraps. . . . . . . . . . . . . . . . . . . . . . . .

Use the recipe for Smoked Turkey Roll-Ups and roll them up in a spinach tortilla that has been spread thinly with whipped cream cheese. Ham, beef, or other sliced meats can be made into similar wraps, with small changes like horseradish sauce for beef and honey mustard for ham instead of cranberry.

# Soy Sauce Dim-Sum Wings

Serve these in their foil packets for guests to open themselves.

1. Combine the peanut oil, garlic, ginger, soy sauce, hoisin sauce, rice vinegar, and sesame oil in a 1-gallon plastic zipper bag and toss the chicken wings in it. Marinate in the refrigerator for 1 hour.

2. While the chicken marinates, cut foil into 3-inch squares, making enough for each wing section.

3. Individually wrap each wing section in a square of foil and place the packets on a baking sheet.

4. Preheat oven to 375°F.

5. Bake the wings for 30 minutes. Remove from oven, turn the wings over with tongs, return to the oven, and bake another 30 minutes.

**SERVES 6**

¼ cup peanut oil
1 tablespoon minced garlic
1 tablespoon minced ginger
¼ cup soy sauce
¼ cup hoisin sauce
2 tablespoons rice vinegar
1 teaspoon sesame oil
1½ pounds chicken wings, tips removed and cut into drumettes and wing segments
Nonstick aluminum foil

# Chicken and Green Lentils Vinaigrette

Serve this salad on individual plates or on one large platter as part of a tapas spread.

1. Put the lentils, water, and bay leaf in a saucepan, bring to a boil, reduce heat, and simmer 20 minutes. Drain in a colander, remove the bay leaf, and let the lentils cool. Put them in a large bowl and set aside.

2. Heat the olive oil in a sauté pan and cook the carrot, celery, and shallots in it over medium heat for about 5 minutes, until tender. Add them with any oil left in the pan to the lentils.

3. Add the chicken, garlic, extra-virgin olive oil, lemon juice, champagne vinegar, lemon zest, thyme, salt, and pepper to the lentils. Toss to combine and chill.

**SERVES 4**

1 cup French green lentils
5 cups water
1 bay leaf
2 tablespoons olive oil
1 carrot, finely chopped
1 stalk celery, finely chopped
2 tablespoons minced shallots
1 cup shredded roast chicken meat
1 teaspoon minced garlic
3 tablespoons extra-virgin olive oil
1 tablespoon lemon juice
1 tablespoon champagne vinegar
1 teaspoon lemon zest
1 tablespoon chopped fresh thyme
Salt and pepper to taste

# Chicken Salad Tarts

**SERVES 6**

2 prerolled pie doughs
2 to 3 cups diced roasted chicken
    meat, cold
1 cup mayonnaise
Salt and pepper to taste
¼ cup diced celery
¼ cup currants
½ cup chopped pecans
½ avocado, diced

The method for blind-baking the tart shells in this recipe doesn't require pie weights or foil.

1. Preheat the oven to 350°F.

2. Cut three circles out of each pie dough. Prick the circles with a fork all over. Turn a muffin tin upside down and spray cooking oil over the bottom. Place the six circles of pie dough over every other muffin tin bottom. Bake for 15 minutes, or until done. Let cool and remove the tart shells.

3. Mix the chicken meat with the mayonnaise, salt, and pepper. Add the celery, currants, and pecans and mix to combine.

4. Fold the avocado into the chicken mixture.

5. Spoon the chicken salad into the tart shells and serve.

# Orange Avocado Chicken Pinchos

**SERVES 4**

1 cup mandarin orange segments
1 avocado, diced
1 cup cooked chicken, large dice
Small bamboo skewers

Use fresh clementines for authentic Spanish pinchos instead of mandarin oranges and segment them with a sharp knife.

1. Thread an orange segment on a skewer.

2. Thread a piece of avocado after the orange.

3. Put a piece of chicken on the end of the skewer after the avocado. Repeat with the remaining ingredients and serve on a tray.

## More Chicken Pinchos . . . . . . . . . . . . . . . . . . . . . .
Grilled chicken with mango chunks, poached chicken with honeydew-melon balls, and roast chicken with red grapes are also good pincho combinations.

# Meat

# Cherry Pork Tenderloin

**SERVES 4**

1 tablespoon olive oil
1 pork tenderloin (1½ pounds)
1 tablespoon kosher salt
1 teaspoon ground black pepper
1 shallot, minced
½ cup dried cherries, chopped
1 tablespoon balsamic vinegar
½ cup cherry preserves

Internal temperature of the tenderloin will go up about 5 degrees after it has been removed from the heat. It should be 155°F when done.

1. Preheat a grill or grill pan on high.

2. Rub 1 teaspoon olive oil on the tenderloin, then sprinkle the kosher salt and black pepper on it.

3. Grill the tenderloin on all sides, for a total of about 10 minutes. Set the tenderloin aside, cover it with foil, and let it rest at least 10 minutes before slicing.

4. Sauté the shallots in remaining olive oil until tender. Remove from heat and stir in the chopped dried cherries, balsamic vinegar, and cherry preserves.

5. Cut the tenderloin in ½-inch-thick slices, arrange the slices overlapping on a platter, and spoon the cherry sauce over them.

## Pitting Cherries . . . . . . . . . . . . . . . . . . . . . . . . . .

There are several ways to pit cherries, one of which is to insert an unfolded paper clip into the end, twist around the seed, and then pull it out. If you are using a manual cherry/olive pitter that works like a paper hole punch, pit them inside a plastic bag to catch the splattering juice that stains.

# Gyro Bites

Serve the gyro bites with Greek Yogurt Cucumber Sauce (tzatziki)
(page 28), diced tomatoes, sliced onions, and lettuce.

1. Preheat oven to 350°F.

2. Combine all ingredients except the olive oil and pita in a bowl with your hands. Shape the mixture into a log and press it into a loaf pan. Brush the top with olive oil.

3. Bake, uncovered, until thermometer inserted in center reads 160°F, about 1 hour. Let the loaf cool and refrigerate it until ready to use.

4. Slice the chilled meat loaf thinly and sear the slices in a hot sauté pan. Cut the pita rounds in half to make six pita pockets.

5. Fill the pockets with seared meat slices and cut each pocket into smaller triangles. Arrange the triangles on a plate and serve with sauce, tomatoes, onions, and lettuce.

**SERVES 4 TO 6**

¼ pound ground beef
¼ pound ground lamb
2 tablespoons minced onion
1 clove garlic, pressed
¼ teaspoon celery salt
½ teaspoon Worcestershire sauce
1 egg white
2 teaspoons chopped fresh
    parsley
2 teaspoons dried oregano
½ teaspoon black pepper
½ teaspoon salt
2 tablespoons oatmeal
2 tablespoons breadcrumbs
2 teaspoons olive oil
3 pita-bread rounds
Accompaniments: tzatziki, diced
    tomatoes, sliced onions,
    shredded lettuce

# Hawaiian Meatballs

SERVES 8

*1 pound ham, ground*

*½ pound fresh pork, ground*

*¾ cup breadcrumbs*

*3 tablespoons buttermilk*

*1 egg*

*¼ cup minced celery*

*2 tablespoons minced Maui sweet onion*

*¼ teaspoon pepper*

*⅛ teaspoon ground cloves*

*⅓ cup brown sugar, firmly packed*

*1 tablespoon vinegar*

*2 tablespoons pineapple juice*

Like a Hawaiian pizza with ham, pineapple, and Maui sweet onions, these meatballs can be served as pinchos with toothpicks or not.

1. Preheat oven to 350°F. Line a baking sheet with nonstick foil.

2. Mix the ham, ground pork, breadcrumbs, buttermilk, egg, celery, onion, pepper, and cloves together.

3. Form into small balls, cocktail meatball size, and place them 1 inch apart on baking sheet and bake for 15 minutes.

4. For the glaze, combine the brown sugar, vinegar, and pineapple juice in a saucepan over low heat. Whisk until combined and cook about 5 minutes.

5. Coat the meatballs with the glaze and serve hot.

## Ham and Melon . . . . . . . . . . . . . . . . . . . . . . . .

The classic combination of salty and sweet make this pairing the perfect appetizer. Simply peel, seed, and slice a cantaloupe into half moons and drape pieces of thinly sliced Serrano ham or prosciutto over them for a salad, or cut the melon into chunks and wrap each chunk with the ham and insert toothpicks for "pinchos."

# Chinese Barbecued Pork

This is the barbecued pork used to make Chinese Barbecued-Pork Buns (page 217) and Chinese Steamed Pork Bao (page 237), and it also can be added to fried rice and soup.

1. Cut pork into 4 × 2-inch strips, 1 inch thick.

2. Mix the hoisin sauce, ketchup, sugar, salt, and soy sauce together, rub it over the pork strips, and marinate in the refrigerator overnight.

3. Preheat the oven to 375°F. Line a roaster pan with foil and set a rack in the roaster.

4. Put the marinated pork strips on the rack and roast for 45 minutes, turning once or twice.

5. Freeze whatever you won't be using right away.

**MAKES 3 POUNDS**

1 (3-pound) pork butt, boneless
2 tablespoons hoisin sauce
4 tablespoons ketchup
4 tablespoons sugar
1 teaspoon salt
1 tablespoon dark soy sauce

# Westphalia Ham Spirals

You can make the ham spirals large enough to fit the cucumber rounds by linking ham slices together to make a larger circumference if necessary.

1. Blend the cream cheese, sour cream, and dill until smooth.

2. Spread the cream cheese mousse on the ham slices and roll them up like a carpet, creating a spiral of ham and mousse. Wrap in plastic and refrigerate for 1 hour, more if possible, to let the rolls firm up.

3. Cut the cucumber into ¼-inch-thick rounds and drain on paper towels before removing the ham logs from the refrigerator.

4. Unwrap and cut the chilled ham rolls into 1-inch-thick slices and place them on the cucumber rounds, cut-side up so the spiral is visible.

5. Arrange spirals on a tray and serve or cover with plastic and refrigerate until serving time.

**SERVES 6**

4 ounces whipped cream cheese, softened
¼ cup sour cream
1 teaspoon dill
½ pound Westphalia ham, sliced
1 cucumber

# Choux Farci Rolls

**SERVES 6**

12 large Savoy cabbage leaves
1 cup cooked rice
¼ cup minced onion
¼ cup toasted pine nuts
¼ cup currants
¾ teaspoon salt
Pepper to taste
½ pound ground beef
¾ pound ground pork
1 tablespoon butter
2 cups tomato sauce
2 garlic cloves, finely minced
1 tablespoon brown sugar

*Choux farci* is French for "stuffed cabbage." The fancy name suggests a dressed-up version with pine nuts and currants in the stuffing.

1. Blanch the Savoy cabbage leaves in boiling water for 4 minutes. Remove and lay flat on a metal tray. Chill in the refrigerator. Remove from the refrigerator and blot with paper towels.

2. In a bowl, combine the cooked rice, onion, pine nuts, currants, salt, and pepper. Add ground beef and pork and mix well. Place about ¼ cup meat mixture on each cabbage leaf. Fold in sides and then roll up leaf to completely enclose filling.

3. In a skillet, melt the butter, add the tomato sauce, garlic, and brown sugar, and stir to combine.

4. Place the cabbage rolls in the tomato sauce, seam sides down. Spoon some of the sauce over the rolls, cover, and cook over medium-low heat for 1 hour. Reduce heat to low and simmer for an additional 20 minutes, adding a little water if needed. Serve hot.

## Cabbage Roll Ups . . . . . . . . . . . . . . . . . . . . .
Blanch cabbage leaves and roll each of them up with a slice of ham and cheese for a simple tapa.

# Cognac Peppercorn Filet

This luxurious tapa is sliced to share. No need for steak knives.
Substitute chopped flat-leaf parsley for the chervil if unavailable.

1. Crack the peppercorns in one layer on a cutting board with the bottom of a heavy pan. Lean on it, don't hammer it. Sprinkle the salt on the filet, then press the meat into the peppercorns to coat both sides.

2. Melt the butter in a small, heavy, stainless steel sauté pan over medium-high heat until very hot. Swirl it around and let it sizzle, then brown the filet in it 4 minutes per side.

3. Remove the filets and keep them in a warm oven while preparing the sauce. On zero heat, add 2 tablespoons of cognac to the pan and carefully ignite the alcohol with a firestick. When the flames die down, turn the heat to medium and stir the liquid in the skillet, scraping up any browned bits from the bottom.

4. Add the cream and bring the pan sauce to a simmer. Cook and swirl until the sauce begins to thicken, maybe 3 minutes. Add the teaspoon of cognac, stir, and taste to see if you need additional salt. Return the filet to the pan, and cook it 30 seconds per side in the sauce.

5. Slice the filet and plate it. Spoon the pan sauce over it and crumble the blue cheese on top. Garnish with the sprigs of chervil.

**SERVES 4**

2 teaspoons black peppercorns
Pinch kosher salt
1 (6-ounce) beef tenderloin filet, 1½ inches thick
1 teaspoon butter
2 tablespoons Cognac plus 1 teaspoon
¼ cup heavy cream
1 ounce Stilton, Gorgonzola, Cabrales, or Roquefort cheese (optional)
4 to 5 sprigs fresh chervil

# Rum Raisin Meatballs

The combination of rum and raisins, as in rum raisin ice
cream, was the inspiration for this savory recipe.

**SERVES 4**

½ cup milk
2 tablespoons rum
1 slice white bread
1 pound ground beef
1 egg
¼ cup minced onion
¼ cup chopped golden raisins
1 teaspoon molasses
½ teaspoon onion powder
1 teaspoon celery salt
¼ cup apple cider
2 tablespoons rum

1. In a bowl, combine the milk and rum and soak the bread in it. Preheat oven to 350°F.

2. Squeeze the liquid out of the bread (discard it) and tear the bread into small pieces.

3. In a large bowl, combine the bread with the ground beef, egg, onion, raisins, molasses, onion powder, and celery salt.

4. Shape the meat mixture into 2-inch balls, with wet hands, and place the meatballs on a nonstick-foil-lined baking sheet with sides. Bake meatballs for 20 minutes.

5. Combine the apple cider and rum, baste the meatballs with the rum mixture, and bake 5 minutes more. Serve hot or warm on small plates.

# Mint Pesto Lamb Lollipops

What goes better on lamb than mint sauce? Mint pesto. Serve with
Greek Yogurt Cucumber Sauce (page 28) for dipping.

1. Combine the garlic, mint, pine nuts, cumin, Parmesan cheese, and
   extra-virgin olive oil in a food processor or mortar and pestle. Set
   aside.

2. Brush the lamb chops with olive oil and season with salt and pepper.
   Preheat a grill or grill pan and grill the chops for 2 minutes on both
   sides. (Cook more or less time to your preference.)

3. Toss the chops in a bowl with the mint pesto, arrange on a plate, and
   serve hot.

## Substitution . . . . . . . . . . . . . . . . . . . . . . . . . . .

Lamb ribs, sometimes called riblets, can also be used to make mint pesto lollipops. Look for them
at purveyors of fine meats or ask for them in butcher shops and at meat counters. Sometimes
they can special order them.

**SERVES 6**

1 clove minced garlic

¼ cup minced fresh mint

2 tablespoons ground pine nuts

¼ teaspoon cumin

2 tablespoons grated Parmesan
cheese

2 tablespoons extra-virgin
olive oil

12 lamb rib chops, Frenched and
trimmed

2 tablespoons olive oil

Salt and pepper to taste

# Pomegranate Lamb Kebabs

SERVES 8

¼ cup dry red wine

½ cup unsweetened pomegranate juice

1 small onion, sliced

2 teaspoons lemon zest

1 tablespoon lemon juice

1 clove garlic, minced

½ teaspoon black pepper

2 teaspoons chopped fresh oregano

½ teaspoon salt

1 pound lamb shoulder or leg, cubed

Pita bread triangles

The exotic flavor of pomegranate juice is in the marinade for this preparation of grilled lamb. To serve, garnish with jewel-like pomegranate seeds.

1. Combine red wine, pomegranate juice, onion, lemon zest and juice, garlic, pepper, oregano, and salt in a bowl. Add lamb to the marinade, toss to coat, cover, and refrigerate 12 hours or overnight.

2. Preheat a grill or grill pan. Thread marinated lamb cubes onto metal skewers.

3. Grill on all sides until cooked through. Take the grilled lamb cubes off the skewers and serve on a plate with pita triangles.

# Mango Pork Medallions

SERVES 4

1 pork tenderloin

1 tablespoon olive oil

1 teaspoon Kosher salt

½ teaspoon pepper

1 tablespoon vegetable oil

½ cup sliced sweet onion

3 cloves minced garlic

½ teaspoon ground cumin

2 tablespoons orange juice

2 tablespoons lemon juice

2 tablespoons lime juice

2 cups diced fresh mango

Chopped fresh cilantro

This sauce can be served cold if you prefer. Just make it ahead of time and then chill it before grilling the medallions.

1. Slice the tenderloin into 1-inch-thick medallions. Rub the olive oil on both sides of each medallion, then sprinkle with kosher salt and pepper. Set aside. Preheat a grill or grill pan.

2. Sauté the onions and garlic in the vegetable oil in a saucepan. Add the cumin, orange juice, lemon juice, lime juice, and mangoes and cook over medium heat for about 15 minutes, stirring occasionally.

3. Grill the pork medallions on both sides, 2 minutes per side.

4. Arrange the medallions on a platter and spoon the mango sauce over them. Garnish with cilantro.

# Barbecued Beef Brisket

For tapas portions, serve brisket-bun sandwiches made from this barbecued brisket and dinner rolls. Put a slice of cheddar cheese and onion on the sandwiches if desired.

**SERVES 12**

1 brisket, trimmed (about 6 pounds)
¼ cup barbecue seasoning or rub
1 can cola
1 bottle porter or dark beer
3 cups water
¾ red onion, sliced
2 cups red barbecue sauce

1. Sprinkle the barbecue seasoning over both sides of the brisket and rub or pat it into the meat. Place the brisket on the rack in a countertop roaster.

2. Pour the cola around the brisket and pour the porter over it into the roaster pan. Add the water and scatter the sliced onions over the meat.

3. Put the lid on the roaster, set it at 250°F, and let it cook for 3 hours.

4. Preheat the oven to 350°F. Put the brisket on a baking-sheet pan and brush ⅓ of the barbecue sauce on it. Bake for 20 minutes. Turn over the brisket and brush half of the remaining sauce on this side and bake for 20 minutes. Take it out, turn it over one more time, and baste it with the remaining sauce. Bake another 20 minutes (1 hour total).

5. Let the brisket rest for 10 minutes, then transfer it to a carving board. Slice and serve.

## Barbecue Rub . . . . . . . . . . . . . . . . . . . . . . . . . .

Make your own barbecue seasoning or rub by mixing together spices and herbs you like best. Try equal portions of paprika, chili powder, oregano, sugar, and kosher salt with a little (or a lot of) garlic powder. Add or substitute spices and herbs of your choosing and try brown sugar and fresh garlic for a moister consistency. Adjust the heat by adding or decreasing the chili powder. Add cinnamon and coriander for an exotic flavor.

# Italian Pot Roast

**SERVES 6**

1 beef chuck shoulder roast (2 to
   3 pounds)
½ teaspoon salt
¼ teaspoon pepper
1 teaspoon oregano
2 tablespoons olive oil
1 cup diced onions
1 cup beef broth
¼ cup Italian salad dressing
3 cloves garlic
2 carrots, peeled and sliced
1 tablespoon tomato paste

Italian Pot Roast can be served a variety of ways, such as over cooked pasta or polenta, as a filling for raviolis, or on hoagie buns for Italian beef sandwiches.

1. Sprinkle the salt, pepper, and oregano over both sides of the roast.

2. Put a frying pan over medium-high heat, add the olive oil, and brown the roast on all sides. Remove the roast to a slow cooker and add the onions to the frying pan over low heat. Scrape up the browned bits on the bottom of the frying pan with the onions and cook for 3 minutes. Add the onions to the slow cooker with the roast.

3. Add the beef broth, salad dressing, garlic cloves, carrots, and tomato paste to the slow cooker, put the lid on, turn the slow cooker on high, and let the roast cook for at least 3 hours, turning it over half way through the cooking time.

4. Remove the roast from the slow cooker and let it rest for 10 minutes.

5. Slice the meat or shred it with two forks, return it to the slow cooker with the cooking liquid, and cook on low for 30 minutes. Serve warm with bread and noodles, mashed potatoes, or polenta.

# Fried Tidbits

# Welsh Rarebit Croquettes

**MAKES 72**

¼ small onion
1 clove
1 bay leaf
1½ cups whole milk
6 tablespoons salted butter
1 cup all-purpose flour
Pinch ground cayenne pepper
Pinch mustard powder
Pinch paprika
1 teaspoon Worcestershire sauce
2½ cups shredded Cheddar
    cheese
1 cup shredded Colby cheese
1 cup grated Parmesan cheese
3 egg yolks
½ cup all-purpose flour
3 egg whites
½ teaspoon salt
1 tablespoon vegetable oil
1 cup dry breadcrumbs
2 cups vegetable oil

Fritters can be kept warm in a 250°F oven after they have been fried, or freeze them and heat them up in a 350°F oven for 15 to 20 minutes.

1. Poke the clove into the quarter onion and place the onion and the bay leaf in a saucepan with the milk. Heat the milk over medium-high to scalding (not quite boiling) and then remove it from the heat. Let steep for 15 minutes, then remove and discard the onion and bay leaf.

2. Meanwhile, melt the butter in another saucepan, add 1 cup of flour, and cook over medium heat for a few minutes, stirring with a wooden spoon. This will make a roux. Gradually add the hot milk to the roux on the heat and whisk with a wire whip to smooth out lumps, for about a minute. The roux will absorb the milk as it cooks and become a very thick béchamel sauce.

3. Remove the béchamel from the heat and stir in the cayenne pepper, dry mustard powder, paprika, Worcestershire sauce, and cheeses with a wooden spoon. Beat in the egg yolks one at a time with the wooden spoon. Spread the mixture onto a plastic-lined baking sheet, cover the top surface directly with plastic wrap, and refrigerate it overnight.

4. Arrange a production line for coating the croquettes by putting the ½ cup flour on a plate, the egg whites in a bowl, and the breadcrumbs on a plate. Add ½ teaspoon salt and 1 tablespoon vegetable oil to the egg whites and whisk them until they are frothy.

5. Remove the plastic from the top of the croquette filling and cut the filling into 36 equal portions. Roll each portion into a ball and then roll it in the flour, dip it in the egg whites, and roll it in the breadcrumbs. Place it on a tray and repeat with the remaining portions. Refrigerate until you are ready to fry them.

6. Put 2 cups vegetable oil in a deep pot or deep fryer and heat it to 375°F. Fry the croquettes in small batches for 3 to 6 minutes, until they are golden brown. Drain on paper towels and serve hot.

# Fertile Crescent Falafel

Serve these hot with toothpicks for Spanish-style pinchos or
with halved pita bread to make pocket sandwiches.

1. Soak the garbanzo beans in 3 cups of water overnight.

2. Drain the garbanzo beans and put them in a food processor with the
   red onion, garlic, salt, pepper, cumin, and cayenne pepper. Pulse until
   everything is combined and the texture is fine, but not a paste.

3. Sprinkle the baking powder and flours over the mixture and pulse
   again until well combined. Refrigerate the mixture for 3 hours.

4. Heat the oil in a deep fryer or large pot to 375°F. Shape falafel mixture
   into small balls and fry four or five at a time. Drain on paper towels.
   Place falafel balls on a plate lined with lettuce and tomatoes. Drizzle
   with yogurt and sprinkle with parsley.

## Substitution . . . . . . . . . . . . . . . . . . . . . .

You may use canned garbanzo beans for this falafel recipe too. Be sure to drain the liquid though.
The resulting falafel will be a little smoother and less crunchy.

**SERVES 6**

1 cup dried garbanzo beans
½ cup chopped red onion
3 cloves garlic, peeled
1 teaspoon salt
1 teaspoon pepper
1 teaspoon ground cumin
Pinch cayenne pepper
1 teaspoon baking powder
3 tablespoons all-purpose flour
3 tablespoons whole wheat flour
2 cups vegetable oil
1 cup chopped fresh tomatoes
1 cup shredded lettuce
6 tablespoons plain yogurt
2 tablespoons chopped fresh
   parsley

# Caribbean Coconut Shrimp

**SERVES 4**

4 egg whites

1 cup cornstarch

1 cup unsweetened grated coconut

1 pound large shrimp, peeled and deveined

3 cups vegetable oil

*If you can't find unsweetened grated coconut, you may use sweetened shredded, but it will burn quicker and turn dark because of the added sugar caramelizing.*

1. Whip the egg whites until frothy and place in a bowl. Put the cornstarch and coconut in separate bowls.

2. Dredge each shrimp in cornstarch, dip in egg whites, and coat with coconut.

3. Heat the vegetable oil in a deep fryer or heavy pot to 365°F.

4. Fry the shrimp in small batches until golden brown, about 2 to minutes.

# Calamari with Lime Aioli

**SERVES 4**

2 limes

¾ cup mayonnaise

1 clove garlic, minced

1 cup rice flour

1 teaspoon salt

½ teaspoon pepper

2 pounds calamari, cut into rings

3 cups vegetable oil

*Traditional French aioli is made in the same manner as traditional Spanish aioli. This is a quick version using commercial mayonnaise, minced garlic, and lime juice.*

1. Grate the zest from one lime and add it to the mayonnaise. Add the juice from the lime and the garlic and mix well. Cut the other lime into wedges. Set aside.

2. Mix the rice flour, salt, and pepper together in a large bowl.

3. Toss a handful of calamari in flour mixture and shake off excess in a strainer.

4. Heat oil to 365°F in a deep fryer or heavy pot and fry the coated calamari until golden brown, about 3 minutes. Drain on paper towels. Repeat with remaining calamari.

5. Serve calamari immediately with lime aioli and lime wedges.

# Chicken Taquitos

Serve these crispy sticks with sour cream, guacamole, and
salsa, or with Mexi-Cali Pepper Jack Fondue (page 59).

1. Toss the chicken with the taco seasoning in a bowl. Add the cheddar
   cheese and toss to mix.

2. Roll a small amount of the chicken mixture tightly in each tortilla and
   place them on a tray.

3. Heat the oil in a skillet over medium heat. Fry the taquitos, seam-side
   down first, in the oil on both sides until crisp. Drain on paper towels
   and serve hot.

Flautas . . . . . . . . . . . . . . . . . . . . . . . . . . . .

Flautas are similar to taquitos, but they are larger and made with flour tortillas instead of cornmeal. *Flautas* means "flutes," which is what they resemble.

**SERVES 4**

*2 cups shredded cooked chicken*
*1 cup shredded cheddar cheese*
*1 package taco seasoning*
*24 corn tortillas*
*1 cup vegetable oil*

# Shrimp Banana Dim Sum

**SERVES 4**

1 firm, ripe banana
3 cups vegetable oil
12 wonton wrappers
12 small cooked shrimp, peeled

I had these off a dim-sum cart in San Francisco, and the combination of
shrimp and bananas was so good I had to recreate them.

1. Peel and cut the banana into three pieces. Cut each piece into four
   sticks.

2. Heat the vegetable oil in a deep fryer or heavy pot to 365°F.

3. Place a wonton wrapper on a work surface in a diamond. Put a banana
   stick and a shrimp in the middle of the wonton wrapper horizontally.

4. Fold the bottom point up and over the filling, fold the side points in,
   place a dab of water on the top point and roll the rest of the way. Press
   the top point into the roll to help the wrapper adhere where the water
   is. Repeat with the remaining wrappers and filling.

5. Fry in small batches for 1 minute and drain on paper towels. Serve
   warm.

## What to Do with Wrappers . . . . . . . . . . . . . . . . . . . .

Take care to freeze wonton, spring roll, and egg-roll wrappers if you are not using them right
away, because the flour in them will oxidize and black spots will speckle the wrappers if you
don't. Thaw them in the refrigerator before using them.

# Chinese Onion Cakes

These onion cakes are cut into wedges and served warm either alone or
with a dipping sauce, such as Hoisin Dipping Sauce (page 34).

1. Cut the loaf of bread dough into six pieces and work with one at a time.

2. Roll one piece of dough out on a lightly floured cutting board to the size of a pancake. Spread 2 teaspoons of sesame oil over the surface of the dough.

3. Sprinkle 1 teaspoon sesame seeds, some cilantro, and a handful of green onions over the dough and press them in with your hands.

4. Roll the dough up from the bottom like a jelly roll. Take one end and press it down on the board, then coil the rest of the roll around it like a snail. Roll the snail out flat into a circle.

5. Heat ⅓ cup oil in a skillet and fry the onion cake on both sides until golden. Drain on paper towels and then cut the cake into six wedges. Repeat with the remaining dough and ingredients. Serve warm.

## Another Method. . . . . . . . . . . . . . . . . . . . . . . . . .

Another way to make onion cakes is to use two large, round gyoza wrappers and fill the middle with green onions like a big ravioli. Pan fry them on each side until crispy and serve whole.

**SERVES 12**

1 loaf frozen bread dough, thawed in refrigerator
4 tablespoons sesame oil
2 tablespoons black sesame seeds
2 tablespoons chopped fresh cilantro
1 cup chopped green onions
2 cups vegetable oil

# Pizza Panzerotti

These pizza turnovers are similar to calzones, except they are
fried, not baked. They are also smaller than calzones.

*16 frozen dinner rolls, unbaked
    dough*

*16 tablespoons (1 cup) pizza
    sauce*

*5 tablespoons diced pepperoni*

*½ cup grated Parmesan cheese*

*1 cup shredded provolone cheese*

*3 cups vegetable oil*

1. Lay the frozen dinner-roll dough out on a plastic-lined baking sheet and cover them with a piece of plastic wrap. Let thaw in the refrigerator overnight. (Spray the plastic wrap with vegetable oil first to prevent sticking.)

2. Roll or press each roll flat and put 1 tablespoon of pizza sauce in the middle of each one. Put about 1 teaspoon of pepperoni and Parmesan cheese and a pinch of provolone cheese on top of the sauce.

3. Fold each dough circle in half over the filling and press down to make a half circle. Use a fork to crimp the edges.

4. Heat the vegetable oil in a deep fryer or heavy pot to 365°F.

5. Fry the panzerotti in batches until they are golden brown. Drain on paper towels and serve warm.

# Japanese Vegetable Tempura

Serve tempura as part of a Japanese-style meal with soy
sauce or Ponzu Dipping Sauce (page 29) for dipping.

**SERVES 4**

¾ cup beer
¾ cup flour
¾ teaspoon salt
2 cups vegetable oil
12 stalks asparagus
12 carrot sticks
4 green onions, trimmed

1. Whisk beer into flour until smooth, then stir in salt.

2. Heat oil to 375°F in a deep fryer or large pot.

3. Dip vegetables individually in batter, let excess drip off, then drop carefully into the hot oil.

4. Cook about 3 minutes, then remove from oil with a slotted spoon, chopsticks, or tongs. Cook in batches.

5. Drain on paper towels and serve immediately.

## Deep-Fried Candy Bars . . . . . . . . . . . . . . . . . .

Tempura batter is a good thing to dip very cold (but not frozen) candy bars in to try your hand at the deep-fried candy-bar craze so popular at British fish and chips stands.

# Polynesian Crab Puffs

These are often called crab Rangoon on restaurant menus. I
consider them the crown jewel of any pupu platter.

**SERVES 4**

1 cup crabmeat

8 ounces cream cheese, softened

1 tablespoon rice wine

2 tablespoons chopped fresh
   chives

16 wonton wrappers

3 cups vegetable oil

1.  Combine the crabmeat, cream cheese, rice wine, and chives in a bowl
    with a wooden spoon.

2.  Lay a wonton wrapper on a work surface and place 1 teaspoon of the
    crab mixture in the middle. Brush two consecutive sides with water
    and fold the wrapper over. Press together, squeezing the air out while
    pinching the sides together, forming a triangle.

3.  Bring the two side corners together and pinch them together with a
    dab of water and set it upright. Repeat with the remaining wrappers
    and filling.

4.  Heat the vegetable oil in a deep fryer or heavy pot to 365°F.

5.  Fry the crab puffs for 1 minute in batches. Drain on paper towels and
    serve warm.

# Pacific Rim Shrimp Toasts

Shrimp toasts are classic dim-sum fare. The crunchy and tasty morsels
are a good hors d'oeuvre before a Chinese, Thai, or Vietnamese meal.

1. Combine the shrimp, fish sauce, butter, shallot, cilantro, egg white, sesame oil, salt, and pepper in a food processor and mix to make a paste.

2. Cut the bread slices in half to make rectangles.

3. Spread the shrimp paste onto one side of each rectangle of bread, dividing it equally among the sixteen pieces.

4. Heat the peanut oil in a skillet and fry the toasts, paste-side down first, on both sides until they are golden brown.

5. Fry in batches dividing the oil accordingly. Drain on paper towels and serve hot.

## Substitution . . . . . . . . . . . . . . . . . . . . . . . . . . . .
Try using slices of baguette instead of sliced white bread for making shrimp toast. They will have a rustic look like bruschetta.

---

**SERVES 4**

10 ounces raw shrimp, peeled

1 tablespoon fish sauce

2 tablespoons cold butter, diced

1 tablespoon minced shallot

1 teaspoon chopped fresh cilantro

1 egg white

1 teaspoon sesame oil

½ teaspoon salt

Pinch white pepper

8 slices thinly sliced white bread, crusts removed

½ cup peanut oil

# Fried Olives

SERVES 4

¾ cup cold pilsner or wheat beer
¾ cup flour
¾ teaspoon salt
¼ teaspoon cayenne pepper
2 cups vegetable oil
1 jar large garlic-stuffed olives,
    drained on paper towels

Olives stuffed with other things, such as cream cheese, blue cheese, anchovies, jalapeños, pearl onions, pimentos, almond, or anything else out there can be made in the same manner.

1. Whisk beer into flour until smooth, then stir in salt and cayenne pepper.

2. Heat oil to 375°F in a deep fryer or large pot.

3. Dip olives individually in batter, let excess drip off, then drop carefully into the hot oil.

4. Cook about 3 minutes, then remove from oil with a slotted spoon.

5. Drain on paper towels and serve immediately.

# Tostones

SERVES 6

2 plantains
3 cups vegetable oil
Kosher salt

Plantains are black when they are ripe, but for this recipe you want to use the almost ripe ones that are yellow with brown speckles.

1. Peel the plantains and cut them into ½-inch-thick slices.

2. Heat the vegetable oil in a deep fryer or heavy pot to 365°F.

3. Fry the plantains until they start to get golden and drain them on paper towels.

4. After they've cooled, smash the once-fried plantains between two pieces of waxed paper with a smooth meat pounder. Fry the plantain discs in oil until they are golden brown. Drain them on paper towels and salt them.

5. Serve them warm as is or as a garnish to Cuban black beans and rice.

# Portuguese Salt-Cod Fritters

Try frying these in olive oil, like they do in Spain with croquetas, for a different flavor. Serve with lemon wedges.

**SERVES 8**

2 baking potatoes, peeled
½ pound salt cod, prepared by
    soaking and cooking
½ cup minced onion
1 clove minced garlic
2 tablespoons chopped fresh
    parsley
1 egg
Pepper to taste
3 cups vegetable oil

1. Cut the potatoes into chunks, put them in a pot of cold water, bring to a boil, and simmer for 15 minutes, until tender. Drain and mash the potatoes.

2. Put the mashed potatoes, prepared cod, onion, garlic, parsley, pepper, and egg in a mixing bowl and mix well with the paddle attachment of a stand mixer or a wooden spoon.

3. Form the mixture into balls.

4. Heat the vegetable oil in a deep fryer or heavy pot to 365°F.

5. Fry the balls until golden brown, drain on paper towels, and serve hot.

Soaking Salt Cod. . . . . . . . . . . . . . . . . . . . . . . .

To cook with salt cod, it must be soaked overnight to remove the excess salt that is used to preserve it. Soak it in cold water, changing it several times. Drain and rinse it and it will be ready to cook. Simmer the cod in milk (2 cups per 1 pound of salt cod) and water to cover for 20 minutes. Drain the cod, separate it into flakes, and remove any bone or skin. Your salt cod is now ready to use in recipes.

# Artichoke and Fennel Pakoras

You may try this with artichoke bottoms if you can find them,
and garnish them with a dab of béarnaise sauce.

**SERVES 4**

½ cup chickpea flour

¼ cup self-rising flour

¼ teaspoon cumin

¼ teaspoon curry powder

¼ teaspoon turmeric

Pinch cayenne pepper

¾ cup cold water

¾ teaspoon salt

2 cups vegetable oil

8 baby artichokes, thinly sliced

1 fennel bulb, thinly sliced

1. Combine the chickpea and self-rising flours with the spices. Whisk water into flour mixture until smooth, then stir in salt.

2. Heat oil to 375°F in a deep fryer or large pot.

3. Dip artichoke and fennel slices individually in batter, let excess drip off, then drop carefully into the hot oil.

4. Cook about 3 minutes, then remove from oil with a slotted spoon or tongs. Cook in batches and don't overcrowd.

5. Drain on paper towels and serve immediately.

## Artichoke Leaf Pakoras . . . . . . . . . . . . . . . . . . . .

Steam a whole artichoke and then let it cool. Pull the leaves out and lay them on paper towels to dry any moisture off them. Dip the edible ends into pakora batter and fry them in the same manner as above, but for only 1 minute. Don't eat the whole leaf, just the battered end.

# Samosas

These crispy, potato-filled triangles are excellent alone or
served with Mango Chutney (page 31) for a dipping sauce.

1. Bring 3 cups water to a simmer and add the turmeric. Cook the potatoes in the liquid for 5 minutes, strain them, and lay them out in one layer to cool.

2. In a bowl, combine the cooled potatoes, frozen peas, paprika, curry powder, cumin, coriander, salt, and lemon pepper to make filling.

3. Lay the wonton wrappers flat on a work surface. Put 1 tablespoon of the filling in the middle of each wrapper. Brush the edges of the wrapper with egg.

4. Fold each wrapper over, corner to corner, to make a triangle encasing the filling. Press down on the outer edges with your fingers to seal.

5. Heat the vegetable oil in a deep fryer or heavy pot to 365°F. Fry samosas in batches until golden brown. Drain on paper towels and serve hot.

**SERVES 6**

¼ teaspoon turmeric
1 cup diced frozen potatoes
¼ cup frozen peas
1 teaspoon paprika
¼ teaspoon curry powder
¼ teaspoon cumin
¼ teaspoon coriander
½ teaspoon salt
¼ teaspoon lemon pepper
18 wonton wrappers
1 egg, beaten
3 cups vegetable oil

# Vegetable Spring Rolls

**SERVES 6**

2 cups cole slaw mix (cabbage
    and shredded carrots)
1 teaspoon sesame oil
1 tablespoon soy sauce
Pinch sugar
½ teaspoon salt
¼ teaspoon pepper
18 spring roll wrappers
1 egg, beaten
3 cups vegetable oil

Spring rolls are smaller than egg rolls and they have more delicate
wrappers that are crisp and flakey when fried. These are filled with a
light vegetable mixture that is slightly sweet and fresh, not heavy.

1. Mix the cole slaw mix with the sesame oil, soy sauce, sugar, salt, and
   pepper.

2. Lay a spring roll wrapper flat with the points facing like a diamond
   shape.

3. Put 1 to 2 tablespoons of the filling on the bottom third of the wrapper.
   Fold up the bottom corner over the filling, fold in the two side corners
   over the filling. Brush the top corner with the beaten egg and roll the
   rest of the way tightly, encasing the filling in the wrapper. Repeat with
   the remaining wrappers and filling.

4. Heat the oil in a deep fryer or heavy pot to 365°F. Add the rolls and fry
   until golden. Remove from the oil and drain on paper towels.

5. Combine ½ cup soy sauce and ¼ cup rice-wine vinegar and serve with
   the hot spring rolls for dipping.

## Stir-Fry Filling . . . . . . . . . . . . . . . . . . . . . . . .

You may stir-fry the cabbage filling if you prefer a more cooked filling in your spring rolls. Combine the ingredients for the filling, heat a wok, add a little peanut oil, and stir-fry the filling mixture briefly. Transfer the filling to a baking-sheet pan and spread it out to cool. Roll the cooled
filling up in the spring-roll wrappers and fry the same way.

# Fried Oyster Tostadas

Feel free to vary the garnish on these by adding diced jalapeños, salsa, or lemon zest. Chipotle pepper instead of cayenne will add an interesting smoky flavor.

1. Heat the oil in a deep fryer or heavy pot to 365°F.

2. Toss the oysters with the rice flour, shake off the excess through a strainer, and fry the oysters until golden brown, 1 to 2 minutes. Drain on paper towels.

3. Combine the tartar sauce and cayenne pepper.

4. Spread a bit of guacamole on each tortilla chip. Place an oyster on top of the guacamole, and top each oyster with a dab of spicy tartar sauce.

5. Serve immediately while the oysters are warm.

**SERVES 4**

2 cups vegetable oil
12 fresh oysters, shucked
1 cup rice flour
2 tablespoons tartar sauce
¼ teaspoon cayenne pepper
2 tablespoons guacamole
12 round tortilla chips

# Baked Noshes

CHAPTER

17

# Vegetable Empanadas

2 rounds pie dough

½ cup diced onion

½ cup corn kernels

¼ cup diced roasted red bell peppers

1 tablespoon seasoning salt

1 egg, beaten with 1 tablespoon water

Empanadas are usually filled with meat, often beef, but these are full of vegetables instead.

1. Cut 3-inch circles out of the pie dough. Preheat oven to 350°F.

2. Combine the onion, corn, peppers, and seasoning salt. Put a spoonful of the mixture in the middle of each dough circle.

3. Brush the edges of the dough circles with beaten egg, fold the dough over to make a half circle, and press the edges to seal. Use a fork to crimp the edges.

4. Place the empanadas on a baking sheet lined with parchment paper and brush the tops with the beaten egg.

5. Bake for 20 to 25 minutes, until the tops are golden. Serve warm.

### Dessert Empanadas . . . . . . . . . . . . . . . . . . . . . . . . .
Various fruit fillings, such as cherry, apricot, raspberry, and peach, can be used to make dessert empanadas. After they are baked, dust them with powdered sugar for a great tapas dessert.

# Chinese Barbecued-Pork Buns

You may use purchased Chinese barbecued pork instead
of your own. If you don't have access to a Chinatown
market, you can purchase it from a restaurant.

**SERVES 8**

16 frozen dinner rolls, unbaked
    dough
1 tablespoon oyster sauce
2 teaspoons ketchup
2 teaspoons soy sauce
2 teaspoons sugar
2 teaspoons cornstarch
1 tablespoon peanut oil
½ cup diced onion
2 teaspoons rice wine
¼ cup chicken broth
½ teaspoon sesame oil
¾ cup Chinese Barbecued Pork
    (page 189)
1 egg, beaten with 1 tablespoon
    water

1. Lay out the frozen (uncooked) dinner rolls on a plastic-lined baking sheet and cover with a piece of plastic wrap. Let thaw in the refrigerator overnight. (Spray the plastic wrap with vegetable oil first to prevent sticking.)

2. Mix the oyster sauce, ketchup, soy sauce, sugar, chicken broth, and cornstarch together. Set aside.

3. Heat the peanut oil in a wok over medium-high heat. Add the onion and stir-fry until tender. Add the rice wine and cook until it reduces a bit. Add the soy sauce mixture and cook until the sauce thickens. Stir in the sesame oil and barbecued pork and remove from heat. Cool to room temperature and then refrigerate to chill completely.

4. Roll or pat each dough circle flat and place a spoonful of chilled filling in the center of each one. Fold the dough up and around the filling and pinch it closed. Place the buns, seam side down, on a baking-sheet pan lined with parchment paper. Cover with a damp towel and let the buns rise in a warm place for about 1 hour.

5. Preheat the oven to 350°F. Brush the tops of the buns with beaten egg and bake them for 20 minutes. Serve warm.

# Chinese Vegetable Buns

**SERVES 8**

16 frozen dinner rolls, unbaked
    dough
1 tablespoon oyster sauce
2 teaspoons ketchup
2 teaspoons soy sauce
2 teaspoons sugar
2 teaspoons cornstarch
½ teaspoon sesame oil
¼ cup chicken broth
2 tablespoons peanut oil
½ cup diced tofu
½ cup diced onion
½ cup diced carrots
¼ cup diced celery
2 teaspoons rice wine
1 egg, beaten with 1 tablespoon
    water

Plan ahead when making this recipe, because it requires the filling be made ahead and chilled. The buns can be baked ahead and reheated in a warm oven.

1. Lay the frozen dinner-roll dough out on a plastic-lined baking sheet and cover them with a piece of plastic wrap. Let thaw in the refrigerator overnight. (Spray the plastic wrap with vegetable oil first to prevent sticking.)

2. Mix the oyster sauce, ketchup, soy sauce, sugar, and cornstarch together. Set aside.

3. Heat the peanut oil in a wok over medium-high heat. Add the onion, carrots, and celery and stir-fry until tender. Add the rice wine and cook until it reduces a bit. Add the soy sauce mixture and cook until the sauce thickens. Stir in the sesame oil and tofu and remove from heat. Cool to room temperature and then refrigerate to chill completely.

4. Roll or pat each dough circle flat and place a spoonful of chilled filling in the center of each one. Fold the dough up and around the filling and pinch it closed. Place the buns, seam-side down on a baking-sheet pan lined with parchment paper. Cover with a damp towel and let the buns rise in a warm place for about 1 hour.

5. Preheat the oven to 350°F. Brush the tops of the buns with beaten egg and bake them for 20 minutes. Serve warm.

## Substitutions. . . . . . . . . . . . . . . . . . . . . . . . .
If frozen dinner-roll dough is unavailable, frozen bread dough can be divided into pieces and used in the same manner. You may even try breadstick, biscuit, or bread dough that comes in a refrigerated can. If all else fails, make the dough used in the Catalan Flatbreads recipe (page 45).

# Chorizo Empanadas

Empanadas are often fried, but this version is baked, making them less oily, which helps when chorizo sausage is the filling.

**SERVES 6**

2 rounds pie dough
1 cup diced chorizo (hard)
1 egg, beaten with 1 tablespoon water

1. Cut 3-inch circles out of the pie dough. Preheat oven to 350°F.

2. Put a spoonful of diced chorizo in the middle of each dough circle.

3. Brush the edges of the dough circles with beaten egg, fold the dough over to make a half circle, and press the edges to seal. Use a fork to crimp the edges.

4. Place the empanadas on a baking sheet lined with parchment paper and brush the tops with the beaten egg.

5. Bake for 20 to 25 minutes, until the tops are golden. Serve warm.

# Cornish Pasties

Pasties are meat pies, or turnovers, that miners in Cornwall originally took down in the mines with them for lunch. These are appetizer-size pasties.

**SERVES 4**

2 rounds pie dough
½ cup diced onion
¼ cup diced carrots
½ cup cooked ground beef, cooled
¼ cup diced cooked potatoes
1 tablespoon flour
1 teaspoon Worcestershire sauce
1 teaspoon seasoning salt
1 teaspoon thyme
1 egg, beaten with 1 tablespoon water

1. Cut 3-inch circles out of the pie dough. Preheat oven to 350°F.

2. Combine the onion, carrots, cooked beef, potatoes, flour, Worcestershire sauce, seasoning salt, and thyme in a bowl. Put a spoonful of the mixture in the middle of each dough circle.

3. Brush the edges of the dough circles with beaten egg, fold the dough over to make a half circle, and press the edges to seal. Use a fork to crimp the edges.

4. Place the pasties on a baking sheet lined with parchment paper and brush the tops with the beaten egg.

5. Bake for 20 to 25 minutes, until the tops are golden. Serve warm.

# Tex-Mex Pasties

These appetizer pasties have the flavors of Tex-Mex burritos in a bite size.

**SERVES 4**

2 rounds pie dough
¼ cup diced onion
½ cup cooked ground beef, cooled
½ cup refried beans
½ cup shredded cheddar cheese
1 tablespoon taco seasoning
1 egg, beaten with 1 tablespoon water
Sour cream
Salsa

1. Cut 3-inch circles out of the pie dough. Preheat oven to 350°F.

2. Combine the onion, cooked beef, refried beans, cheddar cheese, and taco seasoning in a bowl. Put a spoonful of the mixture in the middle of each dough circle.

3. Brush the edges of the dough circles with beaten egg, fold the dough over to make a half circle, and press the edges to seal. Use a fork to crimp the edges.

4. Place the pasties on a baking sheet lined with parchment paper and brush the tops with the beaten egg.

5. Bake for 20 to 25 minutes, until the tops are golden. Serve warm with sour cream and salsa.

## Make It a Meal . . . . . . . . . . . . . . . . . . . . . . . . .

You can make the Tex-Mex Pasties larger by cutting out bigger circles and then filling each with a larger quantity of the same filling. Then cover them with enchilada sauce and cheese and bake them again until the sauce is heated and the cheese is melted.

# Miniature Focaccias

You may top these with whatever you like to make
them into tiny pizzas, but they are great as is.

**SERVES 8**

*16 frozen dinner rolls, unbaked
dough*
*¼ cup green onions*
*2 tablespoons olive oil*
*8 teaspoons tomato paste*

1. Lay the frozen dinner-roll dough out on a plastic-lined baking sheet and cover them with a piece of plastic wrap.

2. Let thaw in the refrigerator overnight. (Spray the plastic wrap with vegetable oil first to prevent sticking.)

3. Preheat the oven to 400°F. Combine the green onions with the olive oil.

4. Press each roll flat, press your fingers down to make indentations and put a teaspoon of tomato paste in the middle of each one.

5. Spread it around to cover the dough. Add the green onions to the focaccias and bake them on a baking-sheet pan for 12 minutes. Serve hot, warm, or cold.

# Blue Cheese Honeycomb Crostini

**SERVES 8**

1 baguette loaf French bread
8 ounces blue cheese
2 tablespoons heavy cream
1 half honeycomb

*If you prefer, you may drizzle honey over the toasts instead of using honeycomb.*

1. Preheat oven to 350°F. Slice the baguette into ¼-inch-thick rounds and lay them out on a cookie sheet. Toast them in the oven for about 5 minutes. Turn them over and toast the other side. Remove from oven and set aside.

2. In a bowl, combine blue cheese and heavy cream and mix well to a spreadable consistency.

3. Spread each toast round with 1 tablespoon of the cheese mixture.

4. Turn the oven to "broil" and broil the toasts just until they are browned, about 3 minutes.

5. Top each toast with a small piece of the honeycomb and serve warm.

## Honeycomb Truffles . . . . . . . . . . . . . . . . . . . . . .

If you freeze honeycomb and cut it into bite-size pieces, you can make delicious truffles simply by refreezing the pieces and dipping them in melted chocolate. Roll them in unsweetened cocoa powder for the finishing touch.

# Mushroom Cigars

This mushroom filling is a classic French preparation called *duxelles*. If available, black truffles would elevate these cigars to a whole new level of deliciousness.

1. Chop the mushrooms and shallots and sauté them in butter for 10 minutes. Lay the mixture out on a sheet pan to cool.

2. Preheat oven to 400°F and line a baking-sheet pan with parchment paper or a silicone baking-pan liner.

3. Brush walnut oil over a sheet of phyllo dough and place another sheet on top. Repeat the process until all six sheets are on top of each other, brushed with walnut oil.

4. Cut the stack of phyllo sheets in half lengthwise. Spoon the mushroom filling across the long side of the halved sheets of phyllo and roll them up tightly to enclose the filling. Cut the rolls into four, making eight cigars.

5. Place the cigars on the prepared baking-sheet pan, seam-sides down, and brush the cigars with walnut oil. Bake for 20 minutes, let cool. Serve warm.

**SERVES 4**

1 pound fresh mushrooms
2 shallots, peeled
4 tablespoons butter
6 phyllo sheets
½ cup walnut oil

# Shrimp Cigars

**SERVES 4**

½ pound fresh shrimp, peeled and deveined

2 tablespoons tahini

1 teaspoon sesame oil

1 green onion, chopped

1 teaspoon soy sauce

2 teaspoons cornstarch

½ teaspoon minced garlic

½ teaspoon minced ginger

6 phyllo sheets

½ cup melted butter

Serve these crispy shrimp-and-sesame-filled sticks warm, on a bed of greens with Apricot Dipping Sauce (page 38).

1. Purée the shrimp, tahini, sesame oil, green onion, soy sauce, cornstarch, garlic, and ginger in a food processor to a paste.

2. Preheat oven to 400°F and line a baking-sheet pan with parchment paper or a silicone baking-pan liner.

3. Brush melted butter over a sheet of phyllo dough and place another sheet on top. Repeat the process until all six sheets are on top of each other brushed with melted butter.

4. Cut the stack of phyllo sheets in half lengthwise. Spoon the shrimp filling across the long side of the halved sheets of phyllo and roll them up tightly to enclose the filling. Cut the rolls into four, making eight cigars.

5. Place the cigars on the prepared baking-sheet pan, seam-sides down, and brush the cigars with melted butter. Bake for 20 minutes, let cool. Serve warm.

## Dessert Cigars . . . . . . . . . . . . . . . . . . . . . . . . . . .

If you roll up a mixture of ground walnuts and sugar in phyllo like the mushroom and shrimp cigars and bake them, you will have delicious dessert cigars. Brush them with a melted honey and butter mixture after they are baked and they will taste like baklava sticks.

# Gougeres

*Gougeres* are choux paste made with cheese. They are traditionally served while tasting wine in Burgundy. You may try cheddar cheese with a pinch of cayenne pepper to vary this recipe.

**SERVES 8**

1 cup water
4 ounces unsalted butter
½ teaspoon salt
1 cup flour
4 eggs
1½ cups shredded Swiss cheese

1. Preheat oven to 400°F. Line a baking-sheet pan with a silicone baking mat.

2. Put the water, butter, and salt in a saucepan over medium-high heat and bring to a boil. When butter is melted, turn heat to medium and add the flour all at once. Stir constantly with a wooden spoon over medium heat until it is the consistency of mashed potatoes.

3. Remove from heat and beat in eggs one at a time. Use a wooden spoon or an electric mixer. Stir in 1 cup shredded cheese.

4. Scoop dough with two spoons onto greased cookie sheet, into 1-inch mounds, evenly spacing them about 2 inches apart. Sprinkle them with remaining cheese.

5. Bake 15 minutes, reduce heat to 350°F, bake 15 minutes more. Serve warm or room temperature.

# Cheddar, Bacon, and Green Onion Muffins

**SERVES 12**

2 cups flour

⅔ cup sugar

1 tablespoon baking powder

½ teaspoon salt

2 eggs

1 cup milk

3 ounces butter, melted

1 cup grated cheddar cheese

¼ cup bacon crumbles

¼ cup sliced green onions

These savory muffins make a good accompaniment with
soup and they are a nice addition to a brunch selection.

1. Preheat oven to 400°F. Grease a muffin tin or line it with fluted paper cups.

2. Combine flour, sugar, baking powder, and salt in a large bowl using a whisk.

3. Combine eggs, milk, and butter in another bowl using a whisk.

4. Stir the wet ingredients into the dry ingredients, fold in cheese, bacon, and green onions with a spatula, and fill muffin cups with the batter.

5. Bake 15 minutes.

## Substitution . . . . . . . . . . . . . . . . . . . . . . . . .

If you substitute blueberries for the cheddar, bacon, and scallions in the recipe above you will have blueberry muffins. Make mini muffins for a brunch buffet so guests can have a taste and not get filled up. That way they can sample everything else on the buffet too.

# Deluxe Cherry Almond Muffins

Cherries and almonds have an affinity for one another. These muffins have the luscious addition of cherry jam baked into them.

**SERVES 12**

2 cups flour
⅔ cup sugar
1 tablespoon baking powder
½ teaspoon salt
2 eggs
1 cup milk
6 tablespoons butter, melted
1 teaspoon almond extract
1 cup chopped fresh or frozen cherries
12 teaspoons cherry jam
¼ cup powdered sugar
¼ cup sliced almonds

1. Preheat oven to 400°F. Line a muffin tin with fluted paper cups.

2. Combine flour, sugar, baking powder, and salt in a large bowl using a whisk. Combine eggs, milk, butter, and almond extract in another bowl using a whisk.

3. Stir the wet ingredients into the dry ingredients, fold in the cherries with a spatula, and then fill the muffin cups ¾ full with the batter.

4. Top each muffin with cherry jam and sprinkle the batter with powdered sugar and almonds.

5. Bake 15 minutes.

# Apple Cheddar Sausage Pastries

Dried apples add a nice flavor to these savory pastries.
Try adding a pinch of cinnamon for variation.

**MAKES 30**

½ pound ground breakfast sausage
1½ cups biscuit mix
2 cups grated sharp Cheddar cheese
½ cup finely chopped dried apples
2 tablespoons caraway seeds
1 teaspoon Dijon mustard
Pinch black pepper

1. Preheat the oven to 375°F. Line a baking sheet with nonstick foil.

2. Combine all ingredients in a large bowl. Mix well with your fingers, squeezing and kneading the ingredients together to make dough.

3. Pinch the dough off into 1-inch pieces and roll them between the palms of your hands to form balls.

4. Place the balls on the prepared baking sheet. Bake for 18 to 20 minutes, or until golden brown. Serve warm.

# Raspberry Brie Purses

The combination of creamy Brie and tart raspberry preserves is the filling for these bites.

**MAKES 2 DOZEN**

8 ounces Brie cheese
¼ cup shredded Jack cheese
4 ounces cream cheese, softened
1 tablespoon lemon zest
1 tablespoon Chambord
Vegetable-oil cooking spray
24 wonton wrappers
6 ounces raspberry preserves

1. Preheat oven to 375°F.

2. Cut the rind from the Brie, discard it, and cut the remaining cheese into small chunks.

3. Toss the Brie cheese with the Jack cheese in a medium-size bowl. Mix the cream cheese, lemon zest, and Chambord together with a wooden spoon until smooth. Stir in the Brie mixture.

4. Spray muffin tins with vegetable-oil cooking spray. Place one wonton wrapper in each cup and gently press down. Place a teaspoon of cheese mixture in each wrapper. Put a dollop of raspberry preserves on the cheese mixture. Twist tops of wonton wrappers to enclose the filling. Spray each purse with vegetable oil.

5. Bake for 12 to 15 minutes, or until lightly brown. Serve warm.

## Simpler Version . . . . . . . . . . . . . . . . . . . . . . . . . . . . . . .

For a simpler version of Raspberry Brie Purses, just cut the Brie into chunks, leaving the rind on, and place them in the wonton wrappers. Top them with raspberry preserves and proceed as in the recipe. This makes a pure melted Brie bite, instead of a creamy filling.

# Florentine Bagels

Garlicky spinach and cheese enhance these miniature bagels that are named after the city of Florence, Italy. Dishes containing spinach are often dubbed "Florentine."

1. Preheat the oven to 350°F.

2. Melt butter and sauté garlic in it, but don't brown it.

3. Partially cook the spinach in the garlic butter.

4. Fill the holes of the bagels with the spinach and top it with the cheese.

5. Bake in the oven to melt the cheese. Serve warm.

## Bigger Bagels . . . . . . . . . . . . . . . . . . . . . . . . . . .
Make the Florentine bagels with regular-size bagels, and then slice them horizontally and fill them with scrambled eggs for a great breakfast sandwich.

**SERVES 6**

*1 tablespoon butter*
*1 garlic clove, minced*
*½ cup chopped frozen or fresh spinach*
*6 plain mini bagels*
*3 slices Swiss cheese, cut in half*

# Seafood Strudel

This rich seafood strudel is nice to serve as a brunch item
with fruit, green salad, and scrambled eggs.

**SERVES 6**

1 cup crabmeat

1 cup chopped peeled shrimp,
    chopped

½ cup chopped smoked salmon

8 ounces cream cheese, softened

1 tablespoon milk

2 tablespoons chopped parsley

¼ cup chopped green onions

Juice and zest of 1 lemon

Salt and pepper to taste

6 phyllo-dough sheets

¾ cup melted butter

¾ cup dry breadcrumbs

1. Combine the crabmeat, shrimp, smoked salmon, cream cheese, milk, parsley, green onions, and lemon juice and zest in a bowl with a wooden spoon. Season with salt and pepper, mix, and set aside.

2. Preheat oven to 350°F and line a baking sheet pan with parchment paper or a silicone baking pan liner.

3. Brush melted butter over a sheet of phyllo dough, sprinkle with 2 tablespoons breadcrumbs, and place another sheet on top. Repeat the process until all six sheets are on top of each other with butter and breadcrumbs.

4. Spoon the seafood filling across the length of the top sheet of phyllo and roll it up to enclose the filling. Place the roll on the prepared baking sheet pan, seam-side down, and brush the roll with melted butter.

5. Bake for 20 minutes, let cool 10 minutes, then cut into slices. Serve warm.

# Steamed and Boiled Snacks

# Pumpkin Ravioli

SERVES 4

½ cup cooked pumpkin purée

1 egg, beaten

Pinch nutmeg

2 tablespoons bread crumbs

2 amaretti, crushed into crumbs

1 tablespoon chopped dried apricot

1 teaspoon honey mustard

12 gyoza wrappers

1 egg, beaten with 1 tablespoon water

¼ cup melted, browned butter

1 teaspoon chopped sage

2 tablespoons grated Parmesan cheese

These ravioli are called mezzaluna, because of their half-moon shape. You may make them ahead, refrigerate them, and then cook them to order.

1. Combine the pumpkin purée with one beaten egg, nutmeg, bread crumbs, amaretti crumbs, dried apricot, and honey mustard.

2. Put one spoonful of filling in the middle of each gyoza wrapper. Brush the edges of the wrapper with eggwash and then fold it over to make a half moon. Press the edges down to seal.

3. Bring a large pot of salted water to a boil, then add the ravioli and cook for about 1 minute. Drain and put the ravioli on a platter.

4. Drizzle the browned butter over the ravioli, sprinkle with sage and Parmesan cheese, and serve hot.

# Pierogi

Pierogi are Polish dumplings that come in a variety of fillings in the freezer section of supermarkets. They can be boiled, but this recipe steams and crisps them using a baking method.

1. Preheat oven to 350°F.

2. Spread soft butter in the bottom of a casserole dish and place the frozen pierogi on top in one layer.

3. Scatter the onions and bell peppers over the pierogi and pour the melted butter over the top.

4. Cover and bake for 45 minutes to 1 hour.

5. Serve with black pepper and sour cream.

## Sweet Pierogi . . . . . . . . . . . . . . . . . . . . . . . . . .
Sometimes you will find sweet fillings in pierogi, often made by Polish churches for fundraising. Sweet fillings may be apricot, prune, or poppyseed.

**SERVES 4**

1 tablespoon butter, softened
1 package frozen potato pierogi, about 12
½ cup diced onions
½ cup sliced bell peppers
¼ cup melted butter
Black pepper, freshly ground
¼ cup sour cream

# Potato Gnocchi

SERVES 4

*1 large baked potato,
    about 1 pound*
*¾ cup flour*
*½ teaspoon salt*
*1 egg, beaten*
*2 tablespoons olive oil*
*¼ cup grated Parmesan cheese*

These Italian potato dumplings can be boiled without the step of rolling them down the tines of a fork, either as is or just put a thumb indentation in each one instead.

1. Scoop the cooked potato flesh out of the skin and mash it with a fork, or put it through a potato ricer or food mill. Toss the potatoes with the flour and salt in a bowl with your hands. Use a light touch.

2. Make a well in the center of the potato mixture and put the egg in it. Gradually incorporate the potato mixture into the egg to make a dough that comes together. Roll dough into 1-inch-thick logs and cut 1-inch pieces off the logs.

3. For the traditional indentations, roll each piece down the tines of a floured fork and flick it off with your thumb.

4. Bring a pot of salted water to a boil, add the gnocchi, stir, and then cook until they float to the top, about 5 minutes.

5. Drain the gnocchi and put them in a serving dish. Toss the gnocchi with olive oil to coat. Sprinkle the Parmesan cheese over them and serve immediately.

# Sweet-Potato Gnocchi

Like the potato gnocchi, these sweet-potato dumplings can be
boiled without the step of rolling them down the tines of a fork,
either as is or just put a thumb indentation in each one instead.

1. Scoop the cooked sweet-potato flesh out of the skin and mash it with a fork, or put it through a potato ricer or food mill. Toss the potatoes with the flour and salt in a bowl with your hands. Use a light touch.

2. Make a well in the center of the sweet potato mixture and put the egg in it. Gradually incorporate the potato mixture into the egg to make a dough that comes together. Roll dough into 1-inch-thick logs and cut 1-inch pieces off the logs.

3. For the traditional indentations, roll each piece down the tines of a floured fork and flick it off with your thumb.

4. Bring a pot of salted water to a boil, add the gnocchi, stir, and then cook until they float to the top, about 5 minutes.

5. Drain the gnocchi and put them in a serving dish. Toss the gnocchi with the melted browned butter and sage to coat. Sprinkle the Parmesan cheese over them and serve immediately.

## Substitution . . . . . . . . . . . . . . . . . . . . . . . .

Gnocchi can be made with other things besides potatoes and sweet potatoes. Butternut squash is a good one. Spinach can be added to regular potato gnocchi, and ricotta cheese is another delish gnocchi.

**SERVES 4**

1 baked sweet potato,
    1 pound
¾ cup flour
½ teaspoon salt
1 egg, beaten
¼ cup melted and browned
    butter
1 teaspoon chopped sage
¼ cup grated Parmesan cheese

# Mushroom Ravioli

**SERVES 6**

24 wonton wrappers

2 cups finely chopped
mushrooms

1 tablespoon olive oil

Pinch nutmeg

Pinch salt

2 tablespoons cream cheese

1 egg, beaten with 1 tablespoon
water

½ cup heavy cream

¼ cup grated Parmesan cheese

1 tablespoon truffle oil

¼ cup shaved Parmesan cheese

These dumplings are large and square shaped, the type of ravioli
that is more traditional than half-moon or round raviolis.

1. Sauté the mushrooms in the olive oil until almost all the liquid evaporates from the pan. Stir in the cream cheese and season with nutmeg and salt. Set aside the filling to cool.

2. Put one spoonful of filling in the middle of a wonton wrapper. Brush the edges of the wrapper with eggwash and then place another wrapper on top. Press the edges down to seal. Repeat with remaining filling and wrappers.

3. Bring a large pot of salted water to a boil, then add the ravioli and cook for about 1 minute. Drain and put the ravioli on a platter.

4. Heat the cream in a sauté pan and add the grated Parmesan cheese. Pour the sauce over the ravioli.

5. Drizzle the truffle oil over the ravioli, scatter the shaved Parmesan cheese over them, and serve hot.

## The Real Ravioli . . . . . . . . . . . . . . . . . . . . . . . . .

Of course you can make ravioli out of Semolina Pasta (page 154) dough instead of wonton wrappers. They will take a little longer to cook because they will be thicker, but you will know they are done when they float to the top of the cooking water.

# Chinese Steamed Pork Bao

These steamed buns are filled with a mixture of Chinese
condiments and slow-roasted Chinese-style barbecued pork.

1. Lay the frozen dinner-roll dough out on a plastic-lined baking sheet and cover them with a piece of plastic wrap. Let thaw in the refrigerator overnight. (Spray the plastic wrap with vegetable oil first to prevent sticking.)

2. Mix the oyster sauce, ketchup, soy sauce, sugar, chicken broth, and cornstarch together. Set aside.

3. Heat the peanut oil in a wok over medium-high heat. Add the onion and stir-fry until tender. Add the rice wine and cook until it reduces a bit. Add the soy sauce mixture and cook until the sauce thickens. Stir in the sesame oil and barbecued pork and remove from heat. Cool to room temperature and then refrigerate to chill completely.

4. Roll or pat each dough circle flat and place a spoonful of chilled filling in the center of each one. Fold the dough up and around the filling, twist and pinch it closed. Place the buns, seam-side down, on waxed-paper squares.

5. Heat water to boiling in a wok to a level just below where the bamboo steamer will be. Transfer some of the buns with their waxed-paper bases to a bamboo steamer, leaving space for them to expand when steamed. (You will need to do this in several batches.) Cover the bamboo steamer with its lid and place it on the wok. Steam buns for 15 to 20 minutes. Remove from heat and serve immediately.

**SERVES 8**

*16 frozen dinner rolls, unbaked dough*
*1 tablespoon oyster sauce*
*2 teaspoons ketchup*
*2 teaspoons soy sauce*
*2 teaspoons sugar*
*¼ cup chicken broth*
*2 teaspoons cornstarch*
*1 tablespoon peanut oil*
*½ cup diced onion*
*2 teaspoons rice wine*
*½ teaspoon sesame oil*
*¾ cup Chinese Barbecued Pork (page 189)*

# Chinese Steamed Tofu Bao

This is a vegetarian filling wrapped in dough, which is then steamed, which gives a moist, spongy texture to the buns.

*16 frozen dinner rolls, unbaked dough*

*2 teaspoons ketchup*

*2 teaspoons soy sauce*

*2 teaspoons sugar*

*¼ cup vegetable broth*

*2 teaspoons cornstarch*

*2 tablespoons peanut oil*

*½ cup diced onion*

*½ cup diced carrots*

*¼ cup diced celery*

*2 teaspoons rice wine*

*½ teaspoon sesame oil*

*½ cup diced tofu*

1. Lay the frozen dinner-roll dough out on a plastic-lined baking sheet and cover them with a piece of plastic wrap. Let thaw in the refrigerator overnight. (Spray the plastic wrap with vegetable oil first to prevent sticking.)

2. Mix the ketchup, soy sauce, sugar, vegetable broth, and cornstarch together. Set aside.

3. Heat the peanut oil in a wok over medium-high heat. Add the onion, carrots, and celery and stir-fry until tender. Add the rice wine and cook until it reduces a bit. Add the soy sauce mixture and cook until the sauce thickens. Stir in the sesame oil and tofu and remove from heat. Cool to room temperature and then refrigerate to chill completely.

4. Roll or pat each dough circle flat and place a spoonful of chilled filling in the center of each one. Fold the dough up and around the filling and twist and pinch it closed. Place the buns, seam-side down, on waxed-paper squares.

5. Heat water to boiling in a wok to a level just below where the bamboo steamer will be. Transfer some of the buns with their waxed-paper bases to a bamboo steamer, leaving space for them to expand when steamed. (You will need to do this in several batches.) Cover the bamboo steamer with its lid and place it on the wok. Steam buns for 15 to 20 minutes. Remove from heat and serve immediately.

## No Running with Scissors. . . . . . . . . . . . . . . . . . . . .

But you can use scissors to cut open the tops of steamed buns like they do in tea houses. Use kitchen scissors to make two snips in an X on top of the steamed buns before eating.

# Vegetable Potstickers

Serve these dumplings warm with the obvious choice—Potsticker
Dipping Sauce (page 34)—as part of a dim sum tapas selection.

1. Combine the napa cabbage, green onion, ginger, cilantro, carrots, sherry, sesame oil, soy sauce, and sugar.

2. Put one spoonful of filling in the middle of each gyoza wrapper. Brush the edges of the wrapper with water and then seal it by pleating and pinching one side to the other flat side. Repeat with the rest of the wrappers and filling.

3. Heat the peanut oil in a skillet and place the potstickers in the oil and cook for 3 minutes. Pour in ¼ cup water and immediately cover.

4. Steam the potstickers, letting the water evaporate, then turn the heat down and cook for 3 more minutes to let the bottoms get browned.

5. Shake the pan to loosen the potstickers, remove, and serve immediately.

**SERVES 6**

2 cups napa cabbage, chopped
2 tablespoons minced green
onion
2 tablespoons minced ginger
2 tablespoons minced cilantro
¼ cup shredded carrots
1 teaspoon sherry
1 teaspoon sesame oil
½ teaspoon soy sauce
1 teaspoon sugar
18 gyoza wrappers
2 tablespoons peanut oil

# Pork Potstickers

As the name says, these dumplings "stick to the pot,"
browning the bottom, but the top is steamed.

**SERVES 6**

5 ounces ground pork

2 tablespoons chopped green onion

1 teaspoon minced ginger

1 teaspoon sugar

1 teaspoon rice wine

1 teaspoon sesame oil

½ teaspoon soy sauce

1 teaspoon oyster sauce

1 tablespoon cornstarch

1 egg, beaten

18 round gyoza wrappers

2 tablespoons peanut oil

1. Combine the ground pork, green onion, ginger, sugar, rice wine, sesame oil, soy sauce, oyster sauce, cornstarch, and half of the beaten egg. Cover and refrigerate overnight.

2. Put a spoonful of filling in the middle of each gyoza wrapper. Brush the edges of the wrapper with the other half of the beaten egg, and then seal it by pleating and pinching one side to the other flat side. Repeat with the remaining wrappers and filling.

3. Heat the peanut oil in a skillet and place the potstickers in the oil and cook for 3 minutes. Pour in ¼ cup water and immediately cover.

4. Steam the potstickers, letting the water evaporate, then turn the heat down and cook for 3 more minutes, to let the bottoms get browned.

5. Shake the pan to loosen the potstickers, remove, and serve immediately.

# Siu Mai

Gyoza wrappers are round. If you can't find them, use wonton wrappers and cut them into circles with a biscuit cutter.

1. Combine all of the ingredients except for the wrappers, peas, and carrots.

2. Put a tablespoon of filling in the center of each wrapper.

3. Bring the sides of the wrapper up around the filling, leaving the top open. Squeeze lightly around the dumpling to make a waistline, and flatten the bottom so the dumplings sit flat. Top each dumpling with one pea or carrot.

4. Line the bottom of a bamboo steamer with cabbage leaves and place the sui mai on top of the leaves. Place the lid on the bamboo steamer.

5. Heat water to boiling in a wok to a level just below where the bamboo steamer will be. Add the bamboo steamer and steam the siu mai for 15 to 20 minutes. Remove from heat and serve immediately.

**SERVES 6**

½ pound ground pork
½ pound chopped raw shrimp, peeled and deveined
¼ cup chopped water chestnuts
1 tablespoon minced green onion
2 teaspoons minced cilantro
1 teaspoon minced ginger
2 teaspoons soy sauce
2 teaspoons sesame oil
2 tablespoons cornstarch
1 tablespoon rice wine
Pinch five-spice powder
Pinch white pepper
½ teaspoon sugar
24 gyoza wrappers
½ cup frozen peas and diced carrots

# Chinese Vegetable Dumplings

These tender dumplings are steamed in a pan so they are crunchy on the bottom. Serve with soy sauce and Indonesian Peanut Sauce (page 33).

**SERVES 8**

16 frozen dinner rolls, unbaked
    dough
½ cup diced zucchini
¼ cup chopped mushrooms
¼ cup frozen peas
1 tablespoon sesame oil
1 tablespoon sugar
2 tablespoons peanut oil

1. Lay the frozen dinner-roll dough out on a plastic-lined baking sheet and cover them with a piece of plastic wrap. Let thaw in the refrigerator overnight. (Spray the plastic wrap with vegetable oil first to prevent sticking.)

2. Mix the zucchini, mushrooms, peas, sesame oil, and sugar together. Put the vegetable mixture in a colander set over a larger bowl, to catch the liquid that will drip. Set aside.

3. Roll or pat each dough circle flat and place a spoonful of the vegetable filling in the center of each one. Fold the dough up and around the filling and twist and pinch it closed.

4. Heat the peanut oil in a nonstick skillet over medium-high heat. Place the dumplings, seam-side down, in the skillet. (Cook in batches.) Pour in ¼ cup water and immediately cover with a lid.

5. Steam the dumplings for 15 to 20 minutes, letting the water evaporate and the bottoms of the dumplings get browned. Serve immediately.

Chopstick Tip . . . . . . . . . . . . . . . . . . . . . .
I like to take a chopstick and use it to poke a hole in the top of a steamed vegetable dumpling before I eat it. Then I pour soy sauce into it and take a juicy bite. Try it!

# Thai Shrimp Dumplings

These dumplings have no wrapper and may be eaten either as is or as part of a curry.

1. Combine all of the ingredients except chicken broth, coconut milk, and curry paste in a food processor to make a paste.

2. Bring the chicken broth, coconut milk, and curry paste to a simmer.

3. Form balls out of the shrimp mixture with oiled hands and drop them into the simmering broth mixture.

4. Simmer until the dumplings float.

5. Serve hot in teacups with a little of the poaching liquid.

**SERVES 8**

8 ounces raw shrimp, peeled and deveined
2 tablespoons minced shallot
1 teaspoon minced garlic
1 teaspoon fresh minced cilantro
1 teaspoon cornstarch
¼ teaspoon sesame oil
1 teaspoon soy sauce
¼ teaspoon pepper
1 egg white
2 cups chicken broth
1 cup coconut milk
1 teaspoon Thai red curry paste

# Steamed Wontons

**SERVES 8**

¾ pound ground pork

1 egg

2 tablespoons minced green
   onion

1 teaspoon minced ginger

½ cup chopped water chestnuts

4 mushrooms, chopped

1 tablespoon soy sauce

1½ teaspoons kosher salt

16 wonton wrappers

2 cups chicken broth

These dumplings can be eaten as is or served in soup. They also can be fried like Polynesian Crab Puffs (page 206) and served with Garlic Dipping Sauce (below).

1. Combine everything except the wrappers and chicken broth in a food processor and mix well.

2. Lay a wonton wrapper on a work surface and place a teaspoon of the pork mixture in the middle. Brush two consecutive sides with water and fold the wrapper over. Press together, squeezing the air out while pinching the sides together, forming a triangle.

3. Bring the two side corners together, pinch them together with a dab of water, and set the wonton upright. Repeat with the remaining wrappers and filling.

4. Line the bottom of a bamboo steamer with cabbage leaves and place the wontons on top of the leaves. Place the lid on the bamboo steamer.

5. Heat water to boiling in a wok to a level just below where the bamboo steamer will be. Add the bamboo steamer and steam the wontons for 15 to 20 minutes.

6. Heat the chicken broth and divide it between eight teacups. Serve wontons in the broth, one per teacup.

## Garlic Dipping Sauce . . . . . . . . . . . . . . . . . . . . . . .
1½ tablespoons soy sauce, 1 tablespoon white vinegar, ¼ teaspoon sesame oil, 1 teaspoon minced garlic: Mix these all together and use as a dipping sauce for wontons.

# Cheese and Green Chili Tamales

Masa harina is cornmeal for tamales. Fresh masa is also a choice for making tamales if you have access to it.

1. Soak the corn husks in warm water for 2 hours to soften.

2. Mix the masa harina with the hot water and set aside. Whip the butter with the baking powder in a stand mixer with the paddle attachment until it is fluffy. Add the masa harina 1 cup at a time, beating it into the butter. Beat in the chicken broth and beat for 1 more minute. Beat in the salt and additional broth if necessary to achieve the consistency of fluffy muffin batter.

3. Take the cornhusks out of the water and lay them out on a clean kitchen towel to drain. Cover each husk with a ½-inch-thick layer of the masa harina mixture, leaving an L-shaped border of 1 inch on two consecutive sides.

4. Put 1 tablespoon of corn kernels, 1 teaspoon of green chilies, and 1 tablespoon of cheese in the middle of the masa harina mixture on each husk. Roll the tamales closed starting with the side with no border. Fold up the other border end to enclose the roll on one end. Place the finished tamales seam-sides down so they don't unroll while you finish the others.

5. Place the tamales in a deep steamer or pasta-cooker basket with their open ends up. Pack them next to each other so they stand up straight. Place the basket in a pot over boiling water, cover with the lid, and steam the tamales for about 35 minutes. Add water if necessary so the pot doesn't run dry. Serve the tamales in their husks; they can be peeled off by each diner.

**SERVES 8**

*16 dried corn husks*
*3 cups masa harina*
*1¾ cups hot water*
*¾ cup unsalted butter*
*1½ teaspoons baking powder*
*¾ cup chicken broth (cold)*
*1 teaspoon salt*
*1 cup corn kernels*
*½ cup diced green chilies (can)*
*1 cup shredded Monterey Jack cheese*

# Combination Tamales

SERVES 8

16 dried corn husks

3 cups masa harina

1¾ cups hot water

¾ cup unsalted butter

1½ teaspoons baking powder

¾ cup chicken broth (cold)

1 teaspoon salt

1 tablespoon olive oil

½ cup cooked chicken meat, shredded

1 cup cooked pork roast meat, shredded

1 teaspoon cumin

2 teaspoons chili powder

1 teaspoon garlic salt

16 dried corn husks

Traditional tamales are wrapped in corn husks or banana leaves, but you may also use parchment paper. Butter is substituted for the traditional lard in this recipe too.

1. Soak the corn husks in warm water for 2 hours to soften.

2. Mix the masa harina with the hot water and set aside. Whip the butter with the baking powder in a stand mixer with the paddle attachment until it is fluffy. Add the masa harina 1 cup at a time, beating it into the butter. Beat in the chicken broth and beat for 1 more minute. Beat in the salt and additional broth if necessary to achieve the consistency of fluffy muffin batter.

3. Mix the meats with the olive oil, cumin, chili powder, and garlic salt and set aside. Take the cornhusks out of the water and lay them out on a clean kitchen towel to drain. Cover each husk with a ½-inch-thick layer of the masa harina mixture, leaving an L-shaped border of 1 inch on two consecutive sides.

4. Put 2 tablespoons of meat mixture in the middle of the masa harina mixture on each husk. Roll the tamales closed starting with the side with no border. Fold up the other border end to enclose the roll on one end. Place the finished tamales seam-sides down so they don't unroll while you finish the others.

5. Place the tamales in a deep steamer or pasta-cooker basket with their open ends up. Pack them next to each other so they stand up straight. Place the basket in a pot over boiling water, cover with the lid, and steam the tamales for about 35 minutes. Add water if necessary so the pot doesn't run dry. Serve the tamales in their husks; they can be peeled off by each diner.

# CHAPTER 10

# Sweets

# Strawberry Torte

SERVES 12

**Crust**
8 ounces unsalted butter, softened
¼ cup brown sugar
1½ cups flour
¼ teaspoon salt
½ cup chopped pecans
**Filling**
8 ounces cream cheese, softened
¾ cup powdered sugar
8 ounces sweetened whipped cream (with vanilla)
**Topping**
4 tablespoons cornstarch
1 cup water
3-ounce package strawberry gelatin
½ cup sugar
Pinch salt
4 cups sliced fresh strawberries

*The crust softens after one day and is more cakey that way. If you want a softer crust, just do the strawberry layer a day later for fresher berries.*

1. Preheat oven to 400°F. For the crust, cream butter and sugar together, then stir in flour, salt, and pecans to form a shortbread cookie-type dough. Press the dough into the bottom of a springform pan. Bake 15 minutes, then cool.

2. For the filling, beat the cream cheese and powdered sugar together, then fold the whipped cream into it. Spread over the cooled crust. Refrigerate at least 2 hours.

3. For the topping, dissolve cornstarch in ½ cup water and combine with gelatin, sugar, salt, and ½ cup water into a saucepan and cook over medium-low heat until thickened. Add sliced strawberries and let mixture cool to room temp.

4. Pour strawberry topping on top of the cream cheese layer and chill well, until firm.

5. To serve, remove the side of the springform pan and cut into twelve slices.

# Ginger Custard

Serve custard with fresh sliced peaches, candied ginger, or
grated chocolate and whipped cream on top.

**SERVES 6**

*1 cup half-and-half*
*2 cups cream*
*1 (4-inch) piece of ginger, cut into
    slices*
*½ cup sugar*
*6 egg yolks*

1. In a sauce pan, heat the half-and-half, cream, and ginger to a simmer and turn off the heat. Let the ginger steep 15 minutes.

2. Preheat oven to 325°F. Put six custard cups in a 2-inch-deep baking dish and set aside.

3. Add the sugar to the cream mixture and bring to a simmer again. Remove from heat and whisk the hot mixture into the egg yolks in a bowl. Strain the custard into a pitcher.

4. Pour the hot custard into the custard cups, dividing it evenly. Pour hot water in the baking dish around the cups to come halfway up the cups. Cover the baking dish tightly with foil.

5. Bake for 30 minutes, then check to see if custard is set. Carefully jiggle the pan and if the custard is not set, cover and bake for 10 more minutes. Remove from oven and then remove the custard cups from the water bath and let cool to room temperature. Refrigerate them until completely chilled, about 2 hours. Serve cold.

## Substitutions. . . . . . . . . . . . . . . . . . . . . . . . . . . .

Substitute a piece of lemongrass for the ginger in the recipe above for a uniquely flavored dessert. Or use a vanilla bean if you prefer vanilla custard. Either way, be sure to remove them before pouring the batter into the custard cups.

# Tropical Toffee

SERVES 12

*20 saltine crackers*
*8 ounces butter*
*1 cup light brown sugar*
*4 cups white chocolate chips*
*1 cup macadamia nuts, chopped*
*1 cup shredded coconut*
*1 tablespoon lime zest*

Make a dessert course for a Southeast Asian–inspired menu
with this candy, sliced fresh fruit, and mango sorbet.

1. Preheat oven to 350°F. Line a sheet pan with sides with nonstick aluminum foil. Lay the crackers out on the foil in four rows of five.

2. Combine the butter and brown sugar in a 2-quart saucepan. Bring to a boil, turn to medium-low, and simmer for 5 minutes, stirring occasionally with a wooden spoon.

3. Pour the hot sugar and butter mixture over the crackers. Spread to cover evenly with a silicone spatula. Bake for 10 minutes. Remove from the oven and let rest about 5 minutes.

4. Sprinkle the white chocolate chips and macadamia nuts evenly over the toffee. Let rest 10 minutes.

5. Smooth the white chocolate out evenly over the top of the toffee with a spatula. Mix the coconut with the lime zest and sprinkle it over the white chocolate, then let the toffee cool completely. When cool and hard, break into pieces and store in an airtight container.

# Cranberry Popcorn

This colorful popcorn is very festive and nibble-worthy. Make a
lime version and combine the two for Cosmopolitan Corn.

**SERVES 8**

¼ cup butter
3 tablespoons corn syrup
½ cup sugar
1 small box cranberry gelatin
8 cups popped corn

1. Preheat oven to 300°F. Line a baking-sheet pan with foil.

2. Melt the butter with the corn syrup in a 6-quart pot over medium heat. Add the sugar and gelatin, stir, and bring the mixture to a boil. Stir occasionally.

3. When mixture comes to a boil, reduce the heat to low and simmer for 5 minutes, stirring occasionally.

4. Remove the mixture from the heat and immediately pour in the popcorn. Toss the popcorn to coat it well and then spread it out on the foil.

5. Bake the coated popcorn for 10 minutes. Cool and break up into smaller pieces. Store in an airtight container.

## Rainbow Colors . . . . . . . . . . . . . . . . . . . . . . . .
If you make several different batches of this popcorn using different flavors (and colors) of gelatin, you can combine them to make a beautiful bowl of rainbow popcorn that is festive and tasty.

# Eggnog Bread Pudding

**SERVES 2**

1 mini-loaf (3.5 ounces)
   panettone bread
1 ounce mascarpone cheese
Nonstick spray oil
½ cup low-fat eggnog
1 tablespoon egg white
1 teaspoon rum, whiskey, or
   brandy
⅛ teaspoon nutmeg

You can use challah bread or brioche in place of the panettone bread in this recipe.

1. Slice panettone vertically into six slices, then spread a little bit of the mascarpone cheese on each piece.

2. Spray an 8" × 8" baking dish with oil. Layer the panettone slices overlapping in the dish, cheese-side up.

3. Combine the eggnog, egg white, and liquor with a whisk in a bowl and pour the mixture over the bread slices.

4. Cover with plastic wrap and refrigerate for from 1 hour to overnight.

5. Preheat oven to 350°F. Take the plastic off the casserole, sprinkle the nutmeg on it, and bake uncovered for 25 minutes.

# Texas Pecan Toffee

Pecan pie and pecan pralines are Tex-Mex dessert staples, so serve this
pecan confection as a sweet ending to a meal of Tex-Mex favorites.

**SERVES 12**

*20 saltine crackers*
*8 ounces butter*
*1 cup light brown sugar*
*4 cups semisweet chocolate chips*
*1 cup pecans, chopped*

1. Preheat oven to 350°F. Line a sheet pan with sides with nonstick aluminum foil. Lay the crackers out on the foil in four rows of five.

2. Combine the butter and brown sugar in a 2-quart saucepan. Bring to a boil, turn to medium-low, and simmer for 5 minutes, stirring occasionally with a wooden spoon.

3. Pour the hot sugar and butter mixture over the crackers. Spread to cover evenly with a silicone spatula. Bake for 10 minutes. Remove from the oven and let rest about 5 minutes.

4. Sprinkle the chocolate chips evenly over the toffee. Let rest 10 minutes.

5. Smooth the chocolate out evenly over the top of the toffee with a spatula. Sprinkle the chopped pecans over the melted chocolate, then let the toffee cool completely. When cool and hard, break into pieces and store in an airtight container.

## Substitutions. . . . . . . . . . . . . . . . . . . . . . . . . . . .

Try hazelnuts instead of pecans, or use half butterscotch chips and half chocolate chips to give the
toffee recipe a twist. You may also substitute Ritz crackers or croissant crackers for the saltines.

# Coconut Rice Pudding

**SERVES 6**

1 cup coconut milk
1 cup heavy cream
½ cup sugar
2 cups cooked long-grain rice
Pinch salt
½ vanilla bean, or 1 teaspoon vanilla extract
1 cup fresh mango, diced
1 tablespoon candied ginger, chopped
6 tablespoons whipped cream

This pudding can be served warm or cold. It can also be chilled in a ramekin that has 2 teaspoons of caramel in the bottom. To serve, run a thin knife around the edge and unmold it onto a plate. The caramel will create a sauce like a flan.

1. Combine coconut milk, heavy cream, sugar, rice, and salt in a saucepan. Split the vanilla bean and scrape the seeds inside into the cream mixture. Add the pod too.

2. Heat the mixture to a simmer over medium heat, stirring occasionally. Reduce the heat to medium-low and cook 20 minutes. Remove the vanilla bean.

3. Spoon the rice pudding into individual serving dishes or one large bowl; cover and refrigerate until cold.

4. Serve with diced mango, candied ginger, and whipped cream.

# Gingerbread Cake

This is delicious with Coffee Caramel Sauce (page 256)
and diced pears, or just with whipped cream.

1. Preheat oven to 350°F. Butter and flour a Bundt cake pan.

2. In one bowl, mix together the sugar, oil, molasses, and boiling water. Set aside. In another bowl, mix together the baking soda, ginger, cinnamon, and flour.

3. Whisk the wet ingredients into the dry ingredients, then mix in the eggs.

4. Pour the batter into the prepared pan and bake for 1 hour. Let cool, unmold, and cool completely.

5. Sprinkle with powdered sugar and cut into slices.

## Hard Sauce . . . . . . . . . . . . . . . . . . . . . . . .
Hard sauce is traditionally served with steamed puddings, but it is delicious on warm gingerbread too. Simply whip these ingredients together: 4 ounces butter, 1½ cups powdered sugar, 1 teaspoon vanilla, 1 ounce orange liqueur, and 1 teaspoon orange zest.

**SERVES 9**

1 cup sugar
1 cup vegetable oil
1 cup molasses
1 cup boiling water
2 teaspoons baking soda
1 tablespoon ground, dried
   ginger
½ teaspoon cinnamon
2½ cups flour
2 eggs, beaten
Powdered sugar

# Coffee Caramel Sauce

**MAKES 3 CUPS**

*1½ cups sugar*
*½ cup brewed coffee*
*½ cup heavy cream*

If you prefer plain caramel sauce, you can substitute heavy cream for the brewed coffee.

1. Dissolve the sugar in ½ cup water in a sauce pan.

2. Heat the sugar mixture over high heat until it caramelizes.

3. Carefully pour in the coffee and cream over medium-low heat. Cook and stir until slightly thickened, then remove from heat and cool. Sauce will thicken more as it cools.

# Tres Leches Donut Holes

If you want variety, you can also make this dessert nosh
with glazed yeast or chocolate cake donut holes.

**SERVES 6**

*2 dozen glazed cake donut holes*
*1 cup whole milk*
*½ cup evaporated milk*
*1 cup sweetened condensed milk*

1. Poke the donut holes with a bamboo skewer several times each. Place them in a container in one layer.

2. Pour the whole milk over the donut holes. Pour the evaporated milk over the donut holes. Pour the sweetened condensed milk over the donut holes.

3. Cover and let the donut holes soak up the liquid for ½ hour. Remove donut holes from liquid and pile on a platter.

## Substitutions. . . . . . . . . . . . . . . . . . . . . . . . . . . . . .

Try *dulce de leche*, cajeta, or any other type of caramel sauce instead of sweetened condensed milk in the Tres Leches Donut Holes recipe. Or substitute coconut milk for the evaporated milk and sprinkle shredded coconut on top before serving.

# Vietnamese Iced Coffee Flan

**SERVES 8**

*Caramel*
*1 cup sugar*
*1⅓ cups water*
*1 tablespoon coffee extract*
*Custard*
*1⅔ cups brewed coffee*
*5 cups sweetened condensed*
  *milk*
*6 eggs*
*6 egg yolks*

Vietnamese iced coffee is brewed in a special drip basket over a glass with sweetened condensed milk in the bottom. It is served over ice. This tastes just like it.

1. Preheat oven to 350°F. For the caramel, dissolve the sugar in ⅓ cup water in a sauce pan. Cook over medium-high heat until the sugar caramelizes to an amber color. Remove from heat and carefully add 1 cup water. Return to heat just to dissolve the caramel remaining on the bottom of the pan. Stir in the coffee extract.

2. Ladle 1 ounce (2 tablespoons) of the coffee caramel into eight ramekins set inside a baking pan with 2-inch-high sides. Set aside. (Save leftover caramel or discard it.)

3. For the custard, heat the coffee and the sweetened condensed milk together in a sauce pan over medium heat. Whisk the eggs and egg yolks together in a bowl and temper the eggs with 1 cup of the hot liquid. Remove the pan from the heat and whisk the egg-yolk mixture into the pan. Immediately strain the custard into a pitcher.

4. Pour the custard into the ramekins, leaving a ½-inch space on top to allow for expansion. Pour hot water into the bottom of the baking pan so it comes halfway up the outside of the ramekins. Cover the baking pan tightly with foil and set it in the oven.

5. Bake for 20 minutes, then check to see if the custard has set by jiggling one of the ramekins. It should move like gelatin and not be liquid in the center. If not done, return them to the oven for 10 minutes, or until they are set. Remove the baking pan from the oven, remove the foil, and carefully lift out the ramekins with tongs and set them on a tray to cool to room temperature. Cover and refrigerate them until they have completely cooled, at least 2 hours.

6. To serve, run a sharp knife around the edge of each ramekin and place a dessert plate on top. Invert the plate and ramekin and give a little shake to release the flan to the plate. Let the caramel run out to form a pool of sauce on the plate.

# Traditional Spanish Flan

This recipe is for individual flans, but if you want one large flan, bake the caramel and custard in a large baking dish for 1 hour and chill for at least 4 hours.

1. Preheat oven to 350°F. For the caramel, dissolve the sugar in ⅓ cup water in a sauce pan. Cook over medium-high heat until the sugar caramelizes to an amber color. Remove from heat and carefully add 1 cup water. Return to heat just to dissolve the caramel remaining on the bottom of the pan.

2. Ladle 1 ounce (2 tablespoons) of the caramel into eight ramekins set inside a baking pan with 2-inch-high sides. Set aside. (Save leftover caramel or discard it.)

3. For the custard, heat the half-and-half, milk, and sugar together in a sauce pan over medium heat. Whisk the eggs and egg yolks together in a bowl and temper the eggs with 1 cup of the hot liquid. Remove the pan from the heat and whisk the egg yolk mixture into the pan. Immediately strain the custard into a pitcher.

4. Pour the custard into the ramekins, leaving a ½-inch space on top to allow for expansion. Pour hot water into the bottom of the baking pan so it comes halfway up the outside of the ramekins. Cover the baking pan tightly with foil and set it in the oven.

5. Bake for 20 minutes, then check to see if the custard has set by jiggling one of the ramekins. It should move like gelatin and not be liquid in the center. If not done, return them to the oven for 10 minutes, or until they are set. Remove the baking pan from the oven, remove the foil, and carefully lift out the ramekins with tongs and set them on a tray to cool to room temperature. Cover and refrigerate them until they have completely cooled, at least 2 hours.

6. To serve, run a sharp knife around the edge of each ramekin and place a dessert plate on top. Invert the plate and ramekin and give a little shake to release the flan to the plate. Let the caramel run out to form a pool of sauce on the plate.

**SERVES 8**

*Caramel*
*1 cup sugar*
*1⅓ cups water*
*Custard*
*4 eggs*
*4 egg yolks*
*¾ cup sugar*
*1 cup half-and-half*
*2 cups whole milk*
*1 teaspoon vanilla*

# Pistachio Rosewater Nougat

**SERVES 10**

¼ cup pistachios

2 tablespoons sugar

¼ cup flour

2 tablespoons unsalted butter

8 ounces cream cheese, softened

1 package instant pistachio
   pudding mix

1 cup sour cream

⅛ teaspoon rosewater

3 cups whipped cream or
   whipped topping

Rosewater is available in some supermarkets and Indian and Middle Eastern food stores. It imparts a delicate flavor that is very subtle. Serve the individual nougats with caramel sauce and sliced mangoes if desired.

1. Preheat oven to 350°F. In a food processor, grind the pistachios with the sugar. Add the flour and mix. Add the butter and process until crumbly. Press the crumb mixture into muffin tins lined with paper liners. Bake for 10 minutes, then let cool.

2. Mix the cream cheese and pudding mix with an electric mixer until combined and fluffy. Add the sour cream and mix thoroughly. Add the rosewater and mix.

3. Fold the whipped cream in with a rubber spatula.

4. Spray the paper liners with cooking oil. Spoon the cream cheese mixture into the paper liners on top of the pistachio crusts. Tap the muffin tin to remove air pockets. Cover with plastic and freeze overnight.

5. Peel the paper liners off the individual nougats and set them on individual plates. Leave them at room temperature for 15 to 30 minutes before serving to soften.

# Coriander Shortbread

These cookies have the delicate flavor of coriander and a
tender texture. Fresh pears are a nice complement with them.

1. Preheat oven to 350°F.

2. Combine butter and sugar in a bowl and mix with a wooden spoon or
   electric mixer.

3. Add vanilla and coriander and mix well.

4. Add flour and salt and mix to form a smooth dough.

5. Press dough into a 9-inch tart pan with a removable bottom, prick
   all over with a fork, and bake for 40 minutes. Remove from oven
   and let cool. Remove the side of the pan and cut the shortbread into
   16 wedges.

## Butter is Better . . . . . . . . . . . . . . . . . . . . . . . . . .

To make plain shortbread, just leave the coriander out of the above recipe. Also, there is no point
in making shortbread if you are going to use margarine. Always use butter in shortbread, because
there are so few ingredients that butter is the star flavor.

**MAKES 16**

*1 pound unsalted butter,*
  *softened*
*1 cup sugar*
*½ teaspoon vanilla*
*1 teaspoon ground coriander*
*4 cups flour*
*¼ teaspoon salt*

# Dulce de Leche Profiteroles

**SERVES 6**

1 cup water

4 ounces unsalted butter

½ teaspoon salt

1 cup flour

4 eggs

6 scoops vanilla ice cream

½ cup dulce de leche or caramel
    sauce, warmed

Powdered sugar

*Dulce de leche* means "milk sweet" in Spanish. It is available in cans or jars in the Mexican foods section of many supermarkets. There is a way to make it out of sweetened condensed milk too, which involves cooking the unopened can in simmering water for 3 hours. It must be cooled completely before opening.

1. Preheat oven to 400°F. Line a cookie sheet with a silicone mat (or grease the pan).

2. Put the water, butter, and salt in a saucepan over medium-high heat and bring to a boil. When butter is melted, turn heat to medium and add the flour all at once. Stir constantly with a wooden spoon over medium heat until it is the consistency of mashed potatoes.

3. Remove from heat and beat in eggs one at a time using a wooden spoon or an electric stand mixer.

4. Scoop the dough with two spoons onto the prepared cookie sheet, into 1-inch mounds, evenly spacing them about 2 inches apart. Bake 15 minutes, reduce heat to 350°F, and bake 15 minutes more. Let cool.

5. Slice the pastries horizontally and place a scoop of ice cream on the bottom of each one. Spoon the warm dulce de leche over the ice cream and place the tops of the pastries on like hats. Dust with powdered sugar and serve immediately.

# Crêpes Noisette

This is street food, Parisian style. Garnish with seasonal
berries when available. Ice cream doesn't hurt either.

**SERVES 8**

2 tablespoons unsalted butter
½ cup milk
½ cup water
2 eggs
½ cup flour
¼ teaspoon salt
Canola oil for frying crêpes
¼ cup melted butter
½ cup hazelnut liqueur
1 cup toasted hazelnuts, chopped
   roughly
Powdered sugar

1. Melt the butter and put it and the milk, water, eggs, flour, and salt into a blender. Blend 30 seconds. Scrape down the blender sides with a rubber spatula and then blend again for 30 seconds. Refrigerate for 1 hour.

2. Remix the chilled crêpe batter in blender for a few seconds before frying.

3. Fry the crêpes in a hot 6-inch nonstick pan brushed with oil, turning once. They don't take but a minute or two. Stack the finished crêpes between waxed paper.

4. Preheat the oven to 325°F. Lay the crêpes out in one layer on cookie sheets, brush them with melted butter, and warm them in the oven for 5 to 10 minutes.

5. Sprinkle the hazelnut liqueur over the crêpes and fold them into quarters. Arrange the crêpe triangles on a platter and sprinkle the toasted hazelnuts over them. Dust with powdered sugar and serve immediately.

## Crêpes Suzette. . . . . . . . . . . . . . . . . . . . . . . . .

Make a compound butter with grated orange zest and powdered sugar and spread it on warm crêpes. Then fold the crêpes in quarters to make triangles. Sprinkle a little orange liqueur over them and dust with powdered sugar for quick Crêpes Suzette.

# Chocolate-Dipped Strawberry Skewers

**SERVES 6**

12 ounces semisweet chocolate

12 large fresh strawberries,
 refrigerated

12 bamboo skewers

Serve these berries as a bouquet by poking the non-strawberry ends of the skewers
in a cantaloupe half that has been set cut-side down on a plate.

1. Chop the chocolate and place it in the top of a double boiler set over hot, but not boiling, water. Melt chocolate and stir with a spatula to a smooth consistency.

2. Put a skewer in the stem end of each strawberry to secure it, but not all the way through the berry.

3. Dip each chilled strawberry into melted chocolate to cover entirely, including part of the skewer. Place them on a piece of waxed paper to set up.

# Banana Egg Rolls

If dulce de leche is unavailable, caramel sauce is a fine
substitute. Alternatively, you may just omit it.

**SERVES 6**

*2 to 3 bananas, depending
  on size*
*6 egg-roll wrappers*
*3 cups vegetable oil*
*½ cup dulce de leche*
*Powdered sugar*

1. Peel and cut the bananas into 3-inch pieces.

2. Lay an egg-roll wrapper flat with the points facing like a diamond
   shape.

3. Place a piece of banana on the bottom third of the wrapper. Fold up
   the bottom corner over the banana, then fold in the two side corners
   over the banana. Dab the top corner with water and roll the rest of the
   way, encasing the banana in the wrapper. Repeat with the remaining
   wrappers and banana pieces.

4. Heat the oil in a deep fryer or heavy pot to 365°F. Add the wrapped
   bananas and fry for 1 minute. Remove from the oil and drain on paper
   towels.

5. Cut the banana egg rolls in half on a diagonal and serve them warm
   on a small plate in a small pool of dulce de leche. Dust the rolls with
   powdered sugar.

# Beverages

# Red Wine Raspberry Sangria

SERVES 4

3 cups Beaujolais wine
½ cup framboise (raspberry liqueur)
½ cup lemon juice, freshly squeezed
½ cup orange juice, freshly squeezed
¼ cup sugar (or more to taste)
1 lemon
1 cup raspberries

This delicious combination of red wine and raspberries can be made into a sorbet or sherbet if you have an ice-cream maker.

1. Combine the Beaujolais wine, framboise, lemon juice, orange juice, and sugar in a pitcher. Stir well and add sufficient ice to chill the mixture without all melting.

2. Slice the lemon into ¼-inch-thick slices and add them to the pitcher. Add the raspberries to the pitcher.

4. Pour a glass for each person and be sure to include several raspberries in each serving.

### Combination Sangria . . . . . . . . . . . . . . . . . . . . . .
You can make sangria with equal parts red and white wine and add lemon-lime soda instead of lemonade, juice, and/or sugar.

# Black Sangria

SERVES 4

3 cups Cabernet wine
½ cup crème de cassis (optional)
¾ cup purple grape juice
¼ cup sugar (or more to taste)
1 cup black grapes
½ cup blueberries
½ cup blackberries
1 lemon
3 purple plums

This is an elegant version of the wine punch sangria. Feel free to try it with any dark wine, such as elderberry, instead of Cabernet.

1. Combine the Cabernet wine, crème de cassis, grape juice, and sugar in a pitcher. Stir well and add sufficient ice to chill the mixture without all melting.

2. Cut the grapes in half and add them and the whole berries to the pitcher.

3. Slice the lemon into ¼-inch-thick slices and add them to the pitcher.

4. Cut the plums in half, remove the pits, and cut each half into wedges and add them to the pitcher.

5. Pour a glass for each person and be sure to include a piece of each fruit in each serving.

# Jamaican Cider

This drink of rum and cider can be served hot or cold. For the hot version, omit the ginger ale and heat and serve it in a mug with the cinnamon stick.

1. Fill a cocktail shaker ¼ full with ice.

2. Pour the apple cider and rum into the cocktail shaker and shake.

3. Strain the drink into a glass.

4. Pour the ginger ale into the glass.

5. Garnish with a cinnamon stick.

**Substitution** . . . . . . . . . . . . . . . . . . . . . . . . .
Spiced rum can be substituted for dark rum in the recipe above.

**SERVES 1**

1 ounce Myers's Rum (Jamaican dark rum)
3 ounces apple cider
2 ounces ginger ale
1 cinnamon stick

# Mojito

This refreshing rum drink is made with fresh lime juice and mint leaves. It is the perfect drink for Cuban and "Floribbean" food.

1. Place the mint leaves, lime juice, rum, and sugar in the bottom of a cocktail shaker and bruise the mint leaves with a muddler.

2. Add ice and shake well.

3. Strain into a tall glass filled with ice and top it off with club soda.

4. Garnish with a stick of sugarcane.

**SERVES 1**

4 fresh mint leaves
1½ tablespoons lime juice
1½ ounces light rum
1 tablespoon sugar
Splash of club soda
1 sugarcane stick (optional)

# Mango Mojito

**SERVES 1**

4 fresh mint leaves

1½ tablespoons lime juice

1½ ounces light rum

1 tablespoon sugar

1 ounce mango purée

Splash of club soda

1 sugarcane stick (optional)

Caribbean food is great with this version of the mojito, but it is equally enjoyable with Mexican, South American, and Pacific Rim cuisines.

1. Place the mint leaves, lime juice, rum, and sugar in the bottom of a cocktail shaker and bruise the mint leaves with a muddler.

2. Add mango purée and ice and shake well.

3. Strain into a tall glass filled with ice and top it off with club soda.

4. Garnish with a stick of sugarcane.

More Mojitos . . . . . . . . . . . . . . . . . . . . . . . . . . . . . . . . . .
More flavors of mojitos can be made with fruit purées, such as guava, strawberry, peach, papaya, and so on.

# Margarita

**SERVES 1**

2 lime wedges

Kosher salt

1 ounce tequila

½ ounce triple sec

1½ ounces lime juice

The most famous tequila drink there is! It is simple and just right in hot climates. You may serve it frozen, up, or on the rocks, with or without salt, but always use fresh lime juice if possible.

1. Run a lime wedge around the rim of a stem glass, then dip the rim in kosher salt. Squeeze the same lime wedge into the glass.

2. Fill a cocktail shaker ¼ full with ice.

3. Add the tequila, triple sec, and lime juice to the shaker and shake.

4. Strain into the glass.

5. Garnish with a lime wedge.

# Watermelon Margarita

This is a slushy frozen watermelon version of the classic margarita,
perfect for cooling the summertime heat anywhere.

1. Run a lime wedge around the rim of a stem glass, then dip the rim in sugar.

2. Put the tequila, watermelon chunks, and lime juice into a blender. Be sure the lid is on tight!

3. Purée it in the blender until smooth.

4. Pour into the glass and serve.

## More Margaritas. . . . . . . . . . . . . . . . . . . . . . . . .
Other kinds of margaritas can be made with different frozen fruits, such as mangoes, strawberries, raspberries, and pineapple.

**SERVES 1**

*1 lime wedge*
*Sugar*
*1½ ounces tequila*
*5 seedless watermelon chunks, frozen*
*2 tablespoons lime juice*

# White Chocolate Sake

This drink is served like a martini, but made with white
chocolate and sake instead of vermouth and gin.

1. Run a wet paper towel around the rim of a stem glass, then dip the rim in sugar.

2. Fill a cocktail shaker ¼ full with ice.

3. Add the white chocolate liqueur, sake, vanilla vodka, and cream to the shaker and shake well.

4. Strain the drink into the glass.

5. Garnish with an orange twist.

**SERVES 1**

*Sugar*
*1 ounce white chocolate liqueur*
*1 ounce sake*
*1 ounce vanilla vodka*
*½ ounce cream*
*1 orange twist*

# Chocolate Martini

**SERVES 1**

*Sweetened cocoa powder*
*1½ ounces chocolate liqueur*
*1½ ounces vanilla vodka*
*½ ounce cream*
*1 maraschino cherry*

This decadent martini is the one to have when you are drinking dessert. To make sweetened cocoa powder, mix equal parts cocoa powder and powdered sugar.

1. Run a wet paper towel around the rim of a stem glass, then dip the rim in the sweetened cocoa powder.

2. Fill a cocktail shaker ¼ full with ice. Add the chocolate liqueur, vanilla vodka, and cream to the shaker and shake well.

3. Strain the drink into the glass. Garnish with a maraschino cherry.

### Mint Chocolate Martini . . . . . . . . . . . . . . . . . . .
Add a shot of crème de menthe to the chocolate martini recipe for a delicious mint chocolate treat. Try to use white crème de menthe, because green will give the drink a muddy, army-green color.

# Limoncello Cooler

**SERVES 1**

*2 ounces limoncello*
*4 ounces lemon-lime soda*
*1 lemon twist*

Limoncello is a delightful and refreshing Italian liqueur made from lots of lemons steeped in vodka.

1. Fill a glass with ice.

2. Pour the limoncello and soda over the ice and stir.

3. Garnish with a lemon twist.

# Mint Julep

Serve these minted whiskey drinks with Oven-Fried Chicken Drumsticks (page 177) and American Deviled Eggs (page 126) for a southern-style Kentucky Derby party.

**SERVES 1**

6 fresh mint leaves
2 ounces Kentucky bourbon
1 teaspoon sugar
1 mint sprig

1.  Place the mint leaves, bourbon, and sugar in the bottom of a cocktail shaker and mash the mint leaves with a muddler.

2.  Add ice and shake well.

3.  Strain into a tall glass filled with ice and garnish with mint sprig.

## Simple Syrup . . . . . . . . . . . . . . . . . . . .
Simple syrup is a neutral sweetener often used in mixed drinks instead of sugar. Make it by bringing equal parts of sugar and water to a boil, then turn off the heat. Let it cool and use it to sweeten iced tea and mixed drinks.

# Hot Buttered Rum

Hot buttered rum is a comforting and soothing hot beverage with a kick. It is the perfect après-ski drink.

**SERVES 2**

2 ounces unsalted butter, softened
2 tablespoons honey
⅓ cup brown sugar
Pinch cloves
¼ teaspoon cinnamon
Pinch nutmeg
1 cup water
3 ounces gold rum
2 cinnamon sticks

1.  Whip the butter with the honey, brown sugar, cloves, cinnamon, and nutmeg with an electric mixer until fluffy.

2.  Bring the water to a boil.

3.  Combine the rum, boiling water, and butter mixture and stir until melted.

4.  Pour the hot buttered rum into two coffee mugs.

5.  Garnish with cinnamon sticks.

# Blood Orange Mimosa

This is the perfect accompaniment to a tapas brunch.

SERVES 1

2 ounces blood orange juice,
    chilled
3 ounces champagne or
    sparkling wine, chilled

1.  Pour the blood orange juice into a champagne flute.

2.  Add the sparkling wine to the juice and serve.

## Mimosa . . . . . . . . . . . . . . . . . . . . . .
A mimosa is normally made with regular orange juice, but you can try it with tangerine juice for a tangy change.

# White Peach Bellini

If you can't find white peaches and/or Prosecco, you may use yellow peach purée and champagne or sparking wine for this elegant drink.

SERVES 1

1 ounce white peach purée,
    chilled
4 ounces Prosecco Italian
    sparkling wine, chilled
1 strawberry

1.  Pour the peach purée into a champagne flute.

2.  Add the sparkling wine to the flute.

3.  Garnish with a strawberry and serve.

# Cava Bellini

Cava, Spain's sparkling wine, is paired with yellow peach
purée in this version of the Venetian classic, the Bellini.

1. Pour the peach purée into a champagne flute.

2. Add the Cava to the flute.

3. Garnish with the blueberries and serve.

### Origin of the Bellini . . . . . . . . . . . . . . . . . . . . . .
The Bellini was invented at Harry's Bar in Venice, Italy, and variations on the theme are available
everywhere. The original has white peach purée, which may be hard to find, so try it with whatever is available, whether it is yellow peaches or nectarines.

**SERVES 1**

*1 ounce yellow peach purée,
    chilled*
*4 ounces Cava Spanish sparkling
    wine, chilled*
*3 blueberries*

# Raspberry Bellini

Try this first, and then make different variations with
blackberry, mango, strawberry, or even chocolate sorbet.

1. Scoop the raspberry sorbet into a champagne flute.

2. Add the sparkling wine over the sorbet.

3. Garnish with the raspberries and serve.

**SERVES 1**

*1 scoop raspberry sorbet*
*4 ounces sparkling wine*
*3 fresh raspberries*

# Campari Cape Cod

**SERVES 1**

*1 ounce Campari*
*4 ounces cranberry juice*
*1 ounce vodka*
*3 ounces soda water*
*1 orange twist*

Campari, a bitter orange Italian liqueur, complements
the cranberry juice in this refreshing fizzy cocktail.

1. Fill a cocktail shaker ¼ full with ice.

2. Pour the Campari, cranberry juice, and vodka into the cocktail shaker
   and shake.

3. Strain the drink into a glass filled with ice.

4. Pour the soda water into the glass.

5. Garnish with an orange twist.

# Bloody Maria

**SERVES 1**

*2 lime wedges*
*¼ teaspoon celery salt*
*¼ teaspoon Worcestershire sauce*
*⅛ teaspoon pepper*
*Dash of Tabasco sauce*
*1 ounce tequila*
*5 ounces tomato juice*

The bloody Mary goes south-of-the-border with tequila
and lime instead of vodka and celery stalk.

1. Run a lime wedge around the rim of a tall glass, then dip the rim in
   celery salt.

2. Fill the glass with ice and squeeze the same lime wedge into it.

3. Shake the celery salt, Worcestershire sauce, pepper, and Tabasco
   sauce into the glass.

4. Add the tequila and tomato juice and stir well with a long iced tea or
   bar spoon. Garnish with a lime wedge.

## Other Bloody Drinks . . . . . . . . . . . . . . . . . . . . .
A Bloody Mary is made like a Bloody Maria, only with vodka instead of tequila, and a Bloody Bull
is made by adding beef bouillon to a Bloody Mary.

# Lemon Shandy

A lemon wedge is served with wheat beer in Germany, and this drink builds on that combination to make a refreshing cooler.

**SERVES 1**

*4 ounces lemonade, chilled*
*4 ounces wheat beer, chilled*
*1 lemon wedge*

1. Pour the lemonade into a pint glass.

2. Add the beer to the lemonade.

3. Garnish with a lemon wedge.

# Chocolate Monkey

This is a smoothie with liqueur. It can be made fat free if you substitute orange juice for the chocolate milk.

**SERVES 1**

*2 scoops chocolate sorbet*
*½ ripe banana*
*¼ cup chocolate milk*
*1 ounce banana liqueur*

1. Put the chocolate sorbet, banana, chocolate milk, and banana liqueur into a blender. Be sure the lid is on tight!

2. Purée it in the blender until smooth.

3. Pour into a glass and serve.

## Substitution . . . . . . . . . . . . . . . . . . . . . . . . . . .

If you substitute mango, raspberry, or any other flavor of sorbet for the chocolate sorbet, cream for the chocolate milk, and other liqueurs for the banana liqueur in the Chocolate Monkey, you can create a whole new repertoire of smoothie drinks.

# Glossary

**Bake**
Cook by dry heat in the oven.

**Baste**
Brush or spoon liquid over food while roasting.

**Blanch**
Partially boil and then stop the cooking in ice water.

**Boil**
Cook in hot, bubbling liquid at the temperature of 212°F.

**Braise**
Bake, covered, in a small amount of liquid.

**Broil**
Cook with the flame or heat source directly above the food.

**Broth**
The liquid derived from cooking foods in water, also often referred to as bouillon.

**Brown**
Fry food in a small amount of oil briefly, just until it turns brown on the outside.

**Caramelize**
Sauté until natural sugar (or added sugar) in food turns brown.

**Chop**
Coarsely cut into bite-size or smaller pieces.

**Colander**
A perforated bowl-shaped container used to strain liquids from foods.

**Deglaze**
Loosen browned flavor bits from a pan with a liquid.

**Dice**
Cut julienne strips into squares.

**Fold**
A technique used to combine a light and airy ingredient with a heavier ingredient. A spatula is used to gently fold the bottom ingredient to the top in a circular motion, turning the bowl one-quarter turn with each rotation of the spatula until the lighter ingredient is completely incorporated.

**Fry**

Cook in hot fat.

**Grill**

Cook with the flame or heat source directly under the food.

**Mince**

Chop very fine; finer than dice.

**Pimentón**

Spanish smoked paprika.

**Pulse**

To allow a food processor or blender to run in 1-second increments by manually pushing the pulse button.

**Reduce**

Simmer to thicken a liquid by evaporation.

**Roast**

Bake in dry heat, usually meat or vegetables.

**Roux**

Butter and flour mixed together to form a paste for thickening sauces, gravies, soups, and stews.

**Sauté**

A method by which food is cooked quickly in very little oil or fat, usually in a skillet over direct heat.

**Simmer**

Cook in liquid that is barely boiling.

**Steam**

Cook in a basket or on a rack set over boiling water.

**Sweat**

Sauté on low heat until translucent (as in onions) and tender.

**Whisk**

Beat ingredients together using a metal whip.

# Tasting Menu by Country

For your next party, why not try a tapas-style setup and provide a taste of Spain with a selection of some or all of the following recipes, depending on your time and budget. Then move on to the tasting menus from other countries that I have set up here. Mix and match for an international party, or choose just a few recipes for a dinner party.

## Happy Hour Tapas from Spain

- Traditional Aioli   11
- Potatoes Brava   10
- Sizzling Garlic Shrimp   14
- Stuffed Piquillo Peppers   17
- Chorizo Empanadas   219
- Shrimp Paella   19
- Andalusian Almond Meatballs   18
- Chicken Croquetas   21
- Catalan Flatbreads   45
- Spanish Saffron-Poached Pears   69
- Valencia Oranges with Orange-Flower Water   86
- Red Sangria   22
- Traditional Spanish Flan   259

## Hors d'Oeuvres Fête from France

- Gougeres   225
- Orange Niçoise Olives   141
- Peppers Brandade   149
- Provençal Leek Croutons   47
- Ratatouille-Stuffed Mushrooms   147
- Cognac Peppercorn Filet   191
- Shallot Tart   143
- Red Wine Raspberry Sangria   268
- Crêpes Noisette   263

## Antipasto Party from Italy

- Sicilian Eggplant Relish   28
- Tuscan Mushroom Crostini   46
- Calamari with Lime Aioli   200

# Wine Pairings

Here are a few guidelines to get started in matching wine with food, but remember, you can break the rules! White wines, like sauvignon blanc, Chardonnay, Pinot Grigio, and Riesling, are traditionally paired with fish, seafood, and chicken. Red wines, like Rioja, Pinot Noir, Zinfandel, Merlot, and Cabernet Sauvignon, are typically paired with pork, beef, and lamb. Additionally, spicy dishes go well with Riesling and Zinfandel.

## Sauvignon Blanc

- Sizzling Garlic Shrimp   14
- Bouillabaisse   97
- Bay Scallops Gratinee   167
- Crab-Stuffed Chicken Rolls   179
- Orange Avocado Chicken Pinchos   184

## Chardonnay

- Chicken Croquetas   21
- Mango Crab Sushi Rolls   163
- Shrimp Tempura Rolls   173
- Chicken Scampi Bites   180
- Baked Mussels   171
- Caribbean Coconut Shrimp   200

## Pinot Grigio

- Italian Cheese Flight   56
- Mediterranean Shaved Fennel   90
- Steamed Mussels   170
- Calamari with Lime Aioli   200

## Riesling

- Hawaiian Meatballs   188
- Asian Honey Ginger Peanuts   76
- Mango Pork Medallions   194
- Pacific Rim Shrimp Toasts   207

## Rioja

- Andalusian Almond Meatballs   18

# Index

# THE EVERYTHING SERIES!

## BUSINESS & PERSONAL FINANCE

Everything® Accounting Book
Everything® Budgeting Book
Everything® Business Planning Book
Everything® Coaching and Mentoring Book
Everything® Fundraising Book
Everything® Get Out of Debt Book
Everything® Grant Writing Book
**Everything® Guide to Personal Finance for Single Mothers**
Everything® Home-Based Business Book, 2nd Ed.
Everything® Homebuying Book, 2nd Ed.
Everything® Homeselling Book, 2nd Ed.
**Everything® Improve Your Credit Book**
Everything® Investing Book, 2nd Ed.
Everything® Landlording Book
Everything® Leadership Book
Everything® Managing People Book, 2nd Ed.
Everything® Negotiating Book
Everything® Online Auctions Book
Everything® Online Business Book
Everything® Personal Finance Book
Everything® Personal Finance in Your 20s and 30s Book
Everything® Project Management Book
Everything® Real Estate Investing Book
**Everything® Retirement Planning Book**
Everything® Robert's Rules Book, $7.95
Everything® Selling Book
Everything® Start Your Own Business Book, 2nd Ed.
Everything® Wills & Estate Planning Book

## COOKING

Everything® Barbecue Cookbook
Everything® Bartender's Book, $9.95
**Everything® Cheese Book**
Everything® Chinese Cookbook
Everything® Classic Recipes Book
Everything® Cocktail Parties and Drinks Book
Everything® College Cookbook
Everything® Cooking for Baby and Toddler Book
Everything® Cooking for Two Cookbook
Everything® Diabetes Cookbook
Everything® Easy Gourmet Cookbook
Everything® Fondue Cookbook
Everything® Fondue Party Book
Everything® Gluten-Free Cookbook
Everything® Glycemic Index Cookbook
Everything® Grilling Cookbook

Everything® Healthy Meals in Minutes Cookbook
Everything® Holiday Cookbook
Everything® Indian Cookbook
Everything® Italian Cookbook
Everything® Low-Carb Cookbook
Everything® Low-Fat High-Flavor Cookbook
Everything® Low-Salt Cookbook
Everything® Meals for a Month Cookbook
Everything® Mediterranean Cookbook
Everything® Mexican Cookbook
**Everything® No Trans Fat Cookbook**
Everything® One-Pot Cookbook
**Everything® Pizza Cookbook**
Everything® Quick and Easy 30-Minute, 5-Ingredient Cookbook
Everything® Quick Meals Cookbook
Everything® Slow Cooker Cookbook
Everything® Slow Cooking for a Crowd Cookbook
Everything® Soup Cookbook
**Everything® Stir-Fry Cookbook**
Everything® Tex-Mex Cookbook
Everything® Thai Cookbook
Everything® Vegetarian Cookbook
Everything® Wild Game Cookbook
Everything® Wine Book, 2nd Ed.

## GAMES

Everything® 15-Minute Sudoku Book, $9.95
Everything® 30-Minute Sudoku Book, $9.95
Everything® Blackjack Strategy Book
Everything® Brain Strain Book, $9.95
Everything® Bridge Book
Everything® Card Games Book
Everything® Card Tricks Book, $9.95
Everything® Casino Gambling Book, 2nd Ed.
Everything® Chess Basics Book
Everything® Craps Strategy Book
Everything® Crossword and Puzzle Book
Everything® Crossword Challenge Book
**Everything® Crosswords for the Beach Book, $9.95**
Everything® Cryptograms Book, $9.95
Everything® Easy Crosswords Book
Everything® Easy Kakuro Book, $9.95
**Everything® Easy Large Print Crosswords Book**
Everything® Games Book, 2nd Ed.
Everything® Giant Sudoku Book, $9.95
Everything® Kakuro Challenge Book, $9.95
Everything® Large-Print Crossword Challenge Book

Everything® Large-Print Crosswords Book
Everything® Lateral Thinking Puzzles Book, $9.95
Everything® Mazes Book
**Everything® Movie Crosswords Book, $9.95**
**Everything® Online Poker Book, $12.95**
Everything® Pencil Puzzles Book, $9.95
Everything® Poker Strategy Book
Everything® Pool & Billiards Book
**Everything® Sports Crosswords Book, $9.95**
Everything® Test Your IQ Book, $9.95
Everything® Texas Hold 'Em Book, $9.95
Everything® Travel Crosswords Book, $9.95
Everything® Word Games Challenge Book
**Everything® Word Scramble Book**
Everything® Word Search Book

## HEALTH

Everything® Alzheimer's Book
Everything® Diabetes Book
Everything® Health Guide to Adult Bipolar Disorder
Everything® Health Guide to Controlling Anxiety
Everything® Health Guide to Fibromyalgia
**Everything® Health Guide to Postpartum Care**
Everything® Health Guide to Thyroid Disease
Everything® Hypnosis Book
Everything® Low Cholesterol Book
Everything® Massage Book
Everything® Menopause Book
Everything® Nutrition Book
Everything® Reflexology Book
Everything® Stress Management Book

## HISTORY

Everything® American Government Book
**Everything® American History Book, 2nd Ed.**
Everything® Civil War Book
Everything® Freemasons Book
Everything® Irish History & Heritage Book
Everything® Middle East Book

## HOBBIES

Everything® Candlemaking Book
Everything® Cartooning Book
Everything® Coin Collecting Book
Everything® Drawing Book
Everything® Family Tree Book, 2nd Ed.
Everything® Knitting Book
Everything® Knots Book
Everything® Photography Book

Everything® Quilting Book
Everything® Scrapbooking Book
Everything® Sewing Book
**Everything® Soapmaking Book, 2nd Ed.**
Everything® Woodworking Book

## HOME IMPROVEMENT

Everything® Feng Shui Book
Everything® Feng Shui Decluttering Book, $9.95
Everything® Fix-It Book
Everything® Home Decorating Book
Everything® Home Storage Solutions Book
Everything® Homebuilding Book
Everything® Organize Your Home Book

## KIDS' BOOKS

**All titles are $7.95**
Everything® Kids' Animal Puzzle & Activity Book
Everything® Kids' Baseball Book, 4th Ed.
Everything® Kids' Bible Trivia Book
Everything® Kids' Bugs Book
Everything® Kids' Cars and Trucks Puzzle
    & Activity Book
Everything® Kids' Christmas Puzzle
    & Activity Book
Everything® Kids' Cookbook
Everything® Kids' Crazy Puzzles Book
Everything® Kids' Dinosaurs Book
Everything® Kids' First Spanish Puzzle and
    Activity Book
**Everything® Kids' Gross Cookbook**
Everything® Kids' Gross Hidden Pictures Book
Everything® Kids' Gross Jokes Book
Everything® Kids' Gross Mazes Book
Everything® Kids' Gross Puzzle and
    Activity Book
Everything® Kids' Halloween Puzzle
    & Activity Book
Everything® Kids' Hidden Pictures Book
Everything® Kids' Horses Book
Everything® Kids' Joke Book
Everything® Kids' Knock Knock Book
Everything® Kids' Learning Spanish Book
Everything® Kids' Math Puzzles Book
Everything® Kids' Mazes Book
Everything® Kids' Money Book
Everything® Kids' Nature Book
Everything® Kids' Pirates Puzzle and Activity Book
**Everything® Kids' Presidents Book**
Everything® Kids' Princess Puzzle and Activity Book
Everything® Kids' Puzzle Book
Everything® Kids' Riddles & Brain Teasers Book
Everything® Kids' Science Experiments Book
Everything® Kids' Sharks Book
Everything® Kids' Soccer Book
**Everything® Kids' States Book**
Everything® Kids' Travel Activity Book

## KIDS' STORY BOOKS

Everything® Fairy Tales Book

## LANGUAGE

Everything® Conversational Japanese Book with
    CD, $19.95
Everything® French Grammar Book
Everything® French Phrase Book, $9.95
Everything® French Verb Book, $9.95
Everything® German Practice Book with CD,
    $19.95
Everything® Inglés Book
**Everything® Intermediate Spanish Book with
    CD, $19.95**
**Everything® Learning Brazilian Portuguese
    Book with CD, $19.95**
Everything® Learning French Book
Everything® Learning German Book
Everything® Learning Italian Book
Everything® Learning Latin Book
**Everything® Learning Spanish Book with
    CD, 2nd Edition, $19.95**
Everything® Russian Practice Book with CD, $19.95
Everything® Sign Language Book
Everything® Spanish Grammar Book
Everything® Spanish Phrase Book, $9.95
Everything® Spanish Practice Book
    with CD, $19.95
Everything® Spanish Verb Book, $9.95
Everything® Speaking Mandarin Chinese Book
    with CD, $19.95

## MUSIC

Everything® Drums Book with CD, $19.95
**Everything® Guitar Book with CD, 2nd
    Edition, $19.95**
Everything® Guitar Chords Book with CD, $19.95
Everything® Home Recording Book
Everything® Music Theory Book with CD, $19.95
Everything® Reading Music Book with CD, $19.95
Everything® Rock & Blues Guitar Book
    with CD, $19.95
**Everything® Rock and Blues Piano Book
    with CD, $19.95**
Everything® Songwriting Book

## NEW AGE

Everything® Astrology Book, 2nd Ed.
Everything® Birthday Personology Book
Everything® Dreams Book, 2nd Ed.
Everything® Love Signs Book, $9.95
Everything® Numerology Book
Everything® Paganism Book
Everything® Palmistry Book
Everything® Psychic Book
Everything® Reiki Book

Everything® Sex Signs Book, $9.95
Everything® Tarot Book, 2nd Ed.
**Everything® Toltec Wisdom Book**
Everything® Wicca and Witchcraft Book

## PARENTING

Everything® Baby Names Book, 2nd Ed.
Everything® Baby Shower Book
Everything® Baby's First Year Book
Everything® Birthing Book
Everything® Breastfeeding Book
Everything® Father-to-Be Book
Everything® Father's First Year Book
Everything® Get Ready for Baby Book
Everything® Get Your Baby to Sleep Book, $9.95
Everything® Getting Pregnant Book
Everything® Guide to Raising a One-Year-Old
Everything® Guide to Raising a Two-Year-Old
Everything® Homeschooling Book
Everything® Mother's First Year Book
**Everything® Parent's Guide to Childhood
    Illnesses**
Everything® Parent's Guide to Children
    and Divorce
Everything® Parent's Guide to Children
    with ADD/ADHD
Everything® Parent's Guide to Children
    with Asperger's Syndrome
Everything® Parent's Guide to Children
    with Autism
Everything® Parent's Guide to Children with
    Bipolar Disorder
**Everything® Parent's Guide to Children with
    Depression**
Everything® Parent's Guide to Children
    with Dyslexia
**Everything® Parent's Guide to Children with
    Juvenile Diabetes**
Everything® Parent's Guide to Positive Discipline
Everything® Parent's Guide to Raising a
    Successful Child
Everything® Parent's Guide to Raising Boys
**Everything® Parent's Guide to Raising Girls**
Everything® Parent's Guide to Raising Siblings
Everything® Parent's Guide to Sensory
    Integration Disorder
Everything® Parent's Guide to Tantrums
Everything® Parent's Guide to the Strong-Willed
    Child
Everything® Parenting a Teenager Book
Everything® Potty Training Book, $9.95
**Everything® Pregnancy Book, 3rd Ed.**
Everything® Pregnancy Fitness Book
Everything® Pregnancy Nutrition Book
Everything® Pregnancy Organizer, 2nd Ed., $16.95
Everything® Toddler Activities Book
Everything® Toddler Book

Everything® Tween Book
Everything® Twins, Triplets, and More Book

## PETS

Everything® Aquarium Book
Everything® Boxer Book
Everything® Cat Book, 2nd Ed.
Everything® Chihuahua Book
Everything® Dachshund Book
Everything® Dog Book
Everything® Dog Health Book
**Everything® Dog Obedience Book**
Everything® Dog Owner's Organizer, $16.95
Everything® Dog Training and Tricks Book
Everything® German Shepherd Book
Everything® Golden Retriever Book
Everything® Horse Book
Everything® Horse Care Book
Everything® Horseback Riding Book
Everything® Labrador Retriever Book
Everything® Poodle Book
Everything® Pug Book
Everything® Puppy Book
Everything® Rottweiler Book
Everything® Small Dogs Book
Everything® Tropical Fish Book
Everything® Yorkshire Terrier Book

## REFERENCE

**Everything® American Presidents Book**
Everything® Blogging Book
Everything® Build Your Vocabulary Book
Everything® Car Care Book
Everything® Classical Mythology Book
Everything® Da Vinci Book
Everything® Divorce Book
Everything® Einstein Book
**Everything® Enneagram Book**
Everything® Etiquette Book, 2nd Ed.
Everything® Inventions and Patents Book
Everything® Mafia Book
Everything® Philosophy Book
**Everything® Pirates Book**
Everything® Psychology Book

## RELIGION

Everything® Angels Book
Everything® Bible Book
Everything® Buddhism Book
Everything® Catholicism Book
Everything® Christianity Book
**Everything® Gnostic Gospels Book**
Everything® History of the Bible Book
Everything® Jesus Book

Everything® Jewish History & Heritage Book
Everything® Judaism Book
Everything® Kabbalah Book
Everything® Koran Book
Everything® Mary Book
Everything® Mary Magdalene Book
Everything® Prayer Book
**Everything® Saints Book, 2nd Ed.**
Everything® Torah Book
Everything® Understanding Islam Book
Everything® World's Religions Book
Everything® Zen Book

## SCHOOL & CAREERS

Everything® Alternative Careers Book
Everything® Career Tests Book
Everything® College Major Test Book
Everything® College Survival Book, 2nd Ed.
Everything® Cover Letter Book, 2nd Ed.
Everything® Filmmaking Book
**Everything® Get-a-Job Book, 2nd Ed.**
Everything® Guide to Being a Paralegal
**Everything® Guide to Being a Personal
    Trainer**
Everything® Guide to Being a Real Estate
    Agent
Everything® Guide to Being a Sales Rep
Everything® Guide to Careers in Health Care
Everything® Guide to Careers in Law
    Enforcement
Everything® Guide to Government Jobs
Everything® Guide to Starting and Running
    a Restaurant
Everything® Job Interview Book
Everything® New Nurse Book
Everything® New Teacher Book
Everything® Paying for College Book
Everything® Practice Interview Book
Everything® Resume Book, 2nd Ed.
Everything® Study Book

## SELF-HELP

Everything® Dating Book, 2nd Ed.
Everything® Great Sex Book
Everything® Self-Esteem Book
**Everything® Tantric Sex Book**

## SPORTS & FITNESS

Everything® Easy Fitness Book
Everything® Running Book
Everything® Weight Training Book

## TRAVEL

Everything® Family Guide to Cruise Vacations
Everything® Family Guide to Hawaii
Everything® Family Guide to Las Vegas, 2nd Ed.
Everything® Family Guide to Mexico
Everything® Family Guide to New York City,
    2nd Ed.
Everything® Family Guide to RV Travel &
    Campgrounds
Everything® Family Guide to the Caribbean
Everything® Family Guide to the Walt Disney
    World Resort®, Universal Studios®,
    and Greater Orlando, 4th Ed.
Everything® Family Guide to Timeshares
**Everything® Family Guide to Washington
    D.C., 2nd Ed.**

## WEDDINGS

Everything® Bachelorette Party Book, $9.95
Everything® Bridesmaid Book, $9.95
Everything® Destination Wedding Book
Everything® Elopement Book, $9.95
Everything® Father of the Bride Book, $9.95
Everything® Groom Book, $9.95
Everything® Mother of the Bride Book, $9.95
Everything® Outdoor Wedding Book
Everything® Wedding Book, 3rd Ed.
Everything® Wedding Checklist, $9.95
Everything® Wedding Etiquette Book, $9.95
Everything® Wedding Organizer, 2nd Ed., $16.95
Everything® Wedding Shower Book, $9.95
Everything® Wedding Vows Book, $9.95
Everything® Wedding Workout Book
Everything® Weddings on a Budget Book, $9.95

## WRITING

Everything® Creative Writing Book
Everything® Get Published Book, 2nd Ed.
Everything® Grammar and Style Book
**Everything® Guide to Magazine Writing**
Everything® Guide to Writing a Book Proposal
Everything® Guide to Writing a Novel
Everything® Guide to Writing Children's Books
**Everything® Guide to Writing Copy**
Everything® Guide to Writing Research Papers
Everything® Screenwriting Book
Everything® Writing Poetry Book
Everything® Writing Well Book

---